Alice Munro

Twayne's World Authors Series
Canadian Literature

Robert Lecker, Editor
McGill University

TWAS 800

ALICE MUNRO
(1931–   )
Photograph courtesy of R.J. Nephew Photography

Alice Munro

By E. D. Blodgett

University of Alberta

Twayne Publishers
A Division of G. K. Hall & Co. • Boston

meis parentibus

Alice Munro

E. D. Blodgett

Copyright 1988 by G. K. Hall & Co.
All rights reserved.
Published by Twayne Publishers
A Division of G. K. Hall & Co.
70 Lincoln Street
Boston, Massachusetts 02111

Copyediting supervised by Barbara Sutton.
Book production by Patricia D'Agostino.
Book design by Barbara Anderson.

Typeset in 11 pt. Garamond
by Williams Press, Inc. Albany, New York.

Printed on permanent/durable acid-free paper
and bound in the United States of America.

Library of Congress Cataloging-in-Publication Data

Blodgett, E. D.
  Alice Munro / by E.D. Blodgett.

    p.   cm. — (Twayne's world authors series ; TWAS 800. Canadian
literature)
    Bibliography: p.
    Includes index.
    ISBN 0–8057–8232–X (alk. paper)
    1. Munro, Alice—Criticism and interpretation.   I. Title.
II. Series: Twayne's world authors series ; TWAS 800.   III. Series:
Twayne's world authors series.   Canadian literature.
PR9199.3.M8Z57   1988
813'.54—dc19   88–1599
                                                                          CIP

Contents

About the Author

E. D. Blodgett is professor and former chairman of Comparative Literature at the University of Alberta. He has published a number of volumes of poetry and a collection of essays entitled *Configuration: Essays in the Canadian Literatures*. His research interests include classical and medieval literatures, and he has published widely in such journals as *The Classical Journal, Speculum, Canadian Literature, Essays on Canadian Writing*, the *Canadian Review of Comparative Literature*, and *Voix et Images*. Dr. Blodgett is the editorial secretary of the *Canadian Review of Comparative Literature*, director of the Canadian Division of the Research Institute for Comparative Literature at the University of Alberta, and a fellow of the Royal Society of Canada.

. . . and always when I read your writing I find that it operates on me in very much the same way that poetry does . . .

—John Metcalf, *Journal of Canadian Fiction*

I want to find out—not what happens next, but—what she *will say* next.

—Douglas Barbour, *Open Letter*

Preface

Alice Munro would not claim, I think, to be avant-garde in any contemporary sense. She is neither resolutely metafictional—indeed she is manifestly suspicious of the trick of fiction—nor feminist. Her sole preoccupation is her craft and the persistent shaping of an often stubborn material. She sometimes thinks of herself, in fact, as old-fashioned. Nevertheless, her appeal to women—some of whom find feminist concerns in her work—cannot be denied, nor can a growing appeal to those attracted by her subtly self-aware manner of narration. It is this appeal that has gradually made her one of the more profound contemporary writers of the short story in Canada. For this reason I have chosen to address the various issues raised by her narrative voice, her manner of turning the matter of the story into discourse.

Munro has remarked that "[w]riting for magazines . . . isn't important to [h]er artistically."[1] For this reason I have made it my task to examine her work in the form it has taken in her published collections and novels. Although I treat her first two books as works of apprenticeship (to be distinguished from juvenilia), the skills that are developed so consummately in subsequent texts are already displayed. There she learns how narrators may be used and what levels of discourse are. In the following two texts the relation of the other and self to the narrator are more intensely examined. The fifth chapter addresses a theme that is found often in Munro, namely, that of absence, in a text that achieves a level of ethereality that may not have been foreseen in the earlier texts. The final chapter, devoted to her most recent collection, discusses the use of time as it bears upon character and narration.

Naturally, no book is the product of a single hand, and my debt to other readers of Munro is incalculable. I should particularly like to thank my friends and colleagues Shirley Neuman and David Staines for their stimulating and enthusiastic support during various stages of the preparation of this book. The research assistance of Virginia Henning was invaluable, as well as the patience and accuracy of a devoted typist, Linda Pasmore. My gratitude, as ever, is extended to Alice Munro for being who she is.

E. D. Blodgett

University of Alberta

Acknowledgments

I am grateful to the following publishers of Munro's work for their permission to quote from her texts: McGraw-Hill Ryerson, Macmillan of Canada, Knopf, and McClelland and Stewart.

Chronology

1931   Alice Anne Munro (née Laidlaw) born 10 July in Wingham, Ontario.

1937–1939   Attends Lowertown School, Wingham, Ontario.

1939–1944   Attends Wingham Public School.

1944–1948   Attends Wingham and District High School.

1949   Graduated from Wingham and District High School.

1949–1951   Attends University of Western Ontario.

1950   "The Dimensions of a Shadow," her first published *Folio* [University of Western Ontario] 4, No. 4 (April 1950).

1951   Marries James Munro and moves to Vancouver.

1952–1953   Works at Vancouver Public Library.

1953   Sheila Margaret born 5 October.

1957   Jenny Alison born 4 June.

1963   Moves to Victoria and establishes Munro's Books with her husband.

1966   Andrea Sarah born 8 September.

1968   *Dance of the Happy Shades*. Receives Governor General's Award for Fiction.

1971   *Lives of Girls and Women*. Receives Canadian Booksellers Association International Book Year Award.

1972   Returns to Ontario. Writer-in-Residence, University of Western Ontario.

1973   CBC dramatization of *Lives of Girls and Women*. Daughter Jenny plays leading role.

1974   *Something I've Been Meaning to Tell You*. Receives Great Lakes Colleges Association Award for *Dance of the Happy Shades* and shares with Hugh Hood the Province of Ontario Council for the Arts Award.

1976   Marries Gerald Fremlin and moves to farm near Clinton, Ontario. Awarded Honorary D.Litt., University of Western Ontario.

1977   Receives Canada-Australia Literary Prize and National Magazine Awards Foundation Gold Medal Award for "Accident."

1978   *Who Do You Think You Are?*, entitled *The Beggar Maid* in the English and American editions, *Bettelmädchen* in the German version. Receives Governor General's Award for fiction and is runner-up for Booker Prize.

1980   January–April, Writer-in-Residence, University of British Columbia; September–December, Writer-in-Residence, University of Queensland. Receives Periodical Distributors of Canada's Foundation for the Advancement of Canadian Letters' First Prize for Paperback Fiction for *Who Do You Think You Are?*

1981   July, official visit to the Republic of China.

1982   *The Moons of Jupiter.* January–February, tour of Scandinavia.

1986   *The Progress of Love.* Receives Governor General's Award and Marian Engel Prize.

Chapter One
Signifying a Life

"... how am I to know what I claim to know?"[1]

In reading Alice Munro, it is difficult not to suppose that the relation between her life and the fiction she makes must be intimate and profound, and certainly the frequency of her denials concerning the character of that relationship urge one all the more to find some clue to the meaning of her fiction in her life. The most famous of her disclaimers occurs exergually to *Lives of Girls and Women,* in which she asserts: "This novel is autobiographical in form but not in fact. My family, neighbors and friends did not serve as models." Someone must have thought the contrary or the statement would have been superfluous. And indeed someone did think so, notably the editor of Munro's hometown paper, the Wingham *Advance-Times.* Even ten years after *Lives of Girls and Women* was published the *Advance-Times* continued to bewail her depiction of some of the citizens of Wingham, who must, the editor argues, continue to serve as models: "Sadly enough," he states in a tone of hurt pride, "Wingham people have never had a chance to enjoy the excellence of her writing ability because we have repeatedly been made the butt of soured and cruel introspection on the part of a gifted writer."[2] Thus, there cannot be the slightest doubt that Munro's fiction is rooted in a living world of pained, perhaps even outraged, lives. How can it, however, be otherwise for a writer of novels and fictions who undertakes to create the world from which she has emerged, the world she knows more deeply than any other? For this is precisely what Munro has undertaken, but if we do not carefully heed Munro's warnings, we will not permit her writing to escape the limitations of the documentary, which would be what any morally aroused Wingham editor would wish us to do. To believe, however, that Munro is primarily a realist, that her knowledge depends exclusively upon relations with "family, neighbors and friends," and that no transformation from the literal level is possible is to forsake fiction for the kind of self-righteous and self-serving arrogance that small-town journalism cannot live without.

However strange it may appear that the winner of three Governor General awards should require such a defense, it remains, nevertheless, necessary, for Munro always seems to return us to that kind of reality and to carry the reader complicitously with her as she goes. Part of this we may attribute to her success with the first-person speaker, which carries an attractiveness that makes her appear as Munro herself. We do this, however, at our peril, for Munro is publicly very reticent about herself, and her preference is to distinguish the "incidents" of a story from its "core."[3] The full sense of this distinction I shall return to later. This means, of course, that we may, besides *Lives of Girls and Women*, see aspects of *Who Do You Think You Are?* as drawn from Munro's life, as well as such stories as "The Ottawa Valley," which examines her memory of a daughter's reminiscence of a mother who died of Parkinson's disease, and "The Turkey Season," which may have been set in her father's turkey barn. But setting and character are not to be confused with the core. Hence, it would be more profitable to consider Munro's awareness of her life as analogous to that of her fiction, each possessing a core, which is the fundamental matter that they share.

From such a point of view it is possible to state that Munro's life so far may be divided into three parts, namely, her growing up in Wingham; her approximately two years at the University of Western Ontario and departure with her first husband, James Munro, for British Columbia, where she resided for twenty years; and her return to southwestern Ontario, where she has resided since. It is a life, then, that has a certain form, and one that she seems to be aware of as belonging to an order beyond her control, and this is true even in her understanding of her second marriage: "In some way," she remarked to Joyce Wayne, "it was inevitable that I marry a man from home."[4] That she now lives in Clinton, Ontario, itself not far from Wingham, gives a clear sense of cycle to her life that allows us to see it as departure and return, a movement that parallels her fictional enterprise that cannot help but take what is to hand, transform it, and return it sensibly other than it was—and, as her recent collection suggests, inscribe the turn with a sense of destiny and mystery that does not seem inherent in the initial donnée.

Her life began, then, in Wingham as Alice Laidlaw on 10 July 1931. Her mother, apparently celebrated both in "The Ottawa Valley" and "The Peace of Utrecht," died after a long struggle with Parkinson's disease in 1959. Before the depression she was an elementary-school teacher, and her interest in education may be seen reflected in Ada Jordan in *Lives of Girls and Women*. Her father, Robert E. Laidlaw, had been a trapper in his youth and in 1925 began breeding silver foxes. He married Anne Chamney not long after. They had three children, a boy and two girls, of whom Alice was the eldest. Her father gave up the fur business in 1948, and in 1952 started a poultry farm which became a turkey business. It is as the owner of a fox farm that he appears in the first novel. The farm itself lay on the western outskirts of the town within what Heather Murray calls a pseudo-wilderness, a place fraught with ambiguity and characteristically female in its capability for mediation.[5] For a few years between the end of the fox farm and the start of the turkey business, her father took up a position as a night watchman in a foundry and later remarried. His second wife may have served as a model for Flo, Rose's stepmother in *Who Do You Think You Are?*. Toward the end of his life, Laidlaw began gathering material for his own autobiography, and he published a novel posthumously entitled *The MacGregors: A Novel of an Ontario Pioneer Family* (1979).

Munro's initial schooling was in a two-room schoolhouse. A hardworking student, she was advanced a grade while attending public school. Her writing began during lunch hours in high school where she stayed rather than go home. During this time she finished her first novel, which she has described as "imitation *Wuthering Heights*." As she also remarks, it was "[s]trange and occult, all about love that is stronger than death."[6] The Gothic overtones of the novel are reworked at least in paraphrase in *Lives of Girls and Women,* as a subtext to the final chapter. Her first novel was left in her father's basement and later thrown away by her stepmother, an action reminiscent of the neglect of Uncle Craig's manuscript in *Lives of Girls and Women*. Although Munro has confessed occasionally to having written poetry— and Del, the protagonist of *Lives,* herself wrote some—none has been published.

In the fall of 1949 Munro left Wingham to attend the University of Western Ontario as a scholarship student. She majored in English, and her first stories appeared in *Folio,* a university publication. In her second year at university she married James Munro and they both left Ontario for British Columbia. Part of the disparity of their relationship is hinted at in *Who Do You Think You Are?*, and as Joyce Wayne remarks: "Those who knew the Munros in the West say they never met two people as opposite as Jim and Alice: he all prim and proper, the son of an established Oakville family; Alice exactly the opposite, from a dirt-poor fox farm in Huron County."[7] During the fifties Munro strove with difficulty to raise two daughters and to continue writing, selling a few stories for airing on the CBC. In 1961, a *femme de trente ans* indeed, she rented an office in order to devote herself utterly to her career, and for a period of eight months nothing came at all. She persisted, despite that failure, and two years later the family moved to Victoria to establish Munro's Book Shop. It may be that "The Office" is based upon the period of barrenness endured in the office, but this is not the impression the story gives, for it is one that already dramatizes the problems of narrating as they overcome those of living. The work in the bookshop, however, Munro credits with taking her mind away from what appear to be her problems with writing, and the spare time that permitted the shaping of "The Red Dress—1946" seems to have given her career the impetus it required.[8] The stories with which she grappled during her stay in British Columbia were collected in *Dance of the Happy Shades,*[9] all dedicated to her father.

Her second book, *Lives of Girls and Women,* was written in a period of less than two years. Dedicated to her first husband, it marked, nevertheless, the end of their marriage and her life on the coast. She returned to Huron County after its publication, and one of her reasons was to be near her father.[10] This may be understood, then, as a coming-to-terms with herself and the character of her past. Thus it is difficult to distinguish Munro from "family, neighbors and friends," as she would have us do. The move home, however, is significant because it is a material response to the sense that at heart one is always the same, and that the symbolic flight could not change anything. As Munro has put it, "[s]ome core of you never changes. All the things in our lives that we think are so important might not be, because eventually you discover that you are left with the same person ticking away, the same as when you were five years old, responding to very simple things."[11]

Yet she did not return home immediately, but returned to her former university and served a term as Writer-in-Residence, a role that she has taken at various times at other universities, going once to Australia, which provided the setting for her haunting story, "Bardon Bus." Eventually she settled on a farm near Clinton, Ontario, with her second husband, the federal cartographer Gerald Fremlin. In many respects, her second collection of stories, *Something I've Been Meaning To Tell You,* does not give the impression of being particularly autobiographical or exclusively of Huron County, its stories being set on the west coast and told in the third person. Nevertheless, they evince a speaker continually trying to come closer to the matter, as well as to the narrator of the fiction. She is right, therefore, to suggest that proper access to her work is to perceive it as *personal*, not autobiographical,[12] and it is these stories of her return that first powerfully manifest that quality that is unmistakably Munro's: the unremitting struggle the narrator makes with her material to find its truth in herself. Thus the first story is designed as a mystery in which everyone's personal truth continually diffuses into possibility, and the final story concludes with a speculation that turns upon the helplessness and vulnerability of the speaking subject.

Her second novel, *Who Do You Think You Are?*, and two subsequent collections are wonderful testimonies to the literary significance of Munro's return, for the second novel is a reconsideration of the first, just as her second collection is a reexamination of the narrative procedures of the first. Her third and fourth collections continue to embroider upon problems raised by the earlier ones, persistently probing toward a core that appears to be all the more destined and mysteriously elusive. It is at such a point, moments that are everywhere in *The Moons of Jupiter* and *The Progress of Love*, that one ceases to be troubled by the literal prompting of the story, for "a person or a moment could become a lily on the cloudy river water, perfect and familiar."[13] It is also at such moments that the Winghams of the world have the fortune to be distilled into the only permanence they may have, achieving grandeur as fiction, and it is from this point of view that I have chosen to examine her work.

Space limitations prevent me from discussing everything, and the examples I have chosen are drawn solely from her books, most of which were previously published (sometimes slightly revised) in a number of magazines, including the old *Mayfair*, no longer published, *Chatelaine*, *Redbook*, *Ms*, *McCalls*, *The Canadian Forum*, *The Tamarack Review*, *Queen's Quarterly*, and *Grand Street*. In 1977 she published "Royal Beatings" in the *New Yorker* and currently holds a first-refusal contract with that magazine. Both collections and individual stories have been translated into several languages including French, German, Dutch, and the Scandinavian languages, thus making her work available to a wide and varied audience. Finally, it should be remarked that three of her six collections have received Governor General's awards, and recently she was the recipient of a new award for her whole oeuvre, the Marian Engel Prize.

Because of her own hints and denials, it would be tempting to examine Munro's work as it plays against the material world of which she writes. Certainly place plays a distinctive role in her writing, but "place" is a variable term, and one might seize a sense of it in a remark Munro recently made in an interview with Peter Gzowski: "I write about where I am in life."[14] Place, then, bears upon the speaking self, the "I" that produces a certain statement. This suggests that the true matter is the writing and how it is made. Rooted though her work may be in a certain historical time and geographical space, it is an error, I suggest, to argue that Munro is primarily a realist and to insist, as commentators continue to do, that "[h]er photographic or documentary realism is an essential aspect of her art."[15] It would be more valid to say that this is the negative aspect of art, that against which her writing has struggled in the three and a half decades of her engagement with her craft. Hence, paradoxical as it may appear, I want to argue that it is the "photographic" that is the dark core of her work, and that the brilliance of her art is to present the reader with a more illumined world, a world that no document can bear witness to. More than once Munro returns to this problem and in such a way as to make the reader question whether in fact she has any particular respect for what the art of fiction can do. A notable example is the story "Material" in which the narrator, for all her respect for her first husband's ability to capture a former acquaintance so that she is "lifted out of life and held in light,"[16] cannot, finally, take this as the model she seeks. The reason she gives forms a kind of leitmotiv in Munro's writing. Hugo, author of the story, suffers from the fact that he possesses "authority," that he is not "at the mercy" (44). How much this simple phrase is asked to do! What it does is to remind the reader in a persistent fashion that art is not to be trusted, but also (and more important) for Munro the essential aspect bears less upon what is given as theme than upon how the author/narrator is prepared to suffer from the gift.

Hence, the point of departure for Munro's work is deceptively ambiguous, for while the world lies there as gift, it also lies there as a problem in meaning. Her question as an artist is: How is the world to be understood, and is it possible, finally, to do so? Thus, when we read the first sentence of her first collected story, we observe that it begins not with fact, but with pure hypothesis. The narrator's father asks: "Do you want to go down and see if the Lake's still there?" On one level, of course, this is a father speaking affectionately to his daughter. On another level, however, it opens to the child an unknown world, whose enigmas the story explores without wholly illuminating for the child. It is a question that asks, then, what the bases of the world are, how we know the way it is placed, whether its mysteries are within our ken. From such a moment, Munro's manner of telling a story becomes a discovery procedure, inviting the reader to attend upon how certain truths are reached. This is the dominant pursuit in Munro's fiction; therefore, the registers of truth, falsehood, art, feigning, legend, fantasy, and hearsay combine in various ways to make the reader continually ponder how something is known and understood. No small part of the problem is the role the observer plays, how reliable her memory is, how fair she is with her characters, what tricks time may play upon her perceptions.

What needs to be addressed in Munro, then, is what Roland Barthes has called the hermeneutic code, that is, "the various (formal) terms [that] can be distinguished, suggested, formulated, held in suspense, and finally disclosed."[17] He distinguishes this from a number of other codes that bear upon character, action, culture, and symbol. Its object is the discovery of (some) truth, and, as he argues elsewhere, its procedure may be formulated syntactically like a sentence:

The proposition of truth is a "well-made" sentence; it contains a subject (theme of the enigma), a statement of the question (formulation of the enigma), its question mark (proposal of the enigma), various subordinate and interpolated clauses and catalyses (delays in the answer), all of which precede the ultimate predicate (disclosure).[18]

Once one has understood the operation of such a sentence, it becomes possible to liken Barthes's hermeneutic code to Roman Jakobson's poetic code, for "just as rhyme (notably) structures the poem according to the expectation and desire for recurrence, so that hermeneutic terms structure the enigma according to the expectation and desire for its solution."[19] As a consequence, the hermeneutic code is characterized by the "*delays* (obstacles, stoppages, deviations) in the flow of the discourse."[20] It stands between the process of question and answer by which an enigma is laid bare, and the effort of discourse is "to *arrest* the enigma, to keep it open."[21] The reader's expectation is turned, however, toward the truth, that is, disclosure and closure. At the same time, "[t]his design brings narrative very close to the rite of initiation,"[22] a not infrequent tendency in Munro's stories.

The procedures of the hermeneutic code are marked by paradox: they ask for truth, and yet to find it brings the search to an end. It is precisely this—that closure signifies meaning—that led Munro to revise her understanding of her writing after her early stories, and to question whether meaning in any static, permanent form may be reached. Thus her development as a writer may be understood as a struggle with the problem of significance, that is, what the method of signifying might mean. It is here that her brief against art begins, for art is a method that may come to be truth. When that occurs, one of the problems of hermeneutics surfaces, for if "[t]he content of a claim of truth is not separable from the method by which it is vindicated,"[23] it may be that what happens in Hugo's version in "Material" will occur, and truth will be obscured by art. To overcome such a possibility, Munro moved against the clarity of a conclusion that would shed significance in an illuminating word or phrase. She also began to develop with increased care tactics of delay, such that the method would appear to be no method, as if meaning were to be found in the act of postponing. Thus, to a certain extent, Munro's art may be said to coincide with some of Jacques Derrida's thinking in their mutual effort to posit understanding not in the apparently harmonious reconciliation of opposites, but rather in the movement that puts off such coming together. An essential aspect, then, of Munro's art turns upon the awareness that the possibility of likeness that would permit us to see a clear pattern in events is continually worn down by time, by aging, by misperception. Rather than see things neatly conjoining, we are more often struck by the improbability of such a thing happening. At such a point, delay is no longer an aesthetic strategy; it becomes, rather, a primal way of seeing and articulating a world. It is then that the insidious character of its working becomes more apparent, for just as events are postponed, so they are deferred, that is, carried away.

Derrida, of course, returns often to this problem, for this understanding is necessary to an understanding of how linguistics and metaphysics operate. Although it would be inappropriate here to provide a full exposition of what he calls *différance,* it should be observed that it is developed from a French verb that means both to differ and to defer. Its bearing on writing springs from the fact that nothing can be said all at once; and it is a mark of the act of writing, as Derrida distinguishes it from speaking, to separate the narrator from the narrated, to create a kind of distance that differs and defers. Thus what the writer wants to recapture is continually put off with each word that would make an effort to seize it. The real, then, that one has known and experienced, once it enters language, enters a system of signs that depend in their sound and sense upon difference. Furthermore, once it enters discourse, it is inhabited by time as we move through the statement. At what moment can we say that the object of our quest is made present again, that is, re-presented? The object as it becomes written is entrapped by deferral, according to Derrida, in an act of spacing which

is temporization, the detour and postponement by means of which intuition, perception, consummation—in a word, the relationship to the present, the reference to a present reality, to a *being*—are always *deferred.* Deferred by virtue of the very principle of difference which holds that an element functions and signifies, takes on or conveys meaning, only by referring to another past or future element in an economy of traces.[24]

The play of difference is sufficient, then, to allow an interplay of time with space, so that the movement of time, which is inscribed in narrating, carries us through a network of spatial relations, each of which prevents by postponing the presencing of the desired object.

One of the frequent ways in which Munro's stuggle with *différance* manifests itself is in the poignancy of her first-person narrators as they begin to open a space between their former (narrated) and present (narrating) selves. It is here that her observation, "I write about where I am in life," may be said to come most into play, for in the act of writing the self as a whole being, couched in the words "I am," becomes problematic and suggests Derrida's remark "that the subject, and first of all the conscious and speaking subject, depends upon the system of differences and the movement of *différance,* that the subject is constituted only in being divided from itself, in becoming space, in temporizing, in deferral . . ."[25] But awareness of such a plight and its consequences for knowing and writing lead to further problems. So we find the narrator at the conclusion of "The Ottawa Valley" having abandoned method for truth (she does not tell "a proper story"[26]), having spaced time into "a series of snapshots," having evidently deferred closure in her search for her mother, only to discover that she has not been able, finally, to re-present the figure sought. The figure sought, the speaker's mother, is not to be clearly found because she is so much a part of the narrating "I". We are left with the subject, and "[s]ubjectivity," as Derrida argues, "—like objectivity—is an effect of *différance.*"[27]

Thus it has been my desire to allow the narrator to become the object of my reading of Munro, for it is that marvelous, sometimes prismatic, focus that so often represents the problem of knowing, explaining, and as it gradually becomes absorbed by the story as it is made into a text. The narrator, furthermore, is a hermeneutic problem whose presence in the text—separate from her narrated self and vainly trying to re-place herself—exemplifies how hard it is to speak of the presence of the real in Munro, and how every effort to find it is equally vain.

To say as much, however, allows me to return to her "life." We have seen it to be characterized by departure and return, thus describing a circle in space and time. Its significance, however, lies in its being an analogue, perhaps, to the circle of hermeneutics, that is, the method by which a text is construed by continually moving round from part to whole. Not only may we speak of Munro's life so, but we should speak a fortiori of her writing in the same manner, for it is exactly what critics have occasionally faulted her for—the continual elaboration of the similar—that has allowed Munro to make her material the matter of the subject. Thus, rather than photographing the object, she illumines the subject, just as someone who has left his birthplace for some twenty years is a native upon return, but a native displaced. In the same way the meaning that hermeneutics would disclose is displaced by postponement, and the truth of method (art) gives way to the disclosure in the relation of parts. It is the process by which the self becomes a text, falling apart as it does so. But as a text, and it is to this perception of the real that Munro seems inevitably to progress, the self becomes no other than what it is, returning, so to speak, to itself. Within all the play of signifiers of which a text and a self are composed, the finished narration acquires a kind of mark of destiny and perfection, some inescapable core. At least this appears as one of the ineluctable signs of Munro's mature work, in which the narrator gradually glides into the narration, and its arrangement into a certain disposition of parts becomes the narrator's as well, illuminating her at once as giver and receiver of the world remade. "I write about where I am in life": or should we not say that she writes about where she is in the text that her life, finally, is?

My central preoccupation here, then, is how Munro narrates, proceeding from Munro's own marking of the speaker as that center from which story and discourse proceed. For this reason, I have frequently had recourse to problems of focalization in her text. It is, therefore, important that we understand the term and its procedures, for if we do not we may overlook much of the play that Munro makes between past and present as perceived by narrator, protagonist, and other characters. Furthermore, there is the danger of us failing to perceive the complex relationship between Munro as author, implied author, and narrator as such, which would permit us to fall into the trap of mere autobiography and would obscure the degree to which the apparent search for the real in Munro is a search for self. The moment when focalization in narration becomes crucial is when the narrator speaks in the first person and refers to herself in the past, for there are clearly differences between the perception of an adult and a child, while both states are ambiguously held in the pronoun "I." Thus an action may be narrated by an adult narrator, but the perspective may be that of the child. The same would be valid for a narrator and a character, permitting the reader to distinguish perspectives.[28]

My purpose in using the term *focalization* is to describe a narrative process, and by *focalizer* I want to describe the agent of the process. Focalization is the means by which story (events arranged into plot sequence) are presented in narrative discourse. Although the term may appear to be synonymous with *perspective,* it is not. It has the advantage, furthermore, of examining the relationship between aspects of the first-person narrator speaking of herself at the moment of narrating and of herself in the narrated past. Such a narrator primarily identifies herself as *I,* but the referent of the pronoun is two different states of mind, one younger and one more mature. The term *focalizer* is especially useful in assisting us to perceive two perspectives that are, in the act of narrating, kept distinct and still interacting. Unlike perspective, focalization does not carry implications developed in the visual arts that suggest a static position to which the composition relates. It connotes, rather, the continuous adjustments of film, particularly as these adjustments bear upon changing perceptions and cognitions of the focalizing character. The use of such terms are of inestimable value in the analysis of such writers as Alice Munro, who hold past and present, not to speak of even more complicated zones of time in between, in continual suspension. It might be suggested that the more common term *focus* also refers to this function, but this is even more abstract. Characters focus; by doing so they participate in the various focalizations perceptible in the narrative. *Point* of view, finally, suggests a unified sensibility. It is precisely this unity that Munro's understanding of fiction—particularly the narration of the self—makes problematic. To speak, therefore, of a narrator's perspective obscures the fact a narrator's point of view is not single, but often multiple, as it plays upon various moments of the *I*'s self-perception in the narrating *now* and the narrated *then*'s.

The distinctions that the term *focalization* permits also help us with others. When we speak of someone's "story," we mean as much the person's life. But as soon as we prepare the story by means of a certain discourse, voice, and plays with time, proleptically alluding to things to come and explaining with the backward glance of analepsis, we begin to see that story and life are not unchanging entities that will always be the same when we stop talking. They are, as produced by fiction, hermeneutical problems that do not simplify the direct relation one would like to make between word and referent. One might say that the relation of story to life is analogous to that which obtains between our several selves and discourse. The relations are chiastic, and not direct. Thus all returns to past, story ("the way things were"), life ("the way I was") are mediated; and what is characteristic of Munro's method is the use of indirection that makes it palpably clear to the reader that she wants us to see the dominance of mediation. Because, however, of her awareness of this dominance, she also calls to our attention that just as the quest for knowledge may be understood as a sentence, as Barthes suggests, so the full understanding of ourselves may be understood as a matter that can only be understood as a certain syntax of relations. Such an awareness on Munro's part is one that takes her beyond the play of focalization into complex problems of textual propriety, indicating how narrators are part of a text and how they relate to other levels of authorial voice. It is brooding upon these problems that brings Munro home to the complexity of self, and home in such a way as to overcome the sense of chaos and chance that sometimes seems to reign unchallenged in her work.

Thus one can trace three phases in her work that range from what appears to be the arbitrary positing of meaning, characterized by a highly directed narrator, to a period in which the narrator is brought to a heightened sense of her radical vulnerability that springs from what she does not know or what is withheld from her by an implied author. In her most recent work, however, Munro, having carefully attended to the problem of meaning and its deceptions, has so shaped her texts as to make it appear that everyone is somehow subordinate to the destiny of discourse. This would suggest that the vulnerability, which she requires for understanding, passes by analogy from the narrating voice to the author herself, suggesting, if only tautologically, that she is as much in the dark as her narrators. The illumination of her darkness is the signifying act of the text as if—reminding one of Jacques Lacan, the philosopher of psychoanalysis—the self were a text, and a finished text, a destiny of the self. Because it is the author's destiny to go on producing texts, one cannot help but feel that the return to self, no matter how necessary it may (be made to) appear, is itself an illusion and supreme fiction governing the others. So it is, nevertheless, that we are drawn to Munro's work somehow through, away from, and back to, her life, investing her work with the sign of necessity, poignancy, and the knowledge of its impermanence that would find itself again as text only to lose itself in its destiny as other. Words only can "get it," if only for the moment.

Chapter Two
Deferring to Difference
Dance of the Happy Shades

> Instead of splashing the colours out and trusting they will all
> come together, I have to know the design.[1]

The titles of Munro's stories and collections are chosen with precision
and care, and to begin properly with her work, one ought to begin
right there. The titles of her collections serve a dual purpose, for they
possess both a general and particular reference. As a reference to particular
stories, they suggest one of the levels of symbolic and thematic meaning.
As an indication of the collection as a whole, these meanings multiply.[2]
As a title for a first collection, *Dance of the Happy Shades* is a superb
intimation of the author's initial preoccupations, and it was so well
chosen that its meanings appear to proliferate throughout the whole
work.

"Dance of the Happy Shades" is the title of one of the movements
from Gluck's opera, *Orphée et Euridice*. It recalls that moment when
Orpheus in the underworld, through the sheer power of his music,
moves the shades to dance. Inasmuch as Orpheus is the classical archetype
of the poet, we are to assume, I think, that it is music combined with
the spell of language that endows the shades with the semblance of
life. The allusion, then, to Orpheus is in itself happy, for it gathers
into itself both the role of speech and telling, as well as the relation
between this and other worlds of experience, which are the worlds of
life and death, and ourselves in other guises. The shades are happy
insofar as they are blessed by the spell of speech that animates them.
Their dance, finally, may be taken as a metaphor of the movements
they enact, the patterns that they play out within the range of the
teller's voice.

The function of our allusion to Orpheus need not end at such a
point. As Dante tells us, the descent through the underworld is a spiral
in which our vision of the human soul is given with an absolute clarity,
despite the fact that the meaning of the vision is only temporarily true.

14

This means for Dante, at least, that the narrative and the characters it calls into life must reckon both with clarity and meaning, and the fact that each must bear an equivalent value. The center of the *Purgatory* is devoted to such a reckoning, and once the reader has passed that point of the poem's unfolding there can be no doubt that one of the purposes of Dante's art is to put us on the threshold of a certain truth.

To enter Munro's narrative art by way of Dante's may seem like a long and somewhat cumbersome detour. Munro does not pretend to the style, nor to the vision, of epic. Her stories are of moderate length, and two attempts at a novel could not be sustained except in linked stories. My overture to Dante has another purpose. I want to suggest, contrary to some readings of Munro, that her art aims beyond what we might take realism to be.[3] In fact, the dissatisfaction that not only some of her narrators but also Munro herself express is a sign that the problem with writing and language is that they are so deceptive that the core of truth one seeks is frequently deflected by the very language one uses. Whatever this core is, it only appears possible to seize it by indirection: no direct statement will grasp it. Thus, like Dante, one circles toward illumination. This means that whoever tells the story gives it its special stamp, and it is a stamp that is powerfully governed by the moves the speaker seems impelled to take.

The moves acquire their design from Munro's intense preoccupation with time and its passage. Thus it is not enough to evoke "that time," to find the exact diction that gives it voice. What becomes paramount is the dramatization of the speaker's peculiar awareness of transience that permits her to ask in the title of her fourth book, *Who Do You Think You Are?* Time passes through such subtle modes of perception that it appears only natural to wonder what connection might exist between levels of consciousness that would be sufficient to constitute an integrated self. The attraction of the question resides in its mildly deprecating irony, designed to dispel pretension. The irony, however, only enhances what is central in the question: "Do you think you are anyone at all?"

The question springs from the predicament that time poses for the narrator, posed not simply between a past and a present, but within a plurality of presents that unfold in the course of narrating and within the *changed* pasts that spring from the continuous change of insight.[4] The art is to crystallize the insights, and for Munro, in a manner suggestive of James Joyce and Dante, the crystallization in her early stories, at least, almost inevitably leads to closures radiant with epiphany.[5]

This, perhaps, is what John Metcalf endeavors to underline when he observes that Munro "is not a 'realist'; she is a marvellously *poetic* writer."[6] The question we should ask ourselves, then, is how the poetry emerges.

To begin with the first story in the collection, "Walker Brothers Cowboy," is characteristic of Munro's sense of exactly how the "story" relates to its telling.[7] We read: "After supper my father says, 'Want to go down and see if the Lake's still there?' " (1). It is a question that immediately establishes an intimacy between father and narrator. We infer, moreover, that the lake has existed before the teller's first words. Consequently, the initial words, "After supper," point both forward into the narration and elsewhere into the story whose material the narrator organizes. This double perspective acts, then, as a kind of "cut" between moments of implicitly continuous action, and we are led to believe that we as readers are being quietly drawn into that action. This gives the sense of the "natural" that hovers over the narration at all times. The double character established by the opening has, however, other aspects of doubleness. Inasmuch as the story seems to be resumed often, we are also led to infer that what at first appears natural also possesses an artificial aspect. The page itself allows us in effect to see the narrator's constant return to the "story" as she continually reexamines and revises what she is telling. So we read, following the prefatory section on the lake, "[m]y father has a job, selling for Walker Brothers" (3). This statement is preceded by a gap in the text sufficient to indicate that a new section has begun. What the relation between the lake and Walker Brothers means is unclear, but the narrative design is such that we are to see the telling as a method of exploration.

The first problem, then, of Munro's narration is that it assumes the shape of exploration, and the burden for the reader is knowing how to assess the discovery. In her early stories Munro tends to draw the various threads of the narration together in a summary insight, thus giving a weight to the story's closure that is somewhat disproportionate to the apparently more casual construction of the rest of the story.[8] As a consequence, the role of the narrator dominates. She does not dominate, however, simply because she is the teller, but rather because of the intimacy she enjoys in her relation to the protagonist. In "Walker Brothers Cowboy" that intimacy rests upon the fact that the narration is in the first person. The narrator knows because she *was* the figure narrated. I emphasize the verb because it is important to bear in mind that by far the majority of stories of this type are designed to close upon insights that remove a level of innocence from the protagonist's self-understanding. She acquires a changed level of understanding analeptically, *after* the event. Thus the story is marked by how it is told in order to reach the moment that will not only clarify the problem, but also allow the teller to emerge from it into a changed silence. But closure is often as ambiguous as beginning, and so one of the implicit hopes of telling—to exorcise the memory, thus freeing oneself from it—is rarely realized.[9]

Intimacy, however, is at once the object of exploration, as well as the means by which it is for the moment attained. Thus to model the structure of the story on the order of a declarative statement would be insufficient. This is particularly true inasmuch as Munro's narrators are frequently older than the protagonist. Furthermore, they possess all the ambiguity of being who the protagonist was but is no longer. One thinks of Charles Dickens's *Great Expectations* as one method of resolving this issue, but the design of the short story urges one to dispense with a linear frame. What Munro's early narrators endeavor to do is to find the meaning in a story that does not appear to have one. Therefore, a clue might be anywhere, and it might be of use at anytime. To say as much is to suggest how spatial Munro's use of narrative time is,[10] and one can in fact liken it to a game board in which moves may be made at any moment—away or toward the object—that will bring the figure through. Thus time in Munro appears to owe more to chance than anything resembling clock time. Nevertheless, the space within which the figure plays always appears to move along various layers of time, part of the object being to find how these layers relate. No single layer, however, gives the meaning, so one can begin almost anywhere.

We can begin, as the narrator does, by raising a question about the existence of the lake. How careful that question now seems upon rereading. What appears at first to be such an ordinary kind of question between father and daughter, now bids us pause upon the notion of its being "still there." And that is precisely the question that is answered in the closing paragraph of the prefatory section. We learn that once indeed there was no lake, and we may assume that it is perfectly possible for the lake to change again as a result of future geological transformations. This information is preceded by what also appears an ordinary entry into the story—a walk through the town to the outskirts, and then to places where tramps dwell, causing some alarm in the protagonist. Such a passage allows Munro to display the kind of skill at description for which she has acquired her celebrity, but part of the point of this opening sequence is to foreshadow the body of the story, which also draws the protagonist away from the known world of sure convention to a world where she can only guess at meaning and action. Furthermore, the movement is also a movement into the layers of time through which Munro's characters are somehow condemned to move and only by moments find order in. This is announced in what appears to be simply part of a gesture toward the real when she remarks, when they reach a part of the town that is used as a resort, "the part of the town we used to know when we lived at Dungannon and came here three or four times a summer, to the Lake" (2). The lake is not only a resort, it is where the grain boats wallow—"ancient, rusty"—full of their other kinds of pasts. The father's discourse on the lake's history then leads to the narrator's conclusions, focalized in herself as child: "He was not alive when this century started. I will be barely alive—old, old—when it ends. I do not like to think of it. I wish the Lake to be always just a lake, with the safe-swimming floats marking it, and the breakwater and the lights of Tuppertown" (3). Thus, by the end of the section, we discover that the father's question is proleptic in its power to foreshadow, allowing us to see the weight that intimacy must bear. Who the protagonist is as she relates to her father cannot be known directly, nor once and for all, but must be picked up in the same way as the narrator's remembering eyes pick up the Silverwoods Ice Cream signs, the playing children like she is and was, "the humble nameless weeds," "the shifting, precarious path boys have made" (2). We are eased not only into times, but also—and somehow simultaneously—into the winnowed psychological effect these have on the narrator as they are illuminated through her younger self.

The second section appears to forecast the father's life as a traveling salesman, but even that new beginning in a time unspecified with respect to the story's opening movement is interrupted by a turn toward the narrator's mother's attitude to the kinds of songs he sings en route. Through such a shift, the linearity of the narrative is immediately broken in order to provide a perspective on the father, rather than on the daughter. The mother's world, the domestic world, is also not without its dangers, for her mother is not one to conform to her neighbor's way of life: she would be a "lady" (5). Poverty, we are told, is a result of fate, and so we discover that even people are subject to the same inexplicable changes that lakes may undergo. Thus the world of the protagonist that extends from home as far as the mysteries

of the geological past is itself a "shifting, precarious path" that can
lead anywhere danger is.

The trip is finally undertaken, and it is punctuated by various
experiences in the back country beyond the highway. What marks the
first part of the section is its random character: "One yard after another
. . ." (9). It is a world whose definition is provided by the narrator:
"The nineteen-thirties. How much this kind of farmhouse, this kind
of afternoon, seem to me to belong to that one decade in time, just
as my father's hat does, his bright flared tie, our car with its wide
running board (an Essex, and long past its prime)" (8). That the ride
is a compound of others is made apparent by one aside in which he
tries "to make my mother laugh" (8). As a result, one can never escape
the sense that nothing exists free of its implication in something else.
And that sense, finally, is focused in the second section of the journey
in which the protagonist and her brother—her mother left this time at
home—visit with their father one of his old girlfriends. It is this scene
that leads the protagonist to the moment of insight that for that time
holds the several threads of the story in ambiguous suspension.

The significance of the episode lies in the impact it has upon the
protagonist. Her first awareness that it possesses mysterious qualities
emerges when she discovers that her father has gone beyond his assigned
territory. This moment of perception corresponds to the successive
transgressions of frontiers in the initial section, that carry her beyond
the safety of home to the larger risks the outer world and the past
may hold in store. All of these risks are gathered in her growing
awareness of the meaning of the relationship between her father and
Nora, the former girlfriend. Part of the attraction of the scene is the
delicacy with which the narrator suggests the character of the relationship.
In response, for example, to one of the father's remarks, Nora laughs,
"her laugh abrupt and somewhat angry" (11). Are we to infer that
this is a normal tone in her laughter or is she reflecting on an unspoken
regret?[11] When she laughs later, there is no trace of anger, but something
of the same attitude appears toward the end of the scene when the
girl's father observes that he has taken up a lot of Nora's time. Nora's
reply is given "bitterly" (17), and the tone is sufficient to confirm the
first of our inferences. The laughter is not normal and hides a certain
regret. In one word, moreover, when Nora simply says " 'Time' " (17),
we are reminded of the degree to which all the characters are imbedded
in their own time, their separate perceptions of it, and how profoundly
transient they are, all traveling through the precarious paths of their

own territories. Time is what brings them to recognition, and the recognition carries with it the shape, at once shifting and precarious, of their isolation from each other.

The focus of the story, however, belongs to the narrator, and on the return drive she begins to reckon with what has passed. Not wholly aware that what has happened to her father is to be attributed to Nora—perhaps it is, rather, "[t]he whiskey, maybe the dancing" (18)— she becomes gradually aware that the past is a psychological domain that makes of those who appear so intimately ours something other and mysterious:

I feel my father's life flowing back from our car in the last of the afternoon, darkening and turning strange, like a landscape that has an enchantment on it, making it kindly, ordinary and familiar while you are looking at it, but changing it, once your back is turned, into something you will never know, with all kinds of weathers, and distances you cannot imagine. (18)

Thus in a single, gathering metaphor the father locates for the remembering narrator all the mysteries of difference—the levels of time and its passing, varieties of place and the meanings they contain, directions of character that descend through father and mother—that the narrative suggests and discovers.

The next two stories follow a similar method to the first: in each the governing structure is that of a venture into an undiscovered world. The differences between them, however, are important, for they display part of Munro's ease with distinctive modes of insight. The first, "Images," follows the mode of the father as his daughter's guide into a special kind of past, one of which is described in "The Shining Houses" (the second story) as possessing "remembered episodes" that, when told, "emerged each time with slight differences of content, meaning, colour, yet with a pure reality that usually attaches to things which are at least pure legend" (19). Although the primary function of this comment belongs to this story, we may extend it and take it as a general characteristic of the oral tale. Part of the truth-value of the oral tale resides in its ability to merge with a kind of collective memory, issuing from a figure invested with authority.[12] Thus when the father leads the daughter along the lake and subsequently into and beyond his territory, he provides her with the powers that permit the real to acquire its effect through its grounding in legend. This is precisely what happens in "Images."

The story is set in three parts, the first announcing the possible theme of finding a husband for the father's cousin. She has arrived to take care of the protagonist's ailing mother. She also brings into the house an almost alien presence, and at the conclusion of the section the protagonist observes the shadows that she and her father cast. The narrator is clear about what the protagonist is doing: " 'I watched the shadows instead of the people' " (35). The people are not, however, excluded from her vision—the narrator is only emphasizing in a characteristic fashion the shadow. The reason for this is simply stated: "I was trying to understand the danger, to read the signs of invasion" (35). This is the clue, then, that guides the reader into the body of the story when, echoing the opening of "Walker Brothers Cowboy," she observes: "My father said, 'Do you want to come with me and look at the traps?' " (35).

Their venturing forth takes them to the Wawanash River, whose role is as proleptic as the protagonist's presentiments of danger. Its noise, the narrator remarks, "was not loud but deep, and seemed to come from way down in the middle of it, some hidden place where the water issued with a roar from underground" (37). Even rivers are perceived to cast shadows, and in fact the curving of the river causes her to remark that her sense of direction has been lost. And so she becomes, with a sympathy often to be observed in Munro's protagonists, a kind of victim of the place she enters. In this she suggests the figures of romance, both Gothic and medieval, for whom the self is rarely integrated before the closure of the narration, and often only a sign whose articulation is displayed by the world that envelops them. This is another way of thickening the story with orality, by enlarging the character and urging the reader to see her as an avatar of others, allowing her to merge into our memory of similar figures.

In "Images" the girl is separated at a certain moment from her father; it is then that the shadow-figure enters the narrative carrying a hatchet. Far from being shocked, the narrator feels a moment of "recognition" (38). Because he has no specificity as yet for the observing girl, he is a type, a figure that she and all of us know: "All my life I had known there was a man like this and he was behind doors, around the corner at the dark end of a hall. So now I saw him and just waited, like a child in an old negative, electrified against the dark noon sky, with blazing hair and burned out Orphan Annie eyes" (38). The allusions to popular culture, particularly the slightly veiled gesture toward the movie *High Noon,* which conflates curiously with Arthur

Koestler's *Darkness at Noon*, assist both of the similes to generalize, but in a paradoxically precise way. Both stranger and girl become larger, more legendary than their "ordinary" selves. The man, of course, is known to the father: he possesses a name and a past. Because of the legendary qualities with which the narrator has invested him through the perceiving protagonist, the figure now acquires an ironic character, forcing an adjustment to the whole process of discovery with which she is engaged. The world through the protagonist's eyes, however, retains its quality of romance. Because the stranger gives it its significance, she sees she has entered a wasteland of "dead grass" (39) and that, like the river that issues from below ground, the man lives in a cellar.

What she discovers is a figure who in his own madness is so bound to his own solipsistic time that any exchange with him must always accept his fantasy of how the Silases burned his house down. Thus the protagonist's father describes him in the concluding section as " 'Old Joe Phippen that lives up in no man's land beyond the bush' " (43). This locates him in a land of shadow beyond the father's territory, but to which he has, nevertheless, access. The discovery, finally, that Phippen himself burned his house down, that the Silases are his own fantasy, leads the narrator in final statement, however, to the insight that the relationship between the legendary and the real is where the story takes shape, thus suggesting the dependence of story upon figure and shadow, river and depth. She becomes "[l]ike the children in fairy stories who have seen their parents make pacts with terrifying strangers, who have discovered that our fears are based on nothing but the truth, but who come back fresh from marvellous escapes and take up their knives and forks, with humility and good manners . . ." (43). Almost unnoticed in this sentence, the word *our* stands out, prompting us to accept the likeness, apply it to ourselves, and recognize what we take to be the level of the real in the story. It is a real, however, that is reached, as we are plainly told, by means of a simile: the narrator perceives herself at this moment "[l]ike the children in fairy stories," the real emerging from something more archetypal.

The other significant phrase in the sentence is "nothing but the truth," which is a leitmotiv in Munro the significance of which is more fully explored in subsequent texts. I would signal now what I have already mentioned as typical in Munro at this stage, and that is the function of closure to reflect upon the story in order to adumbrate its truth as specific meaning. This is, it would appear, the principal function of Munro's narrators—to suggest the meaning by both indirection and reflection.[13] The penultimate story in the collection, "The Peace of Utrecht," illustrates this point.

The title reminds one of the treaty that concluded the wars of the Spanish Succession (1713). Its pertinence for the history of Canada is seen in the change of power between the French and the English by which the latter acquired Nova Scotia, Newfoundland, and posts on Hudson's Bay. It was the beginning of the end of France's rule in North America. How does this knowledge affect the story? Ostensibly it is the subject of a highschool paper written by the protagonist. The narrative itself analogously reflects a moment in the lives of two sisters and their awkward efforts to come to terms with the nature of their relationship. The story is clearly divided into two parts by the use of numerals (extremely rare in Munro), each of these is further divided by spacing into several reprises, and each part begins by announcing a return visit. Thus it follows the pattern of a movement of discovery. Moreover, the process of discovery, projected into the narrative design, is governed by indirection, and the reader continually wants to know what is being sought. The shape of the story gives no precise reply, and this lack of response is a layer of Munro's craft that is also a thematic level of the story. The reader must follow the narrator, surrendering to narrative unfoldings, perceiving that discovery is a relative process, each insight modified by a new one. This accords well with an implication of the title that no peace is lasting. We may also understand the title in another way. If the real recovers its character of truth in the legendary, the teller must in some way abandon herself to the possibilities of not one but several stories impinging upon each other. Because the meaning that Helen seeks is a function of her relationship with her sister Maddy, as well as their two aunts and dead mother, her story must allow for certain kinds of transgressions. By allowing for them, the meaning she seeks is not wholly centered upon herself, but expands into a larger, familial dimension. This dimension also includes Helen's daughter, and it is through her, her tone of voice in seeing the family house for the first time, that we are reminded of how the real arises from the legendary, and also of the difference between them: her voice "contained the whole flatness and strangeness of the moment in which is revealed the source of legends, the unsatisfactory, apologetic and persistent reality" (197). To reach the real, one must go through legend—snatches of recollection that spring from the moment. Under such circumstances narrating cannot, therefore, proceed in a linear fashion. It can only reach points where present time is suspended. We cannot tell where suspension will lead, and if it leads nowhere—a point marked by gaps in the page—then the story must resume at another point. Meaning is a process of unraveling.

What makes the process of unraveling painful is the belief that the threads that compose the characters' lives are separate, playing off against the gradual perception that they are not. We have seen already how unexpected convergences occur in "Walker Brothers Cowboy" and "Images," and the significance of these convergences lies in the realization of how much we live in our own isolated lines of time, only occasionally touching and being illuminated by those of others. Who Helen is cannot be known without knowing where Maddy fits into her life, but her initial perception of herself in relation to her sister is one of rejection: "as for the past we make so much of sharing we do not really share it at all, each of us keeping it jealously to herself, thinking privately that the other has turned alien, and forfeited her claim" (190). The word "alien," however, is a clue: discovery needs the alien as a means of acquiring an unknown intimacy. Thus the design of successive reprises appears to arise naturally from the differences between the sisters, the apparent dead-ends of their intercourse. The story, then, begins with an effort to assess how Maddy coped with their invalid mother, what arrangement she has made with a married man, and the sense of depression this brings upon the protagonist. The next two sections open Helen to her relationship to the small town of her childhood, forcing her to come to terms with her sense of guilt for abandoning her mother to Maddy. All of this is designed to lead her to some recovery of her mother's meaning for her and who she was for herself some ten years earlier, as if her present sense of self could only be understood through the memory of her younger self at a critical period.

Part of the difference that exists between the real and the legendary and that is apparent in the play between them as they seek accommodation is seen in the ambiguity of the reflecting first-person narrator in the act of recollection. The ambiguity rests in the fact that the referent for "I" is either in the present or the past. When the narrator is in the act of recovering the "I" of the past, she is always coloring it by her present knowledge, thus always implying the unrealized absence of the "I" she is trying to recall. Thus when she remembers her mother's voice, she observes: "It seemed to me that I could not close the door behind me without hearing my mother's ruined voice call out to me, and feeling myself go heavy all over as I prepared to answer it" (198). The movement of focalization in this sentence is significant, for it shows how the role of focalizer shifts between narrator and protagonist, older and younger self, generating a characteristic type of exchange in Munro's narration. "It seemed to me that I" is an utterance that permits focalization to capture the younger self, but the adjective "ruined," coming later in the sentence, seems to shift focalization back to the narrator, the older, commenting self. One might argue that this utterance, however, is ambiguous, that the almost-grown woman of her younger self may have been capable of thinking "ruined." Other sentences make the difference more apparent: "the feelings of hysteria which Maddy and I once dissipated in a great deal of brutal laughter, now began to seem partly imaginary; I felt the beginnings of a secret, guilty estrangement" (201). Here in the same sentence "I" refers to both past and present, and is used to constitute difference, even suggesting that something in the former "I" when seen in retrospect seems "partly imaginary." The act of remembrance that the narrator performs carries, then, a special kind of ambiguity: every effort that the narrator as focalizer makes to recapture herself in former relationships by the use of exact qualification runs the risk of separating past from present, of separating herself from herself. Recalling another moment of her mother's desperation, she notes: "Such theatricality humiliated us almost to death; yet now I think that without that egoism feeding stubbornly even on disaster she might have sunk rapidly into some dim vegetable life" (199). The shift of perspective that arises from the change of focalization, clearly marked by the semicolon, permits what can occur only through separation, and that is a certain kind of reconciliation. Thus the effect of the alien that marks the opening section, as well as the narrative play with the self as other, are both necessary for the kind of understanding that the story seeks. In fact, part of the function of narrative play and the several reprises of the narrative design, along with the gaps they create, is to evoke the shadows that characters leave. Such evocation is the level of legend.

The second part of the story shifts to Helen's relationship with her two aunts. Part of the purpose of evoking the aunts is to reflect on two other sisters and how they could serve as a parody of Helen and Maddy if Helen had stayed at home. As the narrator observes, "I had a fascinating glimpse of Maddy and myself, grown old, caught back in the web of sisterhood after everything else has disappeared, making tea for some young, loved and essentially unimportant relative—and exhibiting just such a polished relationship. . . ." (203). Clearly setting off the aunts in their own section permits not only reflection but also the degree of irony that distance provides when considering what is humorously possible. The aunts intimate, moreover, the legendary to the degree that they fulfill "stylized and simplified roles" (203–4), which prompts the narrator to speculate whether they do it from fear or because they are aware that no genuine communication is after all possible. Such a speculation is sufficient to remind us that theirs is the level of the false legend called into presence through parody. Helen's gropings with Maddy are by contrast all the more real, and therefore fraught with the heavier burden of tangled pasts.

The design of the narrative suggests that meeting with the aunts is necessary to summon forth whatever conclusion the story has. For, following her visit, the narrator returns to confront Maddy again, making the singular gesture of reconciliation that the story contains. The effect is cathartic for Maddy, who confesses her inability to take herself from home and to find a way to see her past from another perspective as Helen has managed to do. The moment is important, no matter how brief it may be, for it enables them to do what the two aunts presumably are incapable of, and it enacts what is symbolically hinted at in the story's title. They reach a peace of sorts.

It would be useful to pause for a moment and consider the character of discovery that is made in these three stories, for they are in many ways emblematic of Munro's technique. Although the level of focalization passes back and forth between protagonist and narrator, establishing an order of internal reflection, another order of reflection is created between protagonist / narrator and other characters. She is a multiple reflector both internally and externally. Thus the closure of "The Peace of Utrecht" shifts the emphasis from Helen to Maddy; and while we see Maddy through Helen's eyes, it is Maddy's recognition of her destiny that casts its shade over the story. It does not displace Helen's, but it reorders our perception of it. It underscores the symbolic meaning of the bipartite structure of the story in which emphasis shifts from Helen as schoolgirl to her role as sister, which is neatly foregrounded in the relationship of the two aunts. Helen has had her experience just before the conclusion of the first part, in which some earlier experience reminiscent of Proust "had been transformed into something curiously meaningful" (202). Helen has for the moment recaptured something of her past, but the design of the story makes it clear that this is not all, nor is it perhaps what she is meant to do. The meaning is not clarified, and the event itself is barely elaborated upon. The story suggests, rather, that the fuller meaning of Helen is in her relationship with her sister.

The same kind of conclusion may be drawn from "Walker Brothers Cowboy" and "Images." In each story the protagonist possesses an intimate, reflective rapport with the narrator, and she—in this double role[14]—is used as a reflector of other experiences in which she participates and whose meanings only become significant through the manner by which they are filtered through her perceiving consciousness. A consequence of this filtering is a pattern of absence and apparent recovery that becomes part of the narrative rhythm of the stories. This pattern is particularly apparent in the relationship of protagonist and narrator, but we may also observe it in the relationship that Ben Jordan in "Walker Brothers Cowboy" has with his former girlfriend and in that which is developed between Maddy and Helen. We may also perceive a second consequence, the sense of which is caught in the question that is used as the title of the third collection, *Who Do You Think You Are?* The stories suggest that no one is sufficient in oneself. Thus the sense of self-absence that a narrator might feel for herself she may also feel for an aspect of herself as someone else. Borders between characters tend to blur in Munro's fiction in the sense that lives (one wants to add "of girls and women,"[15] but perhaps it is not that exclusive) are profoundly implicated in Munro. This is particularly true to the degree that they all turn on some central meaning at various levels of participation. "The Peace of Utrecht" is not solely the paper Helen writes in high school: it is a sign of what all the characters in the story are groping for.

In many respects the second story, "The Shining Houses," follows this pattern, at least insofar as the protagonist serves as reflector, and, through her as focalizer the double world of past and present, symbolized by the imposition of a suburban subdivision upon an older settlement, is played off. Furthermore, an outcast figure, recalling Joe Phippen in "Images," draws into herself all the qualities of a complicated past that reflect morally on those who require "shining houses." As in "Images," the structure of opposition is vertical: the unknown is a lower world, providing the legend of the "real" we see.[16] The story differs, however, in its narrative mode, for the protagonist is not another self of the narrator. The focalization is internal, but the narrator does not seek the protagonist so as to understand her in a retrospective light. As a result, much of the tension present in the first-person stories is reduced, and this has a somewhat negative effect on the conclusion, which disengages the protagonist, already distinct from the narrator, from the story. Failing to persuade her fellow dwellers in the shining houses from destroying the other world below, Mary can only brood. The narrator speaks through her: "There is nothing you can do at present but put your hands in your pockets and keep a disaffected heart" (29).

"The Office," by contrast, succeeds precisely because the play of difference is allowed to operate more carefully between protagonist and narrator. In this story the initial section is a venturing forth, a gesture that would establish another place besides the house. The protagonist is a writer who feels that a place outside the home will give her the freedom to be detached enough to work more efficiently. Ironically, her new landlord never lets her alone, constantly trying to invade her discourse with his. Although he never fully replaces the protagonist, he becomes through her a kind of secondary focalizer. Through him, furthermore, rewriting is not hidden, but becomes part of the writing itself. He forces her to revise not only what she thought an office would be, but also who she thinks she is. This is suggested briefly in her initial depiction of the landlord's wife, which is interrupted by the comment, "How much of this I saw at first, how much decided on later is impossible to tell" (62). On one level, of course, such a statement is not unusual and serves as a timely reminder of authorial fallibility. On another level, it springs directly from Munro's uninterrupted meditation on time and how our self-understanding is buried in our endlessly changing notions of ourselves and others. It marks profoundly the transience of our passage, what trace of meaning we leave, and how, if at all, the traces relate, especially our present self and the self we seek. What the narrator / protagonist discovers is that, as reflector of both self and other, the two become inextricably implicated, each participating in the same search on different planes. And so the narrator broods on the landlord cleaning what he takes to be her mess at the end of her story:

I have to wait at least until that picture fades that I see so clearly in my mind, though I never saw it in reality—Mr. Malley with his rags and brushes and a pail of soapy water, scrubbing in his clumsy way, his deliberate clumsy way, the toilet walls, stooping with difficulty, breathing sorrowfully, arranging in his mind the bizarre but somehow never quite satisfactory narrative of yet another betrayal of trust. While I arrange words and think it is my right to be rid of him. (73–74)[17]

What is the reality she never sees? It is this marvelous last entry of Mr. Malley into the narrator's perception, doing what she can only imagine with sympathetic care, allowing him to form the legend that shapes a reality. The resonant word, however, is "right," recalling the initial gesture to establish an independent place apart, to assume a "right." It is precisely that, she discovers, that is a part of the fiction about herself and Mr. Malley. Her scrubbing with words is just as vain as Mr. Malley's scrubbing with soap and water, and just as ironic in its manner of suggesting a male / female role reversal. Her gesture toward a kind of self-subsistence only results in a deeper involvement with the other.

In varying degrees the pattern of venturing forth and ironic failure to escape relationship is elaborated in "Thanks for the Ride," "An Ounce of Cure," "Day of the Butterfly," "Red Dress—1946," "Sunday Afternoon," and "Dance of the Happy Shades." The most highly realized of these rites of initiation are probably "Day of the Butterfly" and "Dance of the Happy Shades." Both address the problem of childhood, each screening it in a differing fashion. "Day of the Butterfly"[18] is the less filtered, taking the reader with the first sentence directly into what will be the central relationship of the story: "I do not remember when Myra Sayla came to town . . ." (100). The story is the enactment of the narrator's remembering Myra who, as the initial statement intimates, is a foreign body entering the relatively closed community of the narrator's school. She is an outcast figure, and with her brother they both are "like children in a medieval painting . . . like small children carved of wood . . . cryptically uncommunicative" (101). No simile could more clearly establish Myra's difference, as well as the difference between the protagonist and the remembering narrator. It urges the reader to infer that as much as the meaning of Myra is sought, so too is the narrator intent upon finding herself in significant relation to Myra's world. The sense of difference inscribed in such an act of focalization suggests, paradoxically, that Myra and the protagonist share a problem to be unraveled. In the unraveling lies painful revelation: each may share the fate of outcasts, but in poignantly differing ways.

Because Myra is the other, she excites all the pitiless scorn of which her schoolmates are capable. The protagonist as a farm girl is also, but to a significantly lesser degree, an outsider, and it is this, despite risks, that allows them to establish a rapport. Part of the danger that Helen runs lies with the other girls who might alienate her even more. The more profound risk, however, is not a social one, but a moral one, and it is toward this danger that the force of the story gathers. Suffering from leukemia, Myra is taken to hospital; and the teacher, expecting the worst, organizes a premature birthday party. After the party, Myra asks Helen to stay behind, offering her a gift. Once the gift is taken, she finds herself suddenly implicated in a world sensibly larger than what the gift can represent. At that moment the sound of life going on rises from the street which "made Myra, her triumph and her bounty, and most of all her future in which she had found this place for me, turn shadowy, turn dark" (110). Thus difference is posed in the starkest terms possible, and gifts become, in a curious pun, "guilt-edged" (110). Nor can they be accepted, beautifully echoing Helen's initial gestures toward Myra, "without danger" (110). To accept the gift draws Helen perilously close to the "unknown, exalted, ether-smelling hospital world" (110), a world charged with the risks the otherworlds of outcasts possess.

The subtlety of Helen's moral lapse recalls that of Gawain in *Sir Gawain and the Green Knight*. She succumbs to a treachery of the heart. It is a treachery, however, that belongs to time, the world from which Myra is excluded. But treachery is not simply the future; it belongs as well to the risks of transformation through which "her offering perhaps already forgotten, [would be] prepared for legendary uses, as she was even in the back porch at school" (110). Thus what appeared to be a moral lapse on the protagonist's part is in fact inscribed in the act of narration. To have seen the children as "small figures carved in wood" (101) was only the first of a series of treacherous acts that are finally realized as narrative discourse. Thus while it may be said that the core of Munro's art turns upon the loss of innocence, that loss begins with the first word of the story. The consequence is that language is not innocent, nor the time in which it unfolds, for both are contexts of treachery.

This is not the moment to explore the implications of such an assertion. As I shall subsequently indicate, such an awareness becomes a problem in Munro's work, which generates a tension between what can be called truth and art. What is true of narrative art, however, is not true of all art. A special place is reserved, for example, for music in the title story, "Dance of the Happy Shades." Music is exempted from the function of language to intimate truth within its fictions, and under the sign of music an innocence can be invoked in another world beyond treachery. Thus Miss Marsalles, the piano teacher, takes her place with Joe Phippen, Mrs. Fullerton in "The Shining Houses," Myra, and even Nora from "Walker Brothers Cowboy," who each are subject to "legendary uses" and yet remain incapable of the moral treacheries of time. Part of the skill of "Dance" is to make Miss Marsalles appear almost a victim of time, and so the initial section of the story is given over to the carefully graduated history of her decline from the "solidity" of the house in Rosedale to the bungalow on Bank Street, coming to rest on Bala Street, prompting the question, "(Bala Street, where is that?)" (211). Miss Marsalles is the center of that decline, but the decline itself is the object of perception of the mothers and daughters who annually go through the ritual of her end-of-year parties. Thus the decline reflects more on them than on her, and locates them in the fading of time that constitutes the world and character of Munro's protagonists. It belongs to their "allegiance" to themselves and "the ceremonies of their childhood, to a more exacting pattern of life which had been breaking apart even then but which survived, and unaccountably still survived, in Miss Marsalles' living room" (215). What they look back to, then, is transmuted into the narrative act of recollection, an act that accounts for difference—the changes of time, the otherness that Miss Marsalles embodies. It survives "unaccountably" in her because she does not recount it. She is not a problem of language, and this makes her enigmatic in the world for which the narrator speaks.

Miss Marsalles, who still possesses innocence, is given her moment of triumph, just as Myra is, and it is a moment that too casts a shadow. Not only has Miss Marsalles sunk to a level of life that appears too "crude and unmannerly to discuss" (216), thus evoking the vertical apposition of "Shining Houses" and "Images," but she also violates decency by taking in retarded students. It is one of these, however, who is capable of making music that is an "original revelation," a "discovery," and for those who "believe in miracles" (223). The difference between the world of Miss Marsalles and that of the narrator is simply put: "after a few minutes the performance begins to seem, in spite of its innocence, like a trick—a very successful and diverting one, of course, but perhaps—how can it be said?—perhaps not altogether *in good taste*" (223). For Miss Marsalles, the girl's music is a "gift" and a "celebration" (223), and one that significantly is neither unexpected nor a surprise. Thus she can receive it in a way neither her guests nor Helen in "Day of the Butterfly" are capable of. Treachery is unknown to her heart. This is perhaps because she was, even now, "outside the complications of time" (214).

The name of the piece of music is, of course, "The Dance of the
Happy Shades," a title which Miss Marsalles then translates into French,
"which leaves nobody any the wiser" (223). To give the title in the
language of the protagonist as well as in the French version is the
almost imperceptible mark of difference that prepares for the concluding
remarks: "why is it that we are unable to say—as we must have
expected to say—*Poor Miss Marsalles?* It is the Dance of the Happy
Shades that prevents us, it is that one communiqué from the other
country where she lives" (224). So the story, and so the book, concludes,
in a sentence that sends its resonance back through all the stories,
analeptically reminding us of the role of the other, as well as of the
domain where shades dwell. The power of music is to evoke that place
and to remind us of its legendary function. The power of language
resides in the fact that it speaks from time, invoking both time and
the timeless, and inscribing the space that spreads between them. That
space is where revelation dwells, in the perception that if Miss Marsalles
is not to be pitied, then perhaps those who were on the point of doing
so are. The pity, then, is in the telling, in its power to evoke, and in
the evoking, recognizing the difference and the loss.

Language does more, of course, then speak in time. It is the color
of character, as in the way Nora speaks in "Walker Brothers Cowboy"
when she says, simply, "well": "This is a habit of country people, old
people, to say 'well,' meaning, 'is that so?' with a little extra politeness
and concern" (12). This kind of narrative intrusion is not uncommon
in Munro,[19] neatly reminding us of distinctions between story and
discourse. By making such a distinction, she reminds us of a difference
in worlds between reader and character, making the "role" an object
of scrutiny. By looking twice at the role, we lose part of the comfort
of realism. The real becomes other, and we are reminded, as well, of
the propensity of language to establish character as other ("country")
and temporality ("old"). Sometimes a special privileging of certain
words, such as "danger" in "Day of the Butterfly," assists in creating
and altering meanings as they bear upon the moral presence of narrator
and also assists in associating the narrator/protagonist with other characters. Association, however, is often ambiguous, and such an ambiguity
and consequent opening of difference becomes the leitmotiv of "Boys
and Girls," a title which in itself associates only to distinguish.

It could be argued that this story possesses a kind of feminist character
insofar as its theme addresses the problem of acquiring self-awareness
as a girl.[20] For the girl in this story such awareness comes only with

a sense of shame and humiliation. This is complicated by the fact that her dreams of heroism are of a kind not usually attributed to girls, and that her one act of greatness is misconstrued, leaving her marked as "only" a girl. To be only a girl is rejection of a radical kind, for in the world of the rural Ontario farm in the late thirties and early forties aspirations that went beyond those of sexual stereotypes were not simply wrong, they were taboo. They are not corrected by anger, but by a more powerful method, by "good humour" (127). The implication is that to be a girl is a destiny that carries with it a certain stupidity that cannot be corrected.

While all of this lies at the core of the story, the discourse in which it is developed makes the problem more subtle by the manner in which it situates the protagonist in the temporal world. For the larger theme is change—everywhere evident in Munro—and the consequences it carries. The point at which the final action occurs, when the protagonist prolongs the life of the mare who is to be shot to feed the foxes, is in the winter of her eleventh year. This information enters the narrative almost casually as part of a section beginning, "I have forgotten to say what the foxes were fed" (118). The sentence makes it appear as if this were a secondary issue whose omission would be perhaps of no importance. On the contrary, it is of central importance. Thus the story's discourse is given an almost negligent allure, deferring any climax by appearing to be simply an accounting of various moments of the girl's childhood at unspecified times before her eleventh winter. But all of these moments are part of a pattern that is to differentiate the father's world from that of the mother. By so doing, the narrator appears to be arriving at some sense of self-definition, particularly by insinuating herself into the father's world. Nothing gives her, for example, a greater sense of pride than to be introduced by her father as " 'my new hired man,' " a phrase that protects her from the salesman's observation, " 'I thought it was only a girl' " (116). To be a man, at least, is an escape from being branded as neuter. Deferral is the narrative mode of postponing what the narrator knows, while the protagonist can only suspect, must happen. As a consequence, the narrator's discourse is designedly casual, evoking a world that is still prelapsarian, its destiny still before the point of being irrevocable. Thus she even makes it appear as if the protagonist had a choice between house and barn, the two dwellings that symbolize female and male difference. The longer one stays in the barn, the more one can remain, as she says, doing work "in my father's service, [that] was ritualistically important" (117).

Housework, by contrast, is "endless, dreary and peculiarly depressing" (117).

Another kind of postponement, no matter how illusory, is embedded in her dreams of glory involving rescue, protecting schoolteachers from "rabid wolves" (113), and being recognized in Jubilee for unknown acts of heroism by riding into town on a horse. These fantasies are immediately undercut by the narrator's remark that only twice had she been on a horse, the second time she fell, and the horse, perhaps recognizing she is only a girl, "stepped placidly over [her]" (114). Her ability to shoot is described as hardly better. The dreams are implicitly recalled in the event that is at once her triumph and final defeat. Her one act of glory is to set Flora free to prevent her, at least for the moment, becoming food for foxes. As the narrator observes, "I was on Flora's side" (125), an admission that is tantamount to saying that Flora is a displacement for her own intuitive sense of finality. The protagonist is also perfectly aware of the futility of the gesture, that the glory it contains cannot receive any public recognition. At the heart of her gesture, however, is an awareness that a destiny might at least be deferred, and so the act is in clear accord with the narrative strategy of the story. But Flora is finally killed, just as the protagonist becomes, finally, a girl—and nothing more, or less.

I have already suggested how the word *girl* is played upon as a sign in the exchange between the father and the salesman, and throughout the story its connotations are continually suggested. Because of the protagonist's attachment to the father, her mother feels as if there were no " 'girl in the family at all' " (117). At one moment the narrator intervenes in such a way as to stress the semiotic function of the term:

The word *girl* had formerly seemed to me innocent and unburdened, like the word *child;* now it appeared that it was no such thing. A girl was not, as I had supposed, simply what I was; it was what I had to become. It was a definition, always touched with emphasis, with reproach and disappointment. Also it was a joke on me. (119)

To become "girl" is evidently an act of time and language, both of which are charged with differing and deferring. As the word is used in the narrative, it is a means of tracing this complex process, and as it is repeated, one cannot help but feel the process is a fate not to be wished for. When one becomes a girl, qualified as it is twice in the story at its first and final usage by the word "only," it is a state accompanied by a sense of irrevocable separation and loss. The girl appears, in fact, to lose even a kind of corporeal reality, for her fate is sealed in her father's *"words* which absolved and dismissed [her] for good" (127, my italics). What only adds to the sense of dismissal is that everyone, including a casual acquaintance, the foxes, and horses, with the exception of the girl's father and mother, has a name. Just as her parents have done, she must learn that to be a girl is to be dispossessed of choice, of individual identity, and to become what a patriarchal society's language tells one to become.

I have chosen to conclude this chapter with "Boys and Girls" for a variety of reasons. First, it may be seen as anticipation of the family in Munro's second book, *Lives of Girls and Women*. It is more important to observe, however, that this story emphasizes to a greater extent than others in this collection difference rather than similarity. If it may be asserted that the tendency in most of the stories is to assert similarity, to suggest how characters, even in their difference, turn upon a common core of meaning, this story strongly points in an opposing direction. Where outcasts are marginal but still charged with significance in a number of the other stories, in "Boys and Girls" the protagonist herself becomes the outcast. Thus a complex tension begins to develop in Munro's work, continually drawing characters together, but also gradually differentiating them. This is grandly evident in the structure of *Lives of Girls and Women* and more subtly in subsequent collections.

As I have tried to suggest, differentiation is a function of narrative form, the use of time and language, and the interplay of what Munro calls the legendary and the real. As a consequence, one of the central preoccupations of narrative discourse is to arrive at some meaning, but not to appear to do so, so as not to destroy the differing levels of perception that distinguish narrator from protagonist. Thus one may account for the frequently random appearance that Munro's sense of structure possesses. The stories seem to be merely accumulations of reminiscences that go to a certain point, then resume at a different moment. The act, then, of reading Munro forces one to observe the action that comprises the story as planes set at different angles, but all drawn toward some moment of clarity in which the various planes are reilluminated. As we shall see in *Lives of Girls and Women,* these planes of perception may be understood thematically, both as sections of narrative and as uses of language, and their function is to draw each chapter together metaphorically. Thus with the movement of time— the girl growing up—the generation of the metaphor serves to alter our sense of time's linearity and to spatialize it into temporary stasis. But as the girl grows, meanings are made relative, thus embedding the double movement suggested in her first collection in the form of the novel. As we shall also see, this raises a further, more profound problem for Munro. Is it not possible that the narrator, if skillful, can control this double movement so well that the meaning discourse seeks will be covered over by the illusion of fiction? This is a question for which the subsequent collections endeavor to find a suitable response.

Chapter Three

The Trope of Alpha

Lives of Girls and Women

Stories of the past would go like this, round and round and down to death; I expected it.[1]

The working title of *Lives of Girls and Women* was *Real Life.*[2] Neither title has the same suggestive power of the titles of Munro's other books, but *Real Life* has the merit, at least, of alluding to the penultimate sentence of the last chapter before the Epilogue:

Now at last without fantasies or self-deception, cut off from the mistakes and confusion of the past, grave and simple, carrying a small suitcase, getting on a bus, like girls in movies leaving home, convents, lovers, I supposed I would get started on my real life.

Then, in italics, we read: *"Garnet French, Garnet French, Garnet French. Real Life"* (242). While it is possible to invoke James Joyce's *A Portrait of the Artist as a Young Man* as a model for the stance taken in these sentences,[3] we should not overlook the self-deprecating tone of what is being said, which is confirmed by the epilogue.[4] The protagonist does not leave, she only "supposed she would get started." And the supposition is projected into a simile that changes the textual register—"like girls in movies." As it unfolds, the sentence dismantles itself, suggesting that while she has abandoned "fantasies and self-deception" at the beginning, she concludes with a self-displacement into the lives of other girls becoming women in a "grave and simple" gesture. The loss of fantasy is replaced by another, a collective fantasy of freedom. For a moment it appears that the sentence is focalized in the protagonist, but by its conclusion it is perfectly clear that the narrator is focalizing, directing the reader to see how far "real life" belongs to a false dichotomy whose emphatic opposition is "Garnet French." To leave him, however, is not to enter upon real life, but into what the narrator implies is a new level of self-deception.

This is precisely the world of *Lives of Girls and Women:* everywhere we find the ordering gesture quietly brought down, leveled by common sense and unexpected disorder. This, perhaps, is the real in the text. But whatever the real may be, it is subject to the narrator's discourse, which will never allow what appears to be in place to stay as she might wish it to.[5] Munro herself implies that her intent is unremittingly to seize the real: "It seems to me very important to be able to get at the exact tone or texture of how things are."[6] The price of such an effort, however, can never escape the kinds of ambiguity we have signaled. This is particularly true of Munro's efforts to find the past, which can never return "exact," but only reconstructed, and it is in the reconstruction that the precisely real begins to lose its firmness.

Although the book concludes by a clearly announced epilogue, the initial section, "The Flats Road," is not through symmetry called a prologue; nevertheless, it may be read as such. Its function is not only to situate the young Del Jordan in the world of early childhood before moving to Jubilee, but also to initiate kinds of meaning and order that are developed in the rest of the book. Like the subsequent sections or chapters, "The Flats Road" is, as Munro admits, one of a number of "almost self-contained segments."[7] Part of the power of the novel is in the linkage of segments, as well as in the manner by which most of the segments are designed around some central ground.[8] The ground of the first chapter is not Uncle Benny, the outcast figure who is the chapter's major character, but rather the problem that he invokes for the narrator. Uncle Benny is the other, and because of that destiny he permits the gesture that similes make. He assists the narrator in the process of reconstruction by permitting shifts in register. Thus he allows her to write: ". . . lying alongside our world was Uncle Benny's world like a troubling distorted reflection, the same but never at all the same" (25). It is his role, indeed, "his triumph," as she says at the end of the paragraph, "to make us see" (25). His world as "distorted reflection" is designed as a challenge to the order of domesticity of "our world"[9] and makes one wonder at the protagonist's efforts to recapture it by making lists with her brother. This also poses a central narratological question: does the past lie in metonymy, and can it be recounted through linear elaboration?[10] The narrator chooses to play with both the necessity and the futility of metonymy, recounting the things remembered from Uncle Benny's house and then, like him, leaving them about for some "practical use" (4). Thus the lists are mere points of departure: their use lies in their potential for transformation.[11]

The protagonist's enthusiasm is reserved significantly not for Benny's tangible collectibles, but for his old newspapers. Her eye is drawn to language, and particularly those headlines that seize upon the sensationally unexpected:

FATHER FEEDS TWIN DAUGHTERS TO HOGS
WOMAN GIVES BIRTH TO HUMAN MONKEY
VIRGIN RAPED ON CROSS BY CRAZED MONKS
SENDS HUSBAND'S TORSO BY MAIL (5)

What we are to see is that information is like junk—it is capable of working wonders. Thus lists are very early in the novel implicitly shown to be useless in themselves. Like the ice cream sign in "Walker Brothers Cowboy," they are useful only as cues to discovering something as yet unseen. Part of this is elaborated upon in the game of writing out Uncle Benny's address that begins with his name and concludes in *"The Universe"* (11). Reminiscent as this may be of Joyce, it also triumphantly demonstrates how such an address is not precise enough, and how it will never be precise because after the universe is heaven. For " '[y]ou don't ever get to the end of Heaven, because the Lord is there!' said Uncle Benny triumphantly" (11). Uncle Benny is somewhere, but the metonymy of an address turns out to be only a convention whose meaning as miracle can be discovered only in the play of language.[12]

The practical use of the address is to assist Benny in finding a bride. Having done so, he endures a brief, but mad marriage in which the wife becomes the object of excited gossip on the Flats Road. After she leaves, Benny decides to find her in order to rescue the wife's daughter from being seriously maimed. The search is in vain, but this leads to a new story in which everything is recounted in his "meticulously remembering voice, and we could see it, we could see how it was to be lost there, how it was just not possible to find anything, or go on looking" (25). Of course, all the objects are lost, but from them discourse arises, itself acquiring a presence distinct from the reality we suppose it recuperates. Thus, by the conclusion of the story, even Uncle Benny's precision is an object of doubt: "Uncle Benny could have made up the beatings, my mother said at last, and took that for comfort; how was he to be trusted?" (27–28). The consequence is that his wife Madeleine whom everyone had known "was like something he might have made up. We remembered her like a story" (27). This is the function of Uncle Benny's world—to lead us through likeness into narrative. But we are implicitly urged to be wary, to use one of Munro's favorite words, for how can narrators be trusted? What we must trust, as "The Flats Road" implies, is narrative transformation that is made possible through the interplay of two kinds of worlds and two kinds of families sharing sufficient similitude to play against the same ground. Without Benny, Del's understanding and vision would not have acquired the sharpness to see herself and her own world, to be prepared, therefore, for the problems of difference the novel generates.

My reading of "The Flats Road" would be insufficient if I failed to note the final words: " 'Madeleine! That madwoman!' " (27). These words, spoken by everyone as if in chorus to some tragic event, echo elegiacally over the chapter. They form a part of "our strange, belated, heartless applause" (27). In one stroke ("heartless") the narrator distinguishes herself from her childhood, passes judgment upon it, and in the word "applause" reminds us that the novel, while initially dominated by a man, is about the lives of girls and women. To evoke Madeleine at this moment marks an abrupt change in emphasis, dramatically foregrounding women, especially those whose suffering remains tragically inarticulate, if not unexpressed.[13] Inasmuch as she is also "like a story," one cannot help but infer that her name bears an intertextual significance, recalling the little cake in Proust's *Remembrance of Things Past,* which Munro was reading while writing this novel.[14] Thus in the name we are reminded how Benny helps Del acquire vision by providing the texts that it is her role to interpret. The fundamental role of the prologue of the novel, then, is to start the traffic with texts that marks this book in a distinctive fashion. It is the first of several steps that invest the novel with the signs of being a *Künstlerroman,* each of which guide the protagonist toward her later function as narrator.[15] Uncle Benny is the impetus that prepares Del to see the world as textual material.

The first test of Del's vision occurs in the following chapter, "Heirs of the Living Body." The phrase is curiously and profoundly suggestive, and its meaning echoes throughout the whole of Munro's work. Part of its meaning lies in what is Del's mother's most moving commentary on human existence as an answer to her own questions on death and being dead. The answer begins at a starkly material level, in which she argues that a person is mostly water and carbon: " 'Nothing in a person,' " she tells Del, " 'is that remarkable' " (47). What is, however, remarkable is how they combine to form organs: " 'Combine them— combine the combinations—and you've got a person!' " What we do not understand is the meaning of the combinations, and this is because

of our limited human perspective. Were we to look at death from the
vantage of nature, we would not speak of dying, but of changing:
" '. . . all those elements that made the person changing and going
back into Nature again and reappearing over and over in birds and
animals and flowers—Uncle Craig doesn't have to be Uncle Craig! Uncle
Craig is flowers!' " (48). Nothing more emphatically in Munro provides
the relation of human to nature as metaphor.[16] The conclusion of the
mother's demonstration is so triumphant, however, that it is possible
to overlook the matrix of the idea. None of us is who we appear to
be: we are all potentially something else. It is this potentiality that we
all possess that makes almost anything possible in Munro's world. It
suggests that we are in some ineluctable manner personae of the same
living body. Thus part of the power of the metaphor resides also in
its propensity for drama and theatricality. It makes guises as possible
as changes, and both are proleptically foreshadowed in the mother's
speech. The metaphor dominates, however, and it is through metaphor
that each of the chapters is elaborated.

Because of the way metaphor can operate as a shaping force, we are
able to understand more clearly why linear structures are undercut in
Munro. Meaning emerges from change, and change is dramatically
perceived not as moving from one position to another, but, paradoxically,
as likeness. On the level of narrative discourse, then, Munro prefers
metaphor to metonymy. This is one way of understanding why she
refers to her novel as "loose" and "episodic":[17] it persists in the
discontinuous. This is particularly evident in the hardcover edition of
the novel as compared to the softcover one in which the spaces within
the chapters are not simply spaces, but consist, rather, of a design of
five little flowers. The editor wants to underline interrupted linearity.
This reminds the reader that meaning is not simply the accumulation
of fact and detail, but the manner in which they acquire significance
through similarity. One might say, then, that fact and detail, like Uncle
Benny's junk, are elements for Munro that are required not in themselves,
but as the material of transformation.[18]

Uncle Craig serves as an introduction to Del of the function of the
linear text. Toward the end of the chapter an example of his discourse
is set forth. It is a highly detailed reconstruction of how a corner in
the township received its two names. His explanation is summed up
as follows: *"This corner was known either as Headley's Corners or Church
Corners. There is nothing in that location at the present time but the
building of the store, which a family rents and lives in"* (61). Craig's

text is metonymy with a vengeance: one fact leads to another and concludes in a clause that contains nothing new for anyone who was familiar with the township. In that sense it is a neat parody of most local history. It is information, merely, and thus it is incapable of the perception that we find in Del's mother's discourse. In *his* text we become heirs of a dying body. His value for Del is to assist her in distinguishing kinds of discourse. Both her mother and her aunts are of use in helping Del see this, even if the vision is apparent only in Del as narrator. Early in the chapter Uncle Craig is treated with delicate irony. The narrator recalls him at a later moment in her life while reading of Natasha's respect for " '*her husband's abstract, intellectual pursuits*' " in *War and Peace* (32). At the same moment she recalls that her two aunts possessed a similar, but ambivalent awe for Uncle Craig's work: "they could believe absolutely in its importance and at the same time convey their judgment that it was, from one point of view, frivolous, nonessential" (32). And, indeed, the glimpses that we are given of it support the view that, no matter how much one might respect the care that would amass all that material, it does not seem to lead anywhere. He might as well, as the narrator implies through her aunts, be "sorting henfeathers" (32).[19]

In contrast to Uncle Craig's history, the narrator's discourse in the chapter is a superb vindication of her mother's view. Not only is it divided into five clearly demarcated parts, but it is also shaped by two separate threads of metaphorical thinking that combine powerfully at Uncle Craig's funeral. Both threads, furthermore, are of the body and heirs, and both belong to the problem of death as the mother raises it. The first thread is carried by Del's Cousin Mary Agnes, whose birth was complicated by lack of oxygen in the birth canal. She could have died then, and almost died later when some boys left her naked in "the cold mud" (42). Ruminating on Mary Agnes's humiliating experience, the narrator concludes that such an exposure of one's body would not permit her to "live on afterwards" (42). Mary Agnes is for Del part of the problem of being physical, and this is developed with great skill in the scene when they walk by the river and discover a dead cow. The river itself is also part of the chapter's metaphorical design, for it recalls immediately the narrator's recollection of Mary Agnes's loss of oxygen in the birth canal: "the words birth canal made [her] think of a straight-banked river of blood" (39). In that setting they discover the cow, the focus of which is its eye. The narrator perceives it as "a reflection of light. An orange stuffed in a black silk stocking" (44). Her discourse makes it apparent that its "reality" can be captured only if changed by metaphor. Even the spots on its hide are perceived as "floating continents" on the brown of the ocean (44), and she cannot prevent herself from concentrating on their shape as she "would sometimes pay attention to the shape of real continents or islands on real maps, as if the shape itself were a revelation beyond words" (45). The cow is only the guise of something else, a palimpsest of a text that possesses a meaning not yet understood, but eagerly desired. It is also a way of accommodating to the brute fact of the body and death. For Mary Agnes, however, the cow is not a mystery nor, apparently, an object of fear, and she is able, to the dismay of the protagonist, to place her hand on the cow's eye "with a tender composure that was not like her" (45). The affinity between Mary Agnes and the cow is unmistakable, and for Del she is a kind of vicious Hermes, echoing the initiation rites of Munro's first collection, guiding her toward the kingdom of the dead to which she has already had a kind of prior access.

At this moment the first section ends, and Uncle Craig's death is announced. These two events are not conjoined through the linear unfolding of chronological time (metonymy), but within the story's matrix. The dead cow, Mary Agnes's incredible gesture, and Uncle Craig's death leap together synaptically across the space of five sketched flowers. Then we discover the meaning of his death to Del's mother, that now, as her mother asserts, " 'Death as we know it now would be done away with!' " (49). The brief interlude of the mother's profession of faith leads to the third part of the chapter, the funeral itself. Here Mary Agnes as Hermes returns, and Del finds her in the storeroom, a room that one of her aunts always called "tomb." Such a statement is sufficient for the narrator to intervene, suspending the action of the story, and to remark how much she loved how the word sounded when she first heard it: "I did not know exactly what it was," she comments, "or had got it mixed up with womb, and I saw us inside some sort of hollow marble egg, filled with blue light, that did not need to get in from outside" (54). The metaphorical substitution of "womb" for "tomb" cannot be missed, as well as the dramatization of her mother's words in which death is a moment of new life. Even the egg itself, a sign of potential life, suggests the shape of the cow's eye, and holds in the image the play of transformation that the chapter imitates. And there stands Mary Agnes, who offers to lead her to Uncle Craig so that Del might *see* him. As a reply, Del bites Mary Agnes's arm "in pure freedom" (55), tasting blood. It is a marvelous act, asserting Del's hatred of the death that her cousin bears.

Del, however, finally sees her uncle, and in her own way. The room where he lies is described as rich with the smells of lilies and roots, both connoting life and death. In fact, his whole trunk is buried in flowers, and what she sees first are his eyelids that "lay too lightly on his eyes" (58). We cannot forget the cow in this observation, nor can we forget it a moment later when she describes an impulse to poke a finger into his face. The face itself appears "like a delicate mask of skin, varnished, and laid over the real face—or over nothing at all" (59). Such is the guise of death's change, and at the same time as recalling the cow, it also recalls Mary Agnes, whose own skin is described "as dusty-looking, as if there was a thin, stained sheet of glass over it, or a light oiled paper" (39). So Mary, who has returned from death more than once, is metaphorically related to Uncle Craig, and Del's understanding of Mary Agnes enhances her understanding of her uncle. It comes as no surprise, then, that her becoming the heir to his text is problematic at best, and that despite her "tender remorse" at its being ruined by flooding, she is finally overcome by a "brutal, unblemished satisfaction" (63). When we consider that part of Del's role, as she is shaped by her older self, is to learn how the world is produced textually, we can assert that her rejection of Uncle Craig is a rejection of the code of history. The text of history, as her uncle produces it, leads only, like Mary Agnes, to dead ends. Uncle Benny, we recall, teaches her to see; Mary Agnes is firmly associated with dead eyes.

The first sentence of the following chapter, "Princess Ida," reads, "[n]ow my mother was selling encyclopedias" (64). It announces both the central figure and code of the chapter. It introduces not only a new kind of text with which Del must come to terms, but also the most remarkable of the women in the novel. The nom de plume that she adopts, which also serves as the title of the chapter, is drawn from Tennyson and is used as her name when writing letters to the editor.[20] The force of these associations cannot be missed, for they point to a woman deeply immersed in a world of books and marking her eccentricity in the eyes of Jubilee as well as in those of her family. For a while she is even a member of a Great Books discussion group, but fails to keep it up because of the control exercised by the group leaders. The mother plays, however, a very special role for Del, for it appears that she learns from her the way stories are told. The discovery is crucial because it is based on characteristics the mother shares with Uncle Craig and Uncle Benny. Both are obsessive collectors of the past, but the difference is the mother's degree of personal involvement. As the narrator remarks, "she kept her younger selves strenuous and hopeful; scenes from the past were liable to pop up anytime, like lantern slides, against the cluttered fabric of the present" (74). As an arranger of the past, the mother stands in sharp contrast to Uncle Craig. Her world, despite the belief in reason and knowledge, depends upon chance and sudden illumination. No wonder, then, that Del asserts that she is no different from her mother (81), for in her we can see the origin of the narrative style and design. Thus the theme of familial legacy that is ushered in in the second chapter is continued and more clearly realized in the third.

Another, related theme is also developed, and that is the notion of death. Through the mother's eyes, however, something is redeemed in death that is not evident in the previous chapter where death is perceived in all its material brutality, and where Del discovers that "[t]o be made of flesh was humiliation" (57). As we know from the same chapter, the mother firmly opposes this view, and the same opposition persists in her life as Princess Ida. Del's mother does not relate things by laying them side by side; she relates them by making them coterminous with her own life. One of the most poignant examples of this is the evocation of the teacher, Miss Rush, who is the focus of her mother's "new chapter in life" (78) after she moves to town as a young woman. Brief though the passage is, it illustrates, through its use of the anaphora of the *ubi sunt* design, how much the past is a part of her mother's life, and how difficult it is to separate past and present, to see the past as a mere chain of events that prepares the present. So the mother recalls a gift from Miss Rush "('what *became* of it?')" (78) and shortly thereafter the narrator echoes: "What had happened to Miss Rush?" (79). And the paragraph devoted to her is beautifully intertwined with the verbs "taught," "gave," and "loved" forming in their repetitions brief refrains of the mother's loss. Miss Rush is "luminous and loved" (79), despite the fact that her life and that of her baby end in childbirth. Death may be the natural closure of her mother's narration, but something survives of radiance, informing the past with continuous meaning. Thus, in the midst of all the remembered detail, the legendary takes its rise.

Death takes another form in the chapter in the fleeting visit of one of the mother's brothers. His arrival is characteristically unprepared, and the only clue the reader has of him comes midway in a recollection of him as a cruel, fat boy who tortures cats, it is implied, in a sexual fashion. The story is briefly sandwiched into the story of Del's grandmother's death, and it appears to possess no particular function. During his visit her brother in turn reminds Del's mother of how their mother brought in a caterpillar in the fall which, at Easter, emerged as a yellow butterfly. While the mother affects to show little interest in the story because of her antipathy to her own mother's religiosity, the butterfly plays metaphorically over the whole chapter. It is an emblem of the mother's natural tendency not only to envisage death as passage and change, but also to understand that the living body is at once material and transformative. That the brother who is dying of cancer tells the story, however, is significant, for it suggests a certain limitation on the mother's part. With all her knowledge, memory, and love—as well as the ability to discover the relation between Uncle Craig and flowers— her discoveries belong more to her mind than to her feelings. This is partly clarified by the association that is made by the narrator between her mother and the town of Jubilee, "the fort in the wilderness" (69) that would not have been there without her mother's complicity.[21] Such an image is, furthermore, tantamount to suggesting that the mother's world of the mind, signified by the encyclopedias, is a place where a clear line is drawn between civilization and the "other." This line is clearly drawn by the mother already in "The Flats Road" (7). Thus a crucial difference between mother and daughter is illustrated in "Princess Ida." The daughter can cross that line and, by crossing it, rejects in a certain measure the code of knowledge as a central narrative design.

The following chapter, "Age of Faith," is divided into two parts, one reflecting upon the other. In the first, as the title implies, Del makes a trial of the limits of faith. Faith's task is to make ultimate connections, to understand the relation of man to God, and especially to discern in whose image each is made. The mother, a convinced humanist, believes that God is made in man's image. She is consequently deeply hurt to discover that Del has become religiously active. The new narrative code, then, is that of theology, particularly as it relates Christ's Passion in the Anglican mass. Because of her own passion for meaning, Del finds the text irresistible. She is attracted to the Anglican service in particular because of its accent on the theatrical. It provides another world, thus recalling Uncle Benny's world, as well as foreshadowing the next chapter that centers on the school operetta. The focus, however, is God: "If God could be discovered or recalled, everything would be safe" (100). What is curious about Del's desire is the kind of reassurance that she seeks: "Then you would see things that I saw—just the dull grain of wood in the floorboards, the windows of plain glass filled with thin branches and snowy sky—and the strange, anxious pain just seeing things could create would be gone" (100). The discovery of God would endow what she sees with substance. Its subsequent importance for the narrator as related to recapturing the world in writing can only be signaled now. Its immediate significance lies in the suspicion, that forms the closure of the chapter's first section, that it is very possible for the world to have no foundation. What if, the protagonist wonders, Christ in his abandonment on the Cross discovered that truth? And so she exclaims: "To look through the slats of the world, having come all that way, and say what He had said, and then see—nothing" (110). This is precisely, however, the text and the mode of seeing that the minister does not gloss.

The thematic link between the sections of the chapter is the limits of prayer. A darker, metaphorical link is provided by Del's brother's dog, Major, who has taken to killing sheep in his old age. The connection that the text of theology suggests would be between Christ, the Lamb of God (108), the slain sheep, and a distant echo of Mary Agnes ["lamb"]. Munro, however, reverses the symbolism, suggesting that Major, who must be put to death now that he is attracted by the taste of blood, is a kind of sacrificial lamb. For Del, putting Major to death is a violation, a transgression of life itself, that the "natural" killing of the sheep cannot be. Thus one cannot help but see in her outrage the same kind of despair she feels in God's forsaking Christ. Part of her thinking is implicitly related to her mother's rejection of Christianity, the mother finding in God the source of bloodthirstiness at its heart. God, in fact, is accused of Christ's death (107), suggesting that man is most godlike in his killing. So Major is drawn into the horror of Del's new religion, God being replaced by "adults, and managers, and executioners—with their kind, implacable faces" (114). As a result, "[d]eath was made possible" (114), despite her mother's caution, knowledge, and ability to transform. Del cannot fail to wonder, then, whether God is not *"real, and really in the world, and alien and unacceptable as death?"* (115). Such a God would be *"beyond faith"* (115). In making such a discovery, she can do nothing else but reject the code of theology, at least as it is produced by Jubilee's churches. It may contain a narrative, like Uncle Craig's history, and knowledge, like her mother's encyclopedias; it does not contain a relation with truth as Del begins to perceive. God is metaphorically related to death; faith is of no help in finding the substances of things in order to keep them alive.[22]

Although the next chapter concludes in Miss Farris's unexplained, mysterious death, death is not its focus; and so the chapter inaugurates, after death, eros, as the major node of organization in the novel. The opening scene is marked by a sharp attack leveled on Del and her friend Naomi, simply because they are girls. It raises the problem of sexuality at its crudest level, and one can only wonder how such vulgarity will be sustained. Munro sustains it by avoiding it physically. Sex is to be discovered elsewhere: first in books, and later through the school operetta. Love, like history, has its own texts, and those that the two girls initially explore are pale imitations of gothic romance. Tiring of that, they eventually try Sigrid Undset's *Kristin Lavransdatter*. The clear task of the chapter is to discover an appropriate language by which sexuality can be understood. The language of boys is designed to remove "the freedom to be what you wanted" (117); romance restores it to a certain extent by investing men and women with mysterious qualities. Del can think of no man in higher terms than Kristin's lover, "a flawed and dark and lonely horseback rider" (119).[23] The best that Jubilee can offer are Mr. Boyce and Miss Farris, the teachers responsible for the annual operetta.

The two teachers represent the possibility of enhancing the real by creating legend, and "[e]very year there was a hypothetical romance, or scandal, built up between her and Mr. Boyce" (122). They set the manner, then, by which boys and girls learn how to relate. By so doing, they inaugurate the three chapters that constitute the second half of the book, balancing sexuality against death. Although Mr. Boyce suffers from the ordinary, Miss Farris is a perfect model for the mode of romance. She is introduced, furthermore, in such a way as to distance her from the normal woman of Jubilee by underlining her girlish skating costume, and particularly her dated hairstyle, hennaed and "bobbed in the style of the nineteen-twenties" (122). Her clothes in general appear dated, exciting the mild criticism of her fellow citizens. But she is seen clearly and simply as a woman endeavoring to attract a man. She is thus pictured as a parody of a dustjacket for a costume Gothic novel. This is quickly perceived by Del and Naomi, who in turn parody her relationship with Mr. Boyce as Gothic romance, especially in the hypothetical matter of getting rid of Mrs. Boyce:

"Do not distress yourself my sweetest angel I will lock her up in a dark closet infested with cockroaches."

"But I am afraid she will get loose."

"In that case I will make her swallow arsenic and saw her up in little pieces and flush them down the toilet. No I will dissolve them with lye in the bathtub. I will melt the gold fillings out of her teeth and make us a lovely wedding ring."

"O you are so romantic, O my beloved." (126–27)

All the signs of the gothic romance are here, turned to ironic account with the final allusion to the Song of Songs. Nor does Miss Farris fail to satisfy them in the house she designed and inhabits, "designed," as the narrator indicates, "for play, not life" (127). As the chorus of her fellow citizens repeats, its difference is its lack of reality. Miss Farris is not only the screen that tries, at least, to protect the girls against "the anarchy, the mysterious brutality prevalent in that adjacent world" of real sex (134); she is the agent that permits the play of romance to enter, if only temporarily, the real. In that sense, she is at the other end of a continuum inaugurated by Uncle Benny, whose world also lies alongside, but with a kind of terrible unpredictability. Miss Farris permits fantasy, the ability for Del to imagine herself with the operetta's star who would surround her "with the unheard music of his presence" (135). The allusion to Keats is deliberate, for love and sexuality in the text of this chapter is a kind of poetry. If life and fantasy met, they would dispel the dream, and Del never tempts the hero too far. It would be "too dangerous," the protagonist asserts, "to be flung . . . into the very text of [her] dream" (138).

Because it is capable of the kind of parody to which Naomi and Del submit it, Miss Farris's ephemeral presence in their lives is always known, even if against their wishes, to be illusory. But it is precisely the illusory that is sought because of its power to distance, to sanction guises, to become other in a manner analogous to metaphor. Miss Farris is one way of answering Del's mother's notion of life. Through her, transformation is not, however, simply an idea; it is capable of being fact.

The code of romance in the end, however, is found wanting. Illusion is only one mode of change, and it requires a certain innocence to sustain it, an innocence that all of Munro's outcasts possess. But the

disparity between the real and the text of the dream can continue only
so long. Nevertheless, Miss Farris's death, which is never explained,
comes to the narrator as a shock. The impact of her death, however,
reaching the narrator distanced by some years in time, contains no
revelation, and so Miss Farris, drifting in the river, drifts into elegy in
a wonderful paragraph of epiphany and appeal that attempts to draw
her back into memory before she sinks at last from sight. This is
immediately followed by a list of the operettas, focusing her true
existence, and receiving a final commentary: "She sent those operettas
up like bubbles, shaped with quivering, exhausting effort, then almost
casually set free, to fade and fade but hold trapped forever our
transformed, childish selves, her undefeated, unrequited love" (141). In
one word, "bubbles," Miss Farris's death by drowning and her life are
metaphorically conjoined in the style of romance, no longer Gothic but
elegiac, opening the space of difference between the narrator and her
distant, childish self. The code of romance responds to that of history,
and neither is shown quite capable of recuperating the past, only filtering
it through a certain rhetorical mode.

One of the chief characteristics of the school operetta is that it achieves
a temporary timelessness by suspending the normal daily routine. The
text that provides the transition into the next and title chapter is drawn
from the local newspaper. It concerns a photograph of a record snowfall.
As a journalistic text, it returns the reader to the quotidian world, while
echoing romance, at least, by suggesting the heroic world of Jubilee.
One of the women in the picture is Fern Dogherty, a boarder in Del's
house. She also signals a change in attitude from Miss Farris and her
"unrequited love," for she, at least, is having a clandestine affair.
Through her, Del's sexuality becomes at once more sensational (reminding
one of heroic photographs) and more physical.

Two other kinds of texts dominate the chapter. These are sex manuals
and vulgar love letters. The function of these texts is to bring Del's
awakening sexuality closer to earth than gothic romance, but they also
provide it with a grotesque and somewhat comic distance. The code of
the sex manual, for example, makes male sexuality comprehensible by
permitting humorous translation. Del and Naomi read, for example,
that the erect male organ may attain a length of fourteen inches. This
immediately inspires Naomi to stretch her chewing gum to such a
length and then announce, invoking the name of Fern's lover: " 'Mr.
Chamberlain the record-breaker' " (148). Uncle Craig may be capable
of becoming flowers, but Mr. Chamberlain is little more than gum.

He is also drawn into the same textual register that the chapter begins by announcing, inasmuch as he is a newsman on the local radio. He also reads commercials "with ripe concern" (149). Thus he combines in himself the routine and the occasionally grotesque. Furthermore, because of his particular knowledge of the world (he was in Europe during the war), Del's mother's encyclopedic kind of knowledge is undermined, reducing, for example, her offering of Michelangelo's David to little more than a sex object. The new text that Mr. Chamberlain represents changes Del's fantasy. As opposed to the dream of romance, she now wants something less timeless. And so she fantasizes prostitution, "the skin of everyday appearances stretched over such shamelessness, such consuming explosions of lust" (154).

Just as Mr. Chamberlain is capable of dismantling culture, so Naomi's father, reading the parable of the wise and foolish virgins, makes it appear not to be a parable about morality, but about sex. No text is innocent any longer. Its ambiguity lies in the fact that they not only color the world, but also become insidious guides. When Naomi's father cites the line *"Behold the bridegroom cometh"* (157), it both excites Del's imagination and proleptically announces Mr. Chamberlain's one climactic moment. This is a moment, however, that is carefully deferred, permitting Del's new awareness of sexuality to see the world around her become possessed with new and heightened significance. Thus the way to the "bridegroom" passes through a long sequence in which the two girls try to get "picked up," discover that the cry of the male peacock is a sexual cry, and swing in the trees pretending to be baboons. The function—and wonder—of the sequence is that it is an enactment of the textual strategy in which the chapter is engaged. Del is discovering that the innocence of her mother's encyclopedic culture is no longer unassailable and that Mr. Chamberlain's knowledge makes innocence as relative as worldly wisdom. Wise and foolish virgins no longer dwell apart. The sequence that leads up to Mr. Chamberlain permits the girls to be both innocent, yet guilty enough to atone for their new awareness.

Atonement, like Mr. Chamberlain, comes soon enough. What Del wants from him is put patently enough: rather than "ideas of love, consolation and tenderness" associated with the hero of the operetta, Del now seeks "the secret violence of sex" where there would be "recognition" (162). Mr. Chamberlain's approach is direct and physical. It comes initially as a response to Del's imitation of a seal—suggesting both the baboons and the peacock—for which he rewards her with a sip of whisky and furtive caress. It is not Del, however, whom Mr.

Chamberlain wants. He wants her seal-like, trainable side so that he can induce her to find out whether Fern still has in her possession any of his old love letters that could lead to a suit for breach of promise. Although she does not find them, she is recompensed for her efforts by three bundles of mostly sexual material of both the sex-manual kind and more explicit, vulgar verses. This is the unmistakable inverse of the romance text, and it leads her into a level of language that fundamentally undercuts her own verse on the erotic cries of peacocks. They are texts, however, that are in accord, if on a slightly lower level, with the sex manual that Del and Naomi consult earlier in the chapter.

Like those in the previous chapter, the text is the notation for performance, and it operates on two levels. The first is the level of innocence, in which the girls play at being baboons for each other, and Del becomes a seal for Mr. Chamberlain. The second is the level of vulgarity, at least, in which Mr. Chamberlain performs for Del. He takes her to the woods and masturbates in front of her. It is characteristic of the narrator's discourse that she cannot see it entirely for what it is (whatever that may be), but continually transposes it into simile. At the first sight of Mr. Chamberlain's penis, she notes its dissimilarity to that of Michelangelo's David. Not art, it is "ugly-coloured as a wound" (169) and "playful and naive, like some strong snouted animal" (169). As he performs, everything becomes "theatrical, unlikely" (170), as if a certain level of the real were absent. His face "was blind and wobbling like a mask on stick," and "the whole performance . . . seemed imposed, fantastically and predictably exaggerated, like an Indian dance" (170). The value of Mr. Chamberlain resides not in what he does or who he is, but rather in his potential for transformation. Because, however, of the disparity between the kind of text that Mr. Chamberlain enacts, the kinds of texts tucked away in Fern's packets, and the discourse employed by the narrator to find what she takes to be suitable comparisons, the code of sex as the mechanical activity illustrated in manuals is neatly undercut. Not only is a certain aspect of sexuality found wanting, but also the kind of discourse that narrates it reaches a limit. Almost as an afterthought, Naomi falls ill during this period and "the grosser aspects of sex" (173) are no longer her text for conversation either.

In a felicitous echo of the beginning of the previous chapter, we are informed that Del at the conclusion no longer reads *Kristin Lavransdatter*. She has abandoned the traditional romance for the modern. Still seeking expressions of sexuality through art, her taste now is for something more contemporary. She finds, however, only what she is capable or desirous of witnessing: "Books always compared [sexual intercourse] to something else, never told about by itself" (175). The sentence appears to prepare for the following chapter, making one ask whether, after the continual rejection of several kinds of discourses, the narrator has finally found the mode she seeks.

The title of the next chapter, "Baptizing," reminds the reader naturally of "Age of Faith." It bids one to inquire whether this is an accidental connection or part of a larger design. If we read "The Flats Road" as a prologue completed by an explicit epilogue, it is evident that the body of the novel is divided into six chapters. The first three are dominated by the theme of death; the second three, by sexuality. It is also possible to see further correspondences. We have just examined a chapter that responds to sex as more a matter of knowledge than experience, and it is significant that the final dialogue between Del and her mother reminds one of the latter's theme that brains, not men, are more important to a woman. It recalls immediately the textuality of "Princess Ida" and its emphasis on knowledge. This leaves the two chapters that initiate each sequence, namely, "Heirs of the Living Body" and "Changes and Ceremonies." Both are profoundly concerned with narrative, with the meaningless connections of metonymy and the disillusioning metaphors of romance. This is a design that suggests that the second half of the novel recursively plays over the narrative problems of the first, permitting sexuality to dominate the problem of death. Both the thematic and the discursive problems that are respectively developed would support the validity of such a structure, and such a design accords magnificently with the kind of novel we are addressing, which most critics concur in calling a *Künstlerroman*.

Because of the diachronic unfolding of the novel, however, the final chapter is not exclusively a recuperation of the problems of "Age of Faith." Parts of it perforce continue themes already broached. Thus the initial section continues aspects of the previous chapter in its organization around the raw sexuality of the Gay-la Dance Hall. Del's reaction to such experience is predictable, and her loyalty to a less vulgar world initiates her gradual drawing apart from Naomi. In the process of differentiation that takes place, Del's description of her response to a new text, Bizet's *Carmen,* reminds one of another aspect of the preceding chapter. Her admiration for *Carmen* is that it provides an intertextual hortation, appealing to another text for meaning, that becomes a kind of guide to the rest of the novel. The phrase is *"Et laisser moi [sic]*

passer!" (184). Its value resides in the fact that it contains a necessary
message: "the hero's, the patriot's, Carmen's surrender to the final
importance of gesture, image, self-created self" (184).[24] The text of
romance this may be; it is also an unmistakable foreshadowing of the
image that constitutes the novel's closure. Thus it prepares for the
gathering of the two central elements of the narrator's continual object
of research, which is to find herself as an expression of a certain mode
of telling.[25] Before that, however, she must confirm a rejection already
made and come to terms with another.

The first concerns the humorous episode with Jerry Storey, who shares
with her the honor of being first in the senior class. He incarnates the
code of knowledge, thus recalling the earlier chapters that endeavored
to address this problem. The didactic Mr. Chamberlain is now replaced
by Jerry who, with Del, makes a superb parody of the comic-strip text
of Pogo in order to explore sex together. This text is in turn shown
to be text of the sexual manual, and it issues in the following dialogue:

> "Has I got all the appurtances on in the right places does yo' think?"
> "Ah jes' has to git out my lil ole manual an' check up on that." (204)

The episode ends shortly thereafter with the arrival of Jerry's mother.
It is sufficient to confirm the limits of sexuality as knowledge, and they
explore no further, content with comradeship. The link with Mr.
Chamberlain is also strengthened in their brief discussion on the matter
of sex. Jerry asserts that he was about to perform something, but Del
quickly interrupts to remind him that he was not.

The world of performing and witnessing ends with the arrival of
Garnet French, a converted drinker and fighter, a man of experience.
He too emerges from a text, this time a hymn sung at a revivalist
meeting, and he corresponds to the *"gypsy boy"* who is brought *"News
of Salvation"* (211). For Del, however, what counts is his "dark side"
(220), the side which will initiate her into the mystery of her sexuality.
As she speculates upon this in advance, she imagines sex to be "all
surrender—not the woman's to the man but the person's to the body,
an act of pure faith, freedom in humility" (218). This is a partial
answer, then, to the problem of faith, an answer that continues to reject
the faith of theology. Faith remains implicit in the text of "self-creation."
Her passage into herself, however, differs radically from all the moves
previously made. To do so she must reject language and enter "the

world . . . I thought animals must see, the world without names"
(221). How unassertively the narrator assumes focalization from the
protagonist in this sentence, reminding us that language is abandoned
only for the moment of passage.[26] For in the narrator's telling, the
experience itself sends up curious echoes from the rest of the book.
Her first sexual experience with Garnet occurs in her mother's peony
border, suggesting that it is the mother who is deflowered, metaphorically
implying that knowledge is no longer innocent. Del's translation of the
experience for her mother, who cannot decipher her slang, creates a
new metaphor: the blood is there because a tomcat killed a bird.[27] This
is perhaps the world seen by animals, but the repetition of the word
"blood" throughout the passage evokes especially the mother's earlier
speech in "Age of Faith," decrying the bloodthirstiness of Christian
ritual. At an even further remove, one is reminded of the slaughter of
foxes and horses on her father's fox farm and of Mary Agnes, whose
blood Del tastes and who almost died in her mother's birth canal, "a
straight-banked river of blood" (39). Thus the blood is at once sacrificial
and a mode of sustenance, a sign of both death and (new) life. As
the narrator indicates, it lacks both romance and an anticipated level
of theatricality, "like a curtain going up on the last act of a play"
(227). It is removed, therefore, from the world of culture and sex as
demonstration, taking her somehow into a world without words. In
that silence it would appear that, without the narrator, Del the protagonist
might have disappeared within the core of the process of self-creation.
Almost as if the protagonist fears the possibility of self-loss in silence,
she "had to mention it to somebody" (227), thus regaining herself in
narration.

The title of the chapter refers to its climax in which Garnet tries to
baptize Del. In this scene the two major thematic levels of death and
love conjoin. For Garnet it is a necessary act that precedes marriage.
Del must become a Baptist like him. For Del it is an act that must
be resisted from fear of losing herself, as well as from fear of dying.
And in this scene the two fears are coterminous. Because of the success
of her resistance, their affair ends. It ends in Del's returning to her
own life in a kind of revival that comments ironically on her first
meeting with Garnet at a revival meeting. As an ending, it is the last
of a series of rejections that constitute the awakenings of the preceding
chapters.

Del does not, however, simply resist. It is in the moment of Garnet's
repeated dunkings that she articulates to herself her awareness of her

role in his life. What Garnet appeared not to understand was that all
the powers he possessed were granted by Del "in play" (238). The
moment she tries to explain this to him, she observes, however, that
he does, in fact, know it, and consequently outrage and insult urge
him on. He is unable to compromise his seriousness with her playacting,
unable to reckon with the kind of fictional and theatrical world that
Del inhabits. So long as Del is able to stand apart from herself, she
keeps her self-possession. Indeed, self-possession appears possible only
when one is primarily a subject for oneself, as opposed to being a
subject for another. This is one of the reasons why the world for Del
appears to acquire significance only when perceived as drama, ritual,
and ceremony, which is apparent from her earliest experiences on Uncle
Benny's farm. The intensity of drama, furthermore, builds particularly
in the chapters that address her interest in religion, the operetta, and
includes as well her witnessing of Mr. Chamberlain's performance. Thus
the death that Garnet comes to represent is the act that would destroy
Del's role as witness. For the witness does not merely see; the witness
sees as Uncle Benny taught her how to see by supplying the vision
with its levels of significance. The witness, then, is more than historian,
philosopher, and theologian (the roles offered by the first half of the
novel). The witness is, we should recall, also martyr; the witness must
participate in order to know how significance is acquired. Del differs,
of course, from the religious witness: her faith is placed in herself.

The significance of Del's witnessing is of fundamental importance to
the role she is developing for herself. As the eventual creator of her
autobiography, her story must be as she narrates it. Thus Del the
protagonist cannot exist without Del the narrator. Consequently, the
rejections of the novel are the inverse of the novel's affirmation, but
the affirmation poses a special difficulty for the narrator. Everything
depends upon the kind of relationship she has with herself. It means
that she must remain in some ineluctable fashion as innocent as her
outcast figures, those like Uncle Benny, her mother, and Miss Farris.
But outcasts are condemned not only to a hermetic existence, but also
to a life untouched by time. Time, however, continually cuts through
Munro's text, and to seize the self it is necessary to grasp it in its
changing and fading world. Passion, then, holds ambiguous attractions.
On the one hand, it removes Del from the ordinary world, and it
possesses an innocence of its own. That very removal, on the other
hand, removes her from the passing of time without which significance
is lost. What she wants is the innocence of the outcast, but she wants

it with the heightened awareness of its temporality. Thus she emerges from the Wawanash, washed of her deluded passion, as if she had entered her own Jordan (one cannot miss the pun on her family name) and survived intact but burdened with the choice of her self-possession.[28]

Self-possession is partly marked by the repossession of the world "sober and familiar" in which her "old self—[her] old devious, ironic, isolated self" (240) feels at home. But the final intertextual note of the chapter is drawn from Tennyson's *Mariana,* "one of the silliest poems [she] had ever read" (242), and it is uttered "with absolute sincerity, absolute irony" (241): *"He cometh not, she said"* (242). One cannot help recall from the previous chapter Naomi's father reading with sexual innuendo the biblical text, *"Behold the bridegroom cometh"* (157). In this conjuncture of texts Del puts a coda upon her initiation into the mystery of her sexuality. It is at once a moment of triumph and a moment of profound loss,[29] and it can be met only by her ambiguous emotional response, its significance sanctioned by the ritual of poetry.

I began this chapter by remarking upon the closure of "Baptizing" and particularly the care with which the narrator draws our attention to the shifting of fantasies that goes on within the protagonist's imagination. We would be deceived, I think, if we were to believe that now, like Stephan Dedalus, Del is free. Her choice is not to be free, but to reckon with the ambiguity she cannot escape. This, I would argue, is the point of the concluding chapter, "Epilogue: The Photographer." It is at this point that the writer, on the threshold of moving from her persona of protagonist to narrator, is forced to see the implications of her situation. The first is a problem of vision as a reflection of style.[30] The second is a related issue, and that is the sense, finally, that self-creation must create a space between self as subject and self as witness, a *differance*[31] that writing only continues to enlarge. But who is the photographer, and is he a displacement of the narrator, continually documenting the passage of the world?

The question about the photographer can be answered only by attending to the context that creates him. He is a figure in Del's unfinished novel, a novel about Jubilee at a second remove, "a town [like Uncle Benny's world] . . . lying close behind the one I walked through everyday" (248). Its characters are extremes of physical size, and their speech is "subtle," "evasive," "bizarrely stupid," and crackling with "madness" (247). The time is always summer, and everyone seems submerged in the innocence of their passions. The heroine is based on

Marion Sherriff, who, like Miss Farris, and almost like Del, died by
drowning.[32] Her role is to bestow "her gifts capriciously on men" (246),
and her final lover is a devil figure, the photographer.[33] His ability is
to photograph everyone in the worst possible manner—"[b]rides looked
pregnant, children adenoidal" (247). Marion, alias Caroline, gives herself
readily to the photographer, becomes pregnant, and walks into the river.
Curiously Pre-Raphaelite and gothic as it is, Del is unsure of what to
make of the novel, and sums it up as "[a]ll Pictures" (248), suggesting
that she is the ultimate photographer as narrator. Part of the novel's
problem is that it is "not real but true" (248). It is only later, during
her encounter with Marion's brother Bobby, that we realize that she
had not been thinking about her novel for a fair amount of time,
having lost faith in it. We are to assume that her faith had been
shaken during her experience with Garnet and that nothing had been
done to restore it. Part of that restoration may be attributed to Bobby.

What Bobby shows her is not so much the real but the avenue
through it. Bobby is considered the town idiot, but what he shows her
of himself is an ordinary man who admits that his mental problems
were possibly caused by malnutrition. All her fantasies about the Sherriffs
were, it turned out, "unreliable" (251). And so her problem becomes
one of finding a basis for truth, and the reader is reminded of her
earlier crisis of faith in which she failed to find the substance of the
world as it presents itself. Bobby's role is to lead her back to faith
and substance, and it appears at first that he does so by making of
her a photographer of the real. In the midst of their conversation the
narrator intervenes and observes: "one day I would be so greedy for
Jubilee. Voracious and misguided as Uncle Craig out at Jenkin's Bend,
writing its History, I would want to write things down" (253). This
is followed by a paragraph in which lists of various kinds are announced,
and then she remarks: "The hope we bring to such tasks is crazy,
heartbreaking" (253). We are not to assume that this means that either
Del or Munro are necessarily to be construed as documentary writers
on the strength of such statements.[34] This is, rather, a rejection of Uncle
Craig at a more informed level. Del could not write his "History" (the
capital letter suggests its pretensions), and she is clearly aware of it as
a misguided, crazy enterprise. It is not, however, lists in themselves
that urge this intervention on the narrator's part, but rather her sympathy
for Del the protagonist, who later makes the lists to become the writer.
In that sympathy resides the narrator's sense of loss that suddenly
appears to come over her at this moment, the moment preceding Del's

discovery. The loss is intensified by the reference to lists: the more she writes, the more she tries to recapture her past, the more she feels its loss, the writing itself continually deferring a merging of narrator and remembered self. It is the cause of difference between the narrated and narrating self: one seems lost in the past, and the other is continually moving away into the future. *Différance* is "heartbreaking," rather than the task itself, and indeed her heart is divided into the two selves of the novel. Lists, as the narrator knows, cannot mend this division, nor can they restore or re-present what she wants, which is everything: "every layer of speech and thought, stroke of light on bark or walls, every smell, pothole, pain, crack, delusion, held still and held together— radiant and everlasting" (253). The decision to write breaks her heart, for writing is perceived as the act where loss dwells in time and where it might, against hope, be recovered in order to remain timeless. If lists and History cannot mend the heart, what can?

Bobby—the mad Bobby of fantasy and the ordinary Bobby of the world of proper nutrition—provides the answer, and in his radiant fashion, for in one stroke he draws all the play and effort toward transformation in the novel together. He is Bobby, and he is Bobby in self-transcendence, the timeless incarnate, reflecting the body as spirit, and spirit as body. Thus he mends division. What he does is to pick up her plate, fork, napkin, then

[w]ith those things in his hands, he rose on his toes like a dancer, like a plump ballerina. This action, accompanied by his delicate smile, appeared to be a joke not shared with me so much as displayed for me, and it seemed also to have a concise meaning, a stylized meaning—to be a letter, or a whole word, in an alphabet I did not know. (253–54)

This is the text that Del has sought throughout the novel, and it is for Del the narrator to restructure the protagonist's story so as to make closure with Bobby's text appear an inevitable epiphany. What is important about the letter or word that Bobby incarnates in his dance is that it is not the real. No list, as the narrator knows, could produce it, but it emerges ineluctably from the real. It completes the ordinary with the unexpected, and so fulfills what Del intuits before the event, namely, that "[p]eople's lives, in Jubilee as elsewhere, were dull, simple, amazing and unfathomable" (253). The problem for the writer is to realize how all four qualities conjoin. Because of her taste for the sensational, cultivated already on the Flats Road, Del's initial tendency

is to overlook the dull and the simple. So her initial attempts at a
novel, as the combined discourse of both protagonist and narrator
indicates, overlook the most readily apparent world for another "behind
the one [she] walked through every day" (248). The virtue of this
legendary world, however, is that it seems to contain a truth that she
cannot find in the real. What Del discovers in Bobby is that the two
worlds need to be combined, and Bobby is the catalyst that suggests
the combination.[35] Neither documentary nor Gothic fiction alone is
capable of the kind of amazing life that Bobby possesses.

Thus the search for the right mode of discourse concludes, and it
occurs as a dramatic event, echoing a series of performances throughout
the novel. Del retains her role as witness, but a witness intimately
related to the event; her role as receiver is to understand the code as
it relates to her. Del as narrator knows, however, that such reception
can be tinged with a certain egoism, and to say so marks her as a
witness at a second remove: "People's wishes, and their other offerings,
were what I took then naturally, a bit distractedly, as if they were
never anything more than my due" (254). Thus her final word on the
event and in the novel is a simple " 'Yes,' " not a thank you, and
the affirmation has a marvelous ironic ring.[36] It confirms the egoist, but
also announces the emergence of narrator, who, over and against the
implicit rejections of the several kinds of narrative propositions that are
made in the novel, can now affirm a mode and a vision. With that
one word Munro's apprenticeship comes to an end.

Chapter Four

The Other Revealed

Something I've Been Meaning to Tell You

"I invented you."[1]

Munro's second book concludes in a gesture that is at once discursive and dramatic. Bobby Sherriff's brief pirouette contains a meaning, both "concise" and "stylized," and what that meaning is remains unexplicated. This, at least, appears to be the initial response the narrator wishes to excite through the protagonist. The narrator, however, by having told a story that ends in a dance, reminds us, as in the concluding story of the first collection, that dance is significance, spelling in its undeciphered alphabet a meaning that, in its turn, casts its spell upon the reader. Thus the apparently careless title of the third book, *Something I've Been Meaning to Tell You,* a phrase that seems to interrupt the normal flow of discourse and dialogue, suggests that meaning, however naturally it may come upon us, is a kind of transgression. Meaning breaks in, invading and reordering the known, the categorized, and the habitual. Thus the kinds of problems that were sketched as central in our first chapter—the preoccupation with time, character, and form— are examined again, but this time with an eye upon their new possibilities. The tone, too, has changed. The idyllic title of the first collection and the panoramic movements of the novel are now discarded, as if the author wished to take us more intensely toward the subject as a subject of meaning. And meaning, as the title emphatically indicates, is a function of telling, as well as a relation between narrator and narratee.[2]

Lives of Girls and Women is also framed by Uncle Benny, who teaches vision, and Bobby Sherriff, who teaches action. What distinguishes Munro's subsequent writing is the manner in which seeing is act, for in this conjunction the witness becomes progressively more complicitous. Her seeing becomes a new kind of knowledge that radically dislocates the ordinary assurance of things. Thus the stories of her third book are more exploratory, more skeptical of the hermeneutic code, persistently testing what we know and how we know it. The consequences of this

experimentation may be seen immediately in Munro's understanding of
form and of how character becomes a part of form, as well as how
the narrator understands or somehow does not understand what is meant.
Although these are not new preoccupations with Munro, her manner
of addressing them indicates that to follow the intimations of her initial
work certain assurances must be called into question. One is reminded
of Del's crisis of faith when she wonders how the phenomenal world
acquires substance. For if God cannot be discovered as a center of
meaning, then we are left with "the strange, anxious pain just seeing
things could create."[3] Having chosen to order meaning in narrative
fiction, rather than to accept religious faith, Munro chose to yield to
the fact that she was playing with a fiction that might be only a fiction,
for everything would be dependent upon her for its authority.[4] What,
then, would become of the hidden truth that is the object of Del's
first, hardly written novel?

With this question in mind, I want to examine initially "Walking
on Water," for in its curious fashion it takes us directly to the narrative
problem of how things subsist and what one is to make of them. The
first paragraph is designed to present the protagonist, Mr. Lougheed,
in what appears to be a perfectly conventional manner. It locates his
room in a certain part of the city, gives some hints of his life in
retirement, and explains some of his efforts to avoid becoming a hermit.
Mr. Lougheed has all the characteristics of someone who merely looks
upon the world like the uncanny Tarrou in Albert Camus's *La Peste,*
merely taking note. To avoid this extreme, Mr. Lougheed deliberately
cultivates Eugene, a young man in his twenties, whose life is absorbed
in philosophy and the esoteric. It is he, of course, who has decided to
walk on water. And he does, and he fails, perhaps, encouraged by a
small crowd of skeptics and the faithful. For Mr. Lougheed the experience
is in many ways unbearable. No amount of reasoning before the event
can dissuade Eugene, nor is it possible for Eugene to explain to Mr.
Lougheed's satisfaction why it is worth the attempt.

The story, however, is Mr. Lougheed's, not Eugene's, and therefore
one cannot escape the suggestion that, while Eugene does the performing
in a public sense, Mr. Lougheed is, through his young friend, being
initiated into the experience of a world beyond what he takes to be
his natural element. The story of Mr. Lougheed, then, is the story of
how he is gradually taken away from the way he thinks things are to
another mode of understanding. Part of the removal requires the loosening
of his habitual sense of human and temporal order. Thus the conventional

opening of the story is in accord with the kind of figure Mr. Lougheed thinks he is. Talking with Eugene, while trying to discover the necessity of walking on water, he is confronted with the actual world within which he, Mr. Lougheed, dwells. The narrator interrupts their discussion to remind the reader that during the recent, but indeterminate past Mr. Lougheed had witnessed two of the three hippies living downstairs making love. "A little while after the incident" Mr. Lougheed returns to find "a sign painted on his door" (74). It is described as "like a flower, with thin red petals, inexpertly painted, and black petals in between, tapering the wrong way. A red circle in the middle and a black circle, black hole, inside that" (74). Mr. Lougheed is informed it is not a sign—which he had not taken it to be—but the word is enough for two things to occur. The first is Eugene's explanation that " 'external reality . . . is nothing like so fixed as we have been led to believe' " (75). The other is that it prompts Mr. Lougheed's awareness that external reality is perhaps only a world of signs, like Bobby Sherriff's undeciphered alphabet, that require a certain kind of initiation to understand.

Eugene, then, is one of his guides into the world external reality conceals, and the hippies downstairs are the others. He even wonders how much of what he has learned in the house his contemporaries could bear, no matter how little of it he might comprehend. The morning in which the event is set Mr. Lougheed discovers a dead bird the hippies left outside his door. The act of burying it interrupts for Mr. Lougheed the normal unfolding of time, reminding him of the house's original owner and his parents. The bird becomes a sign that leads him to remember a recurrent dream. The dream itself grew out of a childhood experience of a mad boy who had murdered his parents. In the chase that ensues Mr. Lougheed is not part of the search party. What he knows of the chase is what he has been told, and that story becomes in turn part of his dream. For the narrator, Mr. Lougheed's childhood experience is summed up as "facts" (82). The narrator then observes: "The dream, as far as he could tell, contained but did not reveal them" (82). The role of the narrator in this passage is to lead the reader to a central preoccupation in Munro's fiction, which is the manner in which significance is sought, and why it cannot, finally, be extrapolated from the discourse that produces it. Mr. Lougheed's progress in the dream appears initially confused: "He did not know where he was going and it would not dawn on him until he had gone along for awhile that there was something they were going to find" (82). In

fact, although their initial progress would be good, "often it would be
slowed by confusing and deflecting invisible forces, so that Mr. Lougheed
would find himself separated, doing things such as mixing a prescription
in his drugstore or eating supper with his wife" (82). By taking such
a turn, the dream is capable of containing facts of present and past,
losing whatever meaning it might have as it is transgressed upon by
Mr. Lougheed's waking world. Or does the reverse take place? In the
initial paragraph we are told that Mr. Lougheed is perfectly capable of
conversing about one thing and thinking another, and thus never revealing
what preoccupies him. Now we are told that, in the meanderings of
his dream, "with such too-late desperate regret, through reproachful,
unhelpful neighborhoods, and always some kind of gray weather, not
disclosing much, he would try to get back to where he ought to have
been" (82). This quest is perhaps what holds Mr. Lougheed beneath
his conversation and social life of "external realities," but we are not
told this explicitly. Even where he ought to be is not clearly located,
for there is no distinction made between the dream and the world from
which it grows. Each flows into the other, obliterating the possibility
of acquiring the distance that would allow meaning to free itself from
the discourse of the dream. Indeed, the reality of the dream is that
"[i]t almost seemed to him there must be a place where [his family]
moved with independence, undiminished authority, outside his own
mind; it was hard to believe he had authored them himself" (83). So
powerful is his dream that it "had brought him in touch with a world
of which the world he lived in now seemed the most casual imitation—
in texture, you might say, in sharpness, in authority" (83).

   What gives the play on the word "authority" its particular persua-
siveness is that Munro is careful to remind the reader how often the
retiring Mr. Lougheed senses himself out of place in what is described
as the sixties. But the true sense of displacement, I would argue, is a
function of Mr. Lougheed's surrendering to the authority of which
Eugene has knowledge and he himself has experience. The role of
Eugene and the hippies downstairs is to lead him from the real as
ordinary to the truth of his own life, beneath the surface of what he
merely sees. His fear of Eugene's possible drowning is a fear that dwells
within the dream, and that is not revealed to him until after Eugene's
unsuccessful attempt. There, beneath a bridge, he sees a drowned boy,
perhaps the murderer. Now that this has been recalled, it acts upon
him in the same painful manner as the thought of Eugene's apparent
attempt at suicide. The narrator then observes that suicide would not

have been Eugene's way of describing the morning's performance, which was "only a rehearsal, an imitation" of some further act (91). Thus Eugene and the reality he would seem to represent are drawn into Mr. Lougheed's world, in which the visual world is only a sign, no matter how theatrical, of the shaping world within.

The story is striking not because of the unconscious connection that Mr. Lougheed makes between Eugene and the boy in his dream, but because of the manner in which the connection is made. The design of the story makes it appear that Mr. Lougheed dwells in two worlds simultaneously. As he is drawn more deeply into one, he is given even greater glimpses of the other, until the two fold into each other. It is the function of the visual world, moreover, to awaken him more acutely. As a consequence, Mr. Lougheed's past as dream gradually invests his present with a significance that the present in itself does not possess. This prompts one to ask what world Mr. Lougheed inhabits, and whether his life with Eugene is only an imitation of his dream life, which is for him his true life. If we answer this question affirmatively, it would mean that the dream bears the same relation to the present as the "real" to the fictional. The dream, as we know, has such "authority" that it appears to have an independent life of its own. This would suggest that what we normally call the "real"—the phenomenal world—would be a fiction, a kind of text that is hard to decipher and perhaps has no substance. We cannot, then, put faith in what we see. The implications for those who make fiction of the phenomenal world are, as a result, problematic indeed. Foremost among these is that meaning itself is undermined, and in this instance inverted.

If we recall Del's cousin Mary Agnes, we can see that Eugene plays a similar role for Mr. Lougheed. He is a Hermes figure who leads the older man beneath the surface to the drowned boy he carries within. We may also see a fundamental difference. For Del, death is outside; it is not an intimate presence within her life. Thus Mr. Lougheed is emblematic of Munro's altered and deepened vision. Within the layers of the worlds within which Mr. Lougheed dwells, no position is privileged. This is the truth that Munro's fiction seeks. The truth, then, is in the telling. This means that the relation of narrator to story, and especially the discourse by which it is marked, is inevitably complicitous. This is the central point of the collection's second story, "Material." The story is told by a former wife of a famous author. It begins with the assertion that she does not "keep up with Hugo's writing" (24), and the statement is qualified by a wonderfully guarded paragraph in which the narrator carefully disassociates herself from the kinds of women who would.[5] Part of the point of the paragraph is to establish a perspective in time present from which the narrator speaks, and it would appear that this is a position that allows her to speak with detachment. This seems to be reinforced by the distinction she draws between Hugo and her present husband, who, in contrast to Hugo, "does not disturb [her], any more than he is disturbed himself" (27). As she begins to dwell upon Hugo, however, gazing at his photograph on a recent book, it becomes evident that the pose of detachment is an aspect about herself with which she must reckon. The first level of complicity, then, is within the narrator herself, and the kind of distinction we made with Del Jordan as a name for a double focalizer as protagonist and narrator should be made here. This is somewhat difficult to do, for the narrator refuses to identify herself by name. The assumed anonymity is significant, especially as even the most minor characters have some identity in the story. This nameless speaker, however, is in the process of acquiring identity—even visibility—and she chooses to do it not only by revealing the degree to which she is not detached, but also by suggesting that the meaning she makes for herself is deeply implicated in Hugo's writing and her memory of their past together. Who she is cannot emerge with a precise, self-sufficient clarity. She is, despite her initial disavowals, very much like the women she tries to differ from.[6] The strength, the authority, of her discourse, however, emerges from the same matrix as Mr. Lougheed's, and that is the realization that self-assertion depends upon yielding to who one is and relating that figure to the other figures that constitute both the story and rhetoric of its discourse. So, brooding upon Hugo, she begins to tell of their life together.

The narrator's life with Hugo focuses upon their landlady's daughter, Dotty. Such a focus allows development of the double perspective about her that the narrator and Hugo share. With her husband she allows herself to perceive Dotty as a kind of figure of fiction, a woman whom they dub "the harlot-in-residence," a term that the narrator is perfectly aware contrasts "ironically . . . with Dotty herself" (31). Who Dotty is "herself" emerges only as a figure in the narrator's discourse, thus allowing another level of irony to develop that reflects upon the narrator. Dotty is primarily a sign for the difference that exists between the narrator and Hugo, a sign particularly of Hugo's inability to know women and, as a consequence, his wife. Dotty is also a double creation, one version of which the narrator develops for her own purposes, and another that is given to Hugo. Eventually, Hugo turns her "into Art"

(43), an act by which she becomes subject to the male text. That she is so subject is made abundantly clear through Munro's use of a narrator who works in contrast to Hugo, telling another kind of story, and who is subject herself both to men and to the consequent division in herself that Munro ironically develops.[7] Hugo's skill is to present "Dotty lifted out of life and held in light, suspended in the marvelous clear jelly" that belongs to Hugo's ability to perform magic tricks (43). This may appear to be praise, but the image of someone hanging in jelly is a false view of human life.[8] Furthermore, fiction need not lift its characters "out of life" but, rather, should invest them with life. The narrator underscores this judgment by remarking that her statements constitute "[i]ronical objections" (43), and these are objections that turn precisely upon the kind of failure that Hugo's text contains. It depends upon a trick, one that separates, removing the character from its situation. Situation, as the narrator reminds us repeatedly, is how lives are implicated to such a degree that to see the individual with clarity in Hugo's manner fails to reckon with the donées of human, and more precisely, female existence.[9] Certainly Dotty cannot be separated from the lives of Hugo and his wife, being part of both their arguments and their fantasies. What we cannot tell, however, is precisely how she becomes Art in Hugo's hands. We may infer that, since her story was filtered to Hugo through his wife, a number of things, particularly her gynecological problems, were probably suppressed. What we are told is that Hugo's art is invested with the kind of "authority" (44), no matter how limited and precarious it may be, that he shares with the other male in the story, the narrator's second husband. As the narrator makes emphatically clear, "[t]hey are not *at the mercy*" (44). With this phrase the narrator takes us to the heart of the problems and triumphs of structuring fiction. The narrator is acutely, even bitterly, aware that Dotty has been a shared subject of her and Hugo's often satirical imagination. Nevertheless, such an awareness does not permit dissociation from Dotty, the sign of the subject who is "at the mercy." Thus the narrator's final judgment is announced in italics to mark it as a text intended both for Hugo and for the implied reader over Hugo's shoulder: *"This is not enough, Hugo. You think it is, but it isn't. You are mistaken, Hugo"* (44). This allows her to say immediately thereafter that her attitude toward both the men in her life is to blame, envy, and despise them.

Without confusing the narrator with Munro, it can, nevertheless, be remarked that "Material" was designed to expose the matrix of the storyteller's craft. The title itself signals such a reading, and the narrator's continual revisions about her relationship with herself and Hugo, which are, we are led to believe, left untouched, are all indications that Munro wants us to see where and how significance is produced. What we discover is that true authority is not imposed upon the material. It is acquired by surrendering to it. The mark of the narrator is her vulnerability and, consequently, her inability to control loose ends.[10] Lives are inextricably intertwined, to draw upon another connotation of "material," and thus the turning of such lives into discourse destroys any pretense to objectivity. We are all subjects for one another. Moreover, because we never remain fixed in time, "suspended in . . . clear jelly," our earlier selves are as much material as those figures who appear to be characters distinct from us. Thus, even for the narrator to grasp herself in an earlier guise is problematic, for the more clearly this is achieved, the greater the *différance* that occurs. Thus the narrator is always at the mercy of her discourse, distancing and narrowing the gap between her present and other selves. To draw them all together in some final, disclosing image and metaphor is a temptation that must be both resisted and yielded to. And this is what Munro does, always moving within the extremes of this temptation, endeavoring to locate the meaning that unifies, and yet always wary of it.[11]

Next to other selves, the other itself is also eagerly sought and just as eagerly held at a certain distance. This other is the "you" that is persistently appealed to in these stories. Among the functions of the other, the narratee of the narrator's desire, as we are told in "Tell Me Yes or No," is to provide a link between the self that narrates and the self narrated. Thus she concludes: "If I could kindle love then and take it now there was less waste than I had thought. Much less than I had thought. My life did not altogether fall away in separate pieces, lost" (113). What the story illustrates, however, is not the connection made through the taking of love, but rather the connection that the nameless narrator, exactly as in "Material," tries to establish through the talking of discourse. One of the first steps she takes is to avoid any recognizable links with space and time. The narrator simply begins by addressing another unnamed figure. She says: "I persistently imagine you dead" (106). She then remarks: "You told me that you loved me years ago. Years ago. And I said that I too, I was in love with you in those days. An exaggeration." The simplicity of these sentences contains in one of Munro's most characteristic manners the problem of the story that they introduce. The diction is of a kind everyone employs.

But merely by the use of an anaphora that one might overlook—"years ago. Years ago" and "I too, I was"—we discover that the time of the utterance is eclipsed by the way in which discourse alters meaning continually. If "years ago" modifies "loved" the meaning of the sentence differs from what it means if it modifies "told." In the case of "told," the loving could still continue. In the case of "loved," the implication is that his love is part of the past. When that past is, is not clearly indicated, for it is all, it would appear, a function of the speaker's imagination. Nor should we overlook the parallel response on the speaker's part, which makes the sense of time even more blurred. "I" and "you" are made to complement each other in a discursive game that makes it clear that time is not to be trusted nor, as a consequence, the way things are put. There will always be a deferral between the event and its expression, so as to imply that pure referentiality might suppress a certain level of truth. This is because time for a narrator is a function of memory and also of changes of attitude that occur with respect to specific events. Thus the event begins to take on a plural focus. Accuracy, then, does not spring from a reconstruction of the event as it is, but in the event as it changes in its reconstruction.

The process of reconstruction in "Tell Me Yes or No" begins by an introductory description of events "in those days" when the speaker was married to a university student. It was then she met the story's addressee. Summing up these initial paragraphs, she observes: "You say you were in love with me and I reply that I was in love with you, but the truth was surely different" (108). Such a statement appears to be made in the present, the time of narration. But they are not speaking in the present, for he is either dead or in some other way nonexistent. It is perhaps, then, an imagined dialogue, in the time of his being persistently imagined as dead. The narrator then interrupts her recollection of their initial meetings and begins a new train of recollection in some middle period of time: "I remembered the same day you remembered, when we met two years ago totally unexpectedly where neither of us lived" (108). Thus it appears that the declaration of love lay two years before. Their subsequent conversation returns to the university period, and the narrator recalls how, at that time, she "said to him, 'I was in love'" (109). What the shifts in tense and repetitions indicate is that memory orders time according to its desire and regret. Things occur when they occur in memory. This incurs certain risks. The foremost of these is that "you" will have no independent existence but will become a function of "I." Thus the role with which the other is invested, that is, to link the present self with past selves, is capable of losing credibility. The reality of the other becomes willed, lacking a reliability of its own. This poses a problem for "I," dependent as she is on "you." She seems to know unconsciously that he has no self-motivating function, and so, immediately following her remembering "in those days" that she loved him, she separates her (present) self from her (past) self by asking him: "Would you like to know how I am informed of your death?" (109). Here we might have expected a past tense, but the death of "you" is meant to be perceived as aorist, part of a timeless present. The manner by which the question enters the story, dividing time, also suggests that his death breaks the possible connection the narrator may have acquired through him with herself. But this disconnection is continually deferred, for what it permits is a movement from present back to the middle time ("two years ago") when they met in the city where neither lived. Here he announces that he loved her then, and he loves her now, which is a statement that permits temporal continuity, and leads to the brief union of "I" and "you." The union is followed by a clear break in the text, ironically underlining the fundamental discontinuity that the discourse makes of the story.

The final sections of the story describe her visit to his city to find him somehow again, "searching . . . for some memory of you" (116). Like Del Jordan, she desires "revelations" (116), and she is given them in a curious manner. She goes to his wife's bookstore, and there she is handed a bundle of letters. The wife assumes she is her husband's lover. The first thing the speaker notices is that the handwriting is not hers, and the next day she avers to the wife that the letters are someone else's. This puts her into the poignant position of brooding on this other relationship, and in particular she begins to think of him contemplating her. Finally, she asks: "Am I right, am I getting close to you, is that true?" (124). Then, after recalling his declaration of love, she asks a more disarming complicitous question: "How are we to understand you?" The "we," presumably, refers to the apparent author of the letters received from the wife. No sooner, however, is such a conjecture made than another, and final, observation comes:

Never mind. I invented her. I invented you, as far as my purposes go. I invented loving you and I invented your death. I have my tricks and trap doors, too. I understand their workings at the present moment, but I have to be careful, I won't speak against them. (124)

We do not know, then, whose letters she was given, whether her own or no one's, nor whether the invention of her love is truth or self-protective disavowal. The extent to which self and other are intertwined is evident, however, in the clause "I invented you." The strength of the assertion resides in the speaker's self-awareness and in the necessity to claim herself at a primary level of being. The fundamental value of "you" is as a figure in her discourse, the manner in which she claims herself, along with her tricks and trapdoors. Thus the links with her selves in other times remain her possessions, no matter how much they must carry with them a threat of discontinuity.

The other does not dwell, then, as it does for the most part in "the other country" of *Dance of the Happy Shades,* but in profound relation to the narrator. It is the necessary angel, one might say, of clarification. It is precisely because of this that Munro's stories possess the kind of poignancy they do. The undefined "something" that "I" is "meaning to tell you" springs from the pun on "meaning" that connotes both signifying and desiring.[12] Thus for Munro writing in this collection takes on the role of desiring, and the desire is to find the self through the presence of the other in the discourse of the self. The discovery, however, resides in a collusion of self and other that gradually blurs the outlines of the self.[13] The risk of relationship is that if the other cannot be grasped, neither can the self. This is particularly true in the story that serves as a conclusion to the collection as a whole, "The Ottawa Valley."

The story begins with the speaker thinking of her mother in a variety of places and times, "and more and more often lately," she remarks, "when I look in the mirror" (227). The story consists of a series of brief vignettes that compose a trip taken in childhood with her mother back to her mother's childhood home. The narrator, underlining her peculiar kinship with her mother, is at the time of narration the same age as her mother when the story takes place. One is reminded, then, of the shared focalization of *Lives of Girls and Women,* but in this story the discontinuites of the plot are of such a character as to make us question whether a story is being told or whether the story is simply an occasion for reminiscence on the part of aunts and uncles that continuously throws time out of joint. Their stories simply provide layers of discourse from which the mother, the object that story as a whole endeavors to retrieve, is sought, as if the narrator were trying to rescue her and herself from a shared past. As the conclusion dramatically indicates, their stories set up the narrator so as to be able to reply to them and to examine the fundamental discursive problem of the story as a whole. At the conclusion of the last sketch a break in the text is indicated, and the narrator writes: "If I had been making a proper story of this . . ." (246). One is tempted to see such an intervention as metafictional in some way,[14] but part of the point of the hypothesis is to remind us that there may not have been any intention to be proper, and that in fact another story is being sought that needs to avoid conventions of decorum. It is at this moment that "I" desires to explain the necessity of her desire to reach "you," and this is the desire upon which the fiction of the whole rests. The narrator does not desire her mother merely to pass "into Art," thus remaining satisfied with the kind of fiction Hugo practices in "Material," but "to find out more, remember more . . . to bring back all I could" (246). Hugo's Art not only washes its hands of the subject, but also, through the use of the verb "passed," desires to fix the subject forever in a kind of perfect death. It is possible to speculate, I think, that Munro invests her narration with her own fear of death, refusing, like Del Jordan, to give up the past easily.[15] The point of the refusal is to find a way to set the figure free, thus releasing the narrator from its burden. The more intimate the burden, however, the more difficult is the release. Thus the whole object of the narrator's discourse and the protagonist's journey is to come to terms with the mother, "[t]o mark her off, to describe, to illumine, to celebrate, to *get rid,* of her" (246). But, as she asserts, in this she fails. The burden "is heavy as always, she weighs everything down, and yet she is indistinct, her edges melt and flow" (126).

The problem, then, of Munro's fiction is what it has been from her first collection. The mark of her style is always one of intimacy. Beneath the intimacy there lies both a compassion and desperation that turn upon a paradox. The urge to return, as this story enacts, is suspended between the desire to know the subject as profoundly as possible and not to possess it, but to set it free in some uncanny way, as if it were giving new life to the subject sought. This becomes a struggle on the level of narration because the life Munro seeks is in a fiction that is not "like life," but in a mode of discourse that demonstrates that the problem of life, death, loss, and recuperation must pass into the telling. This suggests that fiction itself might be a kind of fraud, a magic act and an act of faith that obscures a truth. This passion for truth is already present in *Lives of Girls and Women,* and it emerges again in the narrator's appeal to the lover at the conclusion of "Tell Me Yes or No," when she asks: "Am I right, am I getting close to you, is that true?" (124). But truth does not lie wholly in the subject sought, especially when the principal subject of the first-person narratives is the narrator. She is also part of the fiction, but her stance is of one who is not engaged in fiction but in truth, as if the terms stood in some clear opposition.[16] They do not, of course, and part of the secret of Munro's skill is to play with them, allowing her narrators, at least, to appear on the side of a truth that the fiction does not always yield. Thus the narrator breaks into the telling of "Winter Wind," interrupting a shift in focalization from herself as a child visiting her grandmother to herself as narrator, commenting on a secret love of her grandmother's, to say: "And how is anybody to know, I think as I put this down, how am I to know what I claim to know?" (201). What troubles her is that in a certain way she has taken advantage of her characters, to whom she refers as "people" to suggest their referential reality. But now she confesses: "I am not doing that now, I am being as careful as I can, but I stop and wonder, I feel compunction" (201). Her compunction comes, she says, because she has strayed from the facts. With reference to her grandmother she has "implied that she would be stubbornly, secretly, destructively romantic" (201). She has no proof for what she has implied, only her belief, and her belief is "that we get messages another way, that we have connections that cannot be investigated, but have to be relied on" (201).

I have called these statements by the narrator interruptions because they intervene in the narrative movement. Inasmuch as Munro privileges her narrators and their problems, it is perhaps not entirely correct to suggest that these moments when the narrator is focalizing are interruptions so much as reductions of the level of narration to a primary grade. We should not forget, however, that these are formal strategies employed by the author to lend more credibility to the story simply by showing her narrators' efforts to arrive at a certain truth within the fiction. Just as the "legendary" arises out of the "real," so the basis for all utterance is said to be the "true." By employing narrators who engage in issues of knowledge and perception apparently apart from the stories they tell and are engaged in, Munro reminds us how problematic indeed these issues are. As her narrators themselves also remind us, separating self from other, narrator from narration, truth from fiction is a hopeless task, and thus their assertions of special knowledge and desire for truth only underscore the fact that they are as much subject to discourse as the characters they use or try not to use for special purposes.

Thus one feels a certain kind of deception when, toward the end of "The Spanish Lady," one reads of the narrator's traveling companion that he had "vanished as if I had invented him" (189). Does "I" *only* invent? Does their author only invent? These questions are pertinent because they are implicit in the problems that Munro set herself from her initial stories and that become more acute as her craft develops. The problem that most frequently recurs in her work is the relation of past to present. The expression of that problem in writing is one that questions the nature of time. When something is gone in time, no longer present physically, its re-presentation appears impossible. The re-presentation of the mother appears so in "The Ottawa Valley" because she is gone in all but memory, and she cannot be cleared from memory if she is not known sufficiently enough to be herself and not merely a memory. Clearance depends upon the kinds of relations that can be established with the lost figure, and this is the central problem posed by "The Spanish Lady."

The narrator of the story is on a train returning home, trying to reckon with her husband and the woman for whom he has left her. The story begins with the texts of two letters the narrator writes to them. The first is tolerant and understanding. This letter is interrupted by a second, a letter of protest, in which a crucial issue of the story is raised. *"It is terrible,"* she is reported to write, *"when you find out that your idea of reality is not the real reality"* (176). The immediate referent of "real reality" is the deception of Hugh and Margaret. The reconstruction of the story's events follows the differing modes of the two letters as strategies for arriving at a notion of the real. Thus the story operates on a level of various flashbacks, analeptically piecing together the relationship between the three of them. Present time is represented as the journey on the train with a Rosicrucian who infiltrates the pulse of the narrator's recollections. He serves a dual purpose. The first is that he may possibly become a character in a story for Hugh, an act which will, paradoxically, condemn him to a past, thus illustrating through the narrator Munro's concern for loss and transience.[17] On another level, however, he simply shifts from one fictional register to another, deepening the problem of truth and reality. His other role is to illuminate the myth of palingenesis (another kind of re-presentation) held by Rosicrucians. Each of us, he declares, lives for 144 years, a period that includes the years of our life and death. After that given span of time has passed, we return in a new life. Thus he insists that the narrator was with him in Spain before the Conquest of Mexico.

So she becomes on a train from Calgary a woman with a past as the Spanish lady. She too can be invented or discovered in another reality, a possibility that questions the real of reality.

The story urges the reader, then, to consider which level of time invests one with a credible sense of actuality. The arrival in the station presses the story to a climax that continues to undermine the narrator's grasp of the world. She is in the act of recalling how she and Hugh had met in the Vancouver of twenty-one years before. She remembers how they "clung like people surfacing, miraculously rescued" (189), persuading herself that it can happen again. That is exactly what does not happen. At that moment the station is filled with a great cry of "rage and terrorization" from which everyone flees. The cry is of an old man dying, and one might infer that the cry, echoing a howl of protest the narrator makes earlier in the story, links him metaphorically with the narrator. Munro, however, moves in a different direction and has the narrator observe: "By that cry Hugh, and Margaret, and the Rosicrucian, and I, everybody alive, is pushed back. What we say and feel no longer rings true, it is slightly beside the point" (190). The brute reality of death appears to be the reality by which the real and the true are discovered, and so it guarantees the fiction through which the narrator has been moving. The cry, then, is a "message," but one that itself requires confirmation. Thus the narrator asserts: "I really believe it is; but I don't see how I can deliver it" (191).

In this conclusion we are reminded again of the title of the collection, the necessity of its message, and the relating of "I" and "you." When the real has no basis that the narrator can perceive, the message cannot be formulated. This may appear to be a limitation of the first-person narrator. As we have seen, however, Munro's more "omniscient" narrators merely prefer to suggest, rather than disclose all. It is a mark of Munro's scrupulousness that Mr. Lougheed is never permitted to make connections other than with his dream, and the reader is given no special knowledge about Eugene. For if final connections could be made in which true meaning could be found, then stories would not need to be told. To discover at last would destroy the telling, the continual deferring of finality. For Munro, telling is the process of playing off the quest against its object so that the object is absorbed by the quest. While there is for Dorothy, the protagonist of "Marrakesh," "in everything something to be discovered" (163), she does not derive a feeling of release in the discovery. It is a feeling, rather, that pins "her where she was in irritable, baffled concentration" (163). For the reader, the story appears designed to suggest that messages, whether given intentionally or not, may become too intimate to be objectively understood. This is because the message is so deeply interwoven with its context, and the context traced by this story appears to be nothing if not haphazard and random.

"Marrakesh" turns upon the relationship of Dorothy and her granddaughter, Jeanette. Echoing a similar relationship in "Walking on Water," the narrator takes care to suggest the difference between the two generations. For Dorothy, "Jeanette was a problem to understand" (161), and her character as a problem is perceived as "a hieroglyph on her grass" (166). She possesses, then, the same qualities as the cry in the Vancouver Station at the close of "The Spanish Lady," and the problem is that she speaks in a code of ethics and ideology that exceeds the elderly woman's understanding. Thus their relationship is dramatized as one in which Jeanette provides the text, and Dorothy responds with a baffled gloss. As a result, their relationship composes the message that draws them both into a shared configuration. Because of that intimacy, a linear exposition of the story is not particularly necessary, for logical relations are subordinated to relations of possible insight that occur accidentally. Thus the narrator, apparently following the clues of recollection, leads the reader into the story by telling of Jeanette's visit to the cemetery, of how Jeanette since childhood continued to visit Dorothy, of how she appears to dress like a hippie, of Jeanette's gloomy views of the world, of Dorothy's recollections of her own childhood. The story appears to go nowhere, but simply to meander through Dorothy's mind as focalizer, trying to make things fit, and discovering well beyond the midpoint that "the connection [between them] had either broken or gone invisible" (166). The point at which the various threads of the story appear to conjoin is in the conversation between Jeanette and the man from next door about their respective trips abroad, in which Jeanette recounts her adventure with two Arabs in Marrakesh. It is a text, however, that remains unclarified for Dorothy. In the final scene she later witnesses the two of them making love. She wants to cry out to them both a word of warning, for "[b]old as they were, they looked helpless to her, helpless and endangered as people on a raft pulled out in a current" (173). They cannot, like Mr. Lougheed's Eugene on the water, be reached, and like Eugene's performance, what the lovers do is to become transformed into imitation of themselves elsewhere, appearing "[o]n the underside of [Dorothy's] eyelids" as "two welded figures, solid and bright, like those chalked-in drawings she used to put on the blackboard—surprising herself—for festive occasions" (174). The figures rest there as texts in palimpsest for Dorothy to continue to puzzle over.[18]

I have suggested an analogy between Mr. Lougheed and Eugene, on the one hand, and Dorothy and Jeanette, on the other, for their mutual relationships serve as emblems of how meaning is derived, if not always comprehended. On one level, they continue the relation that Bobby Sherriff bears to Del Jordan, and on another, they deepen it, suggesting the extent to which the perceiver is "at the mercy" of the perceived. Thus Mr. Lougheed and Dorothy suffer the same kinds of problems that the narrators do in the other stories we have examined, and the most intricate problem is that of distinguishing "I" from "you," narrator from narratee. We assume that the first-person narrators are all senders trying to reach someone, such as a mother, a husband, a grandmother, a lover. But before assuming the role of sender, they have already been receiving and somehow trying to make out the message in their narratives. Thus Jeanette and Eugene are already senders before the stories make them possible receivers. Because of this uncanny intimacy of "I" and "you," then, in these stories, it is impossible for the reader to translate the message with any clarity, distinguishing the real from the fiction. Thus Munro appears most at home in those stories in which the desperation of her groping narrators is most readily displayed, continually showing themselves at the mercy of the author's concern for the truth that hides and sometimes disappears in language.[19] So the protagonist of "How I Met My Husband" is used to show how we prefer our version of the truth to whatever the truth may be. Because of the levels, however, on which Munro's stories unfold, "truth" can only be the intertwining of versions, texts whose meanings always require revision. Meaning is always subject to narration(s) whose function is to seek conclusion without necessarily finding fulfillment in closure. This is exactly the strategy of the narator / protagonist of the story just mentioned who, while waiting for mail from a man who promised to write, the failed sender, finally marries the mailman. The mailman's version of the story is that she "went after him by sitting by the mailbox everyday." She does not dispute this story because she likes "for people to think what pleases them and makes them happy" (66).

Such an ending may seem cute, but it is in fact a humorous way of addressing knowledge and deferral. The story is in a context of stories, however, whose humor is predominantly ironic, all governed by the title story that initiates most of the issues we have been raising. Its protagonist too fails to convey the message, thus forever delaying

any recognition of her guilt and complicity. This can be attributed to
the kind of character Et is, as well as the implication of the story's
design, which, like "The Ottawa Valley," may be considered as "a
series of snapshots" (246). The function of these glimpses into various
moments of past and present is to so blur continuity that one never
has, as one does in classical tragedy, for example, a sense of the
inevitability of events in their awful succession. Closure, by contrast,
cannot be reached inasmuch as time is arranged spatially, giving one
the illusion of a certain freedom from seeing anything in an ultimate
perspective. This means that all those issues that Munro persistently
broods upon through her narrators—the relation of the real to fiction
and truth, the basis of knowledge, the sense of the transient, language
as recuperation and illusion—are finally subordinate to a central narrative
preoccupation. Above everything else is the relation of narrative discourse
to story and how it controls how we perceive and approach knowledge.

The title story begins with a sentence that draws three of the four
central characters immediately together. As Et remarks to her sister
Char, " 'Anyway he knows how to fascinate the women!' " (1). The
sentence has the same kind of charm as the opening sentence of "Walker
Brothers Cowboy," except for a crucial difference. In the earlier story
we are told of the lake. Here, the focus is on "he," a word of appropriate
vagueness, referring to Blaikie Noble, but figured in a pronoun he is
allowed to float between the two sisters as an object of special purposes.[20]
The narrator then observes: "She could not tell if Char went paler
hearing this, because Char was pale in the first place as anybody could
get. She was like a ghost now, with her hair gone white. But still
beautiful, she couldn't lose it." Et's remark, then, no matter how offhand
it appears, is part of a design. As we later discover, it is the guiding
design of the sisters' relationship. It is a message, and the narrator,
from her position just over Et's shoulder, wants the reader to follow
its course to see if Char grows paler upon receiving it. The reader
cannot tell, but is given a second message in return regarding Char's
unfailing beauty. Et, it would seem, plays a role that corresponds to
that of both Mr. Lougheed and Dorothy, always playing up to a center
of attraction. Et, however, is in many ways more manipulating, constantly
sending messages to see how they will affect her sister. Thus she specifies
more about Blaikie. "Et pressed on" (1), as the narrator puts it, but
Char appears to remain unmoved.

This initial exchange admirably sets the essential character of the two
sisters and their relationship. The first indication of when it takes place—

for the whole story is narrated in the past tense—occurs at the end of
the fourth paragraph: "She and Char had known him in the old days"
(1). This concludes a passage in which the reader is informed of Blaikie
Noble's change of fortune. He is now only a handyman at the local
hotel and driving bus tours. Neither the past nor present time of the
discourse is in any way specified, and Blaikie becomes a sign for the
ease with which Et floats between moments of time. In the next section
we discover that this conversation occurred in "that summer" (3) when
a trip had been canceled because of Arthur's (Char's husband) illness.
From the conversation that ensues among the three of them, it is made
clear that this section occurs prior to the first one, for Et is now
reporting her reunion with Blaikie. It is brought up within the context
of a game they like to play in which Arthur is likened to the king of
many legends. It serves as an occasion to draw out Et's obsession with
relationships when Arthur remarks that his namesake in his time too
was married to the most beautiful woman in the world. Et sharply
reminds him of how the story of Arthur and Guinevere concludes,
allowing the image of Blaikie to emerge suggestively as Lancelot. The
reader is reminded not only of Blaikie's patronym, but also of Char,
suggesting flesh (Fr. *chair*) and death by fire. One is also reminded of
Munro's own preoccupation with the legendary dwelling in the real,
investing the real with qualities that make it timeless. This again removes
from the story a sense of time's urgency, permitting the apparently real
to reflect upon legend in both earnest and game. The same tendency
is present, too, in the earlier story "Images," in which the present is
translated in such a way as to be perceived as fairy tale. Such shifts,
of course, work in Et's favor, creating a screen through which we
perceive Et as merely playing, no matter how dangerously.

The third section concludes the prefatory statements of the story,
taking the reader back to the reunion itself of Et and Blaikie. Thus
in a space of less than three pages the reader is attuned to the particular
relation that narrative discourse has with respect to the story. A normal
paraphrase of the story would reorder the relation of sections that are
now A-B-C into C-B-A. We have already remarked upon some of the
reasons for the order of the narrative. Now that we have observed how
the story is focalized through Et, we can begin to conjecture upon
others. This particular way of relating discourse to story tends to
emphasize Et's relationship with her sister while, at the same time,
preventing us from doing more than guess at motivation. Analepsis in
this instance, continually moving back in time, does not clarify, but

rather defers explanation. Nevertheless, whatever clarification we are given appears intent upon capturing our interest through random reconstruction, as if the secret lay not in logical progression but accident. But we are never permitted to forget that Et will always be near the scene of the accident. Just as the second section concludes with a question about how Blaikie lost possession of the hotel, so section three concludes with Et talking with Blaikie and volunteering the information that Char was married.

The next section begins with a clear shift of time in Et's remembering their childhood and Char's beauty, prompted by an old photograph. We are reminded in a different register of what we discovered in the game that evoked King Arthur, and that is that Char's beauty proves "that the qualities of legend were real" (6). How we discover this takes us through another aspect of time's complexity because of the mode of the recollection. We read: "Et remembered the first time she understood that Char was beautiful. She was looking at a photograph taken of them . . ." (5). We are led to believe that this occurs in the present time of the narrative, during her remembering "now."[21] As the section unfolds, however, it becomes evident that the time of her looking is in the past, not long after the picture was taken. The picture is of the two sisters and their brother Sandy, who has drowned between the moment when the picture was taken and when she compares her sister as picture and reality. Observing the real in the legendary, the narrator also adds that for Et beauty was thought to be "a fictional invention" (6). Such a statement urges the reader to consent to whatever the narrator might say about Et. It enhances our belief that no matter how much Munro's story might be a fiction, the narrator is part of the process that makes the fictional seem real. But if we so consent, we must not forget that the narrator also bears a complicitous relation to Et. She neither follows up her recollections nor probes what she does not reveal. This leaves the reader somewhat suspicious, then, of the real for Et and the extent to which it is shaded by the fictional, such is Et's manner, the air around her always echoing with innuendo. Because she "didn't like contradictions, didn't like things out of place, didn't like mysteries or extremes" (7), she prefers to see them in others, not herself.[22] This does not prevent the narrator from also treating Et the same way, and so, despite Et's preferences, she becomes a figure at the other extreme from Hugo's Dotty in "Material." The vagueness of time helps to make her so, as well as such comments that follow directly upon her dislike of mysteries as that she also "didn't like the bleak notoriety of having Sandy's drowning attached to her" (7). The anaphora of the phrase "didn't like" suggests that there are reasons for her protest, but we are probably not going to be given them.

The move in memory to Sandy's drowning provides the threshold for introducing Blaikie as he was "in the old days," specifying the time as the summer of 1918. It also sketches Blaikie's romance with Char, his sudden elopement with an older woman, and Char's attempted suicide by swallowing poison. Here are clues, at least, of motivation, and we learn from Et's witnessing Blaikie and Char kissing that Char's attraction for him can only be understood as being "at the mercy." The look on her face is like Sandy's face drowned. It is "lost" (11), recalling Jeanette's helplessness in "Marrakesh." The power of the motivation, however, arises not only from what Munro would call the facts, but also from echoes of things we already know. Poison, for example, was introduced in the first section as part of Blaikie's spiel on a bus tour about a woman who poisoned her husband. But the truth of the story is immediately undermined by the implication that it is all hearsay. It occurred, furthermore, in a haunted house, thus lending an air of Gothic mystery to the story. When Et meets Blaikie again in section three, she observes that he might be visiting " 'old haunts,' " to which Blaikie only replies that he is " 'not visiting,' " but " 'haunting' " (5), recalling the initial description of Char as "like a ghost now" (1). What we have already spoken of as a screen, through which characters are perceived, is here projected as a fictional register, through which both narrator and characters play a charade (the pun on Char is suggestive), allowing the reader to believe whatever level is desired.[23] Where, then, does "truth" reside?

Immediately following the episode of Char's attempted suicide, a new section is elaborated in which at a later time Et discovers a bottle of rat poison in Char's pantry. She recalls Blaikie's story, but infers that Char is slowly poisoning her somewhat boring and invalid husband. Et, who does not like mysteries, cannot help, nevertheless, interweaving fiction, gossip, and fact to produce further mysteries. Char's own attempt at poisoning herself is also turned to account. She becomes famous for it, and it assists her entry into the local drama society, playing the role of "the cold and beautiful heroine, or the brittle exquisite young society woman" (15). No one in the story avoids the protection of legend and fiction. Here, in fact, they are most at home and most vulnerable. Thus, when Et reports that now, in the summer of present time, Blaikie has left again, as well as a well-to-do woman at the hotel, the conclusion

that she wants Char to draw is drawn. Suggestion, not fact, is everyone's
true nourishment. It is no surprise that Char dies, nor that the cause
is not made known. The poison bottle is never found, and Et, who
cannot support mystery, can only speculate in a passage in which the
word "perhaps" is repeated three times, introducing her sentences (23).
We are not to know; we are to be left with an unsolved mystery. Nor
is it possible for Et to prevent herself from remembering, when Blaikie
returns a few days later, the similarity between this event and "some
story" (23). The narrator reminds us that the story is Shakespeare's
Romeo and Juliet, each, then, assisting us to transpose the effect of the
death into fiction and legend.

It is perhaps appropriate that all of this takes place in a town called
Mock Hill, a pun on mock kill, always suggesting the false and true
deaths that play off each other in the story. Such a pun is appropriate
for a character like Et and her complicitous narrator. And it is the
reader, finally, who is being mocked to a certain extent, being prepared
for clues that do not materialize. In the final paragraph Et is again on
the verge of telling Arthur what she failed to do earlier, tell him of
Char's attempted suicide over Blaikie. And so "[s]ometimes Et had it
on the tip of her tongue to say to Arthur, 'There's something I've
been meaning to tell you' " (23). But she cannot tell him, preferring
to put it off and enjoying the role of seeming to be his wife. Here we
can understand the accuracy of her name, *et* being Latin for the
conjunction "and," a word that couples, links, and supplements. It is
the sign of deferral, of never quite delivering the message that will
clarify.

No message, however, clarifies, and this is the point of the collection.
For Et to tell Arthur about Char would only put the story on another
level. That kind of message signifies little in itself. Signifying for Munro
depends upon the register in which it is placed. The truth of the
signification, then, can dwell only in the manner in which discourse
plays with story. This means, of course, that the real and the true run
the risk of becoming lost as levels of fiction. But such is the pleasure
of texts, particularly those that continually impose texts and versions
upon other texts. They are not always, however, designed to be primarily
pleasure, and one might also argue that the pleasure masks a certain
pain. The texts play; the narrators do not. This is the importance, I
take it, of the emphatic phrase *"at the mercy"* that is angrily put
forward at the end of "Material" (44). Thus the need to know, to
come across revelations, which is everywhere in Munro, is not merely

to satisfy a pleasure in passive sense, but an active desire inscribed deeply within the narrative voice. It is a voice, furthermore, that indicates that the relation of narration to story can never be direct or "logical" because there is always more than one story. The best the narrator can do is to suggest ways of drawing versions and texts together to indicate, if nothing more, how revelation is sought. This always gives an impression of a certain desperate fragmentation and possible loss of self within the levels of discourse.

It would be tempting to argue that the dominant cause of fragmentation and loss may be attributed to the roles men play in the lives of Munro's women. Certainly this is powerfully suggested by "Memorial," in which a woman attends her nephew's funeral. In the course of it she sleeps with her brother-in-law. The narrator comments: "What Eileen meant to Ewart, she would tell herself later, was confusion" (224). Thus she can be distinguished from her sister, and thus she "with her fruitful background of reading, her nimble habit of analysis . . . can later explain and arrange it for herself. Not knowing, never knowing if that is not all literary, fanciful." She then reflects more specifically on Ewart, seeing him as collectively male:

A woman's body. Before and during the act they seem to invest this body with certain individual powers, they will say its name that indicates something particular, something unique, that is sought for. Afterwards it appears that they have changed their minds, they wish it understood that such bodies are interchangeable. Women's bodies. (225)

A woman is not only reducible to a neuter pronoun, as in "Boys and Girls"; she is simply one among any number of "its." She is not only "at the mercy" of the male, but she is also subject to his discourse.[24] It would appear that, for the sake of their object, men will both conjure its name as special and later speak as if no difference is apparent at all.

The concluding passage of the story, however, addresses discourse from another perspective. The mother of the killed boy reveals to Eileen the true circumstances of his death. The explanation is given, we are told, as an offering. The final image of the two is their reflection in a mirror, showing them as images of themselves. For a moment one supposes that Eileen might reciprocate by a revelation of her own, but she means to say nothing. Her one gesture is to take a sister's hand in token of a kind of bonding, and the narrator suggests that "[a]cts

done without faith may restore faith," something which Eileen "had
to believe and hope . . . was true" (226).

"True," as the final word, cannot help but reverberate through the
story, bidding the reader recall who the characters are, in their reflection,
for each other. It is almost impossible to say, however, to what extent
such a weak character as Ewart can divide the sisters from each other.
Indeed, Eileen as focalizer is the figure that discourses for Ewart, providing
him with attitudes he may or may not have. To say this in no way
mitigates the pain that the story holds. It would be more appropriate
to argue, however, that the pain does not reside in a particular theme.
Other relationships, such as mother and daughter, are equally, if not
more, painful. The pain resides in narrators and such protagonists as
Eileen, Dorothy, and Mr. Lougheed, who play upon our belief in a
truth distinct from fiction. The more appeals are made to the true, the
more one's faith is undermined. Sentences do not, as the title "Material"
implies, return the real with simplicity. They persistently embroider
upon it, drawing it into their various threads. The message has no end,
always woven into another message. How is one, then, to have faith;
how is one to know?

Chapter Five
The Self Unraveled

Who Do You Think You Are?

"Words are all shameful."[1]

It would appear upon initial reading that *Who Do You Think You Are?* is in many respects a revision and extension of *Lives of Girls and Women*.[2] Like the earlier text, it is a bildungsroman; it carries a central relationship between mother and daughter, and pays close and painful attention to the deceptions of love. This returning movement, that is also evident in the relationship between the two collections of short stories, serves a fortiori to suggest that the same material is constantly being reworked. Munro can be criticized for a certain monotony in this regard, especially if the reader is reluctant to see that her attention to the matter of her text is guided by a specific intent. The intent, as we have seen, bears upon the endless consideration of where meaning lies, how the teller ushers that meaning forth from the zones of nonmeaning where it dwells, and whether meaning can, in the end, be reached. Thus, while the matter of her stories is not subordinate to her intent, for without the matter her purpose would have neither passion nor poignancy, her intent illuminates the matter so as to make what appears to be real an object of semiotic and epistemological inquiry. The real becomes real, so to speak, in Munro because, paradoxically, so many questions are raised about it. But the questions always seem to turn upon similar situations,[3] and in this respect Munro calls to mind Isaiah Berlin's distinction between writers who are either hedgehogs or foxes. The hedgehog is characterized by his ability to relate everything to "a single, universal, organizing principle in terms of which alone all that they are and say has significance."[4] The fox, by contrast, pursues "many ends, often unrelated and even contradictory."[5] It may be that Munro's protagonists appear to be foxes, but Munro herself comes closer, I would argue, to what Berlin calls the centripetal intent of the hedgehog. This would put Munro in a certain tradition that includes Dante, Dostoyevski, Ibsen, and Proust as opposed to Molière, Goethe, Balzac, and Joyce.

Such a distinction acquires even more validity when we consider the wonderfully gnomic character of the question that forms the title of the volume.[6]

The most obvious use of the question is to be seen in the manner by which it is brought into the text. It is initially used in the first chapter, "Royal Beatings," as a way of exposing the protagonist's rude behavior. By coming early in the book it establishes the significance of a complex theme that ranges from mere rudeness to levels of pretension that pose very difficult problems of characterization. The same question is raised in the final and title story, thus framing the novel and returning explicitly to an initial field of inquiry. The return is made even more emphatic inasmuch as Rose, the protagonist, is in each instance viewed in her adolescence and being scolded by her stepmother and teacher, respectively. But reverberations of meaning do not end there. It occurs also in the chapter "Half a Grapefruit," which takes its title from a moment of daring in which Rose tries to distinguish herself as somehow different from her humble origins. Indeed, much of the story turns upon Rose's growing awareness of difference, of her desire to transcend her origins, and especially the pain it will cause. At one point in the chapter Rose exchanges stories with her stepmother, Flo, telling of a girl who is having sexual intercourse with a boy in the dark under her front porch. It is part of a joke that two of the boys are playing on a third, but the victim of the joke is the girl who must suddenly ask of her second partner, thinking he is the first boy: *"Then who the hell are you?"*[7] This question immediately changes the meaning of the first question, and the sense of the new meaning is implicitly developed in Flo's story in which she recalls a time in her youth close to the age of Rose and her school acquaintances. She tells how she was working for the pretentious wife of a farmer. The woman requests her to take the husband's dinner out to the field where he is working. When the husband asks for the pie he was expecting for dessert, Flo replies "in the exact words and tone of her mistress when they were packing the dinner," saying, " 'If you want any pie you can make it yourself' " (43). The story neatly exemplifies Flo's talent for imitating others, but in its context of exchanged anecdotes it leads the reader to perceive an important implication of the title question. Not only are we invited to see the thematic usage of the question as it illuminates pretension in the text, but also, and more emphatically, we are to consider the problem of imitation itself.[8]

We have already observed Munro's preoccupation with imitation, most notably in Bobby Sherriff's final moment in *Lives of Girls and Women* in which his self-transcendent dance guides Del into the alphabet of the real. Pantomime, the adoption of a persona, is ineluctably related to the act of narration, and this is, perhaps, the primary level upon which Munro's preoccupation with imitation turns. There is, however, another level to which we will later return. That is, the act of imitation reflects as much on the actor as on the dramatized scene, and at this level the apparently simple question, who do you think you are?, raises ontological considerations. The emphasis falls on the verb "are," and it bids us examine to whom "you," in fact, refers. It makes us ask what the referential real is, finally, for actors and mimics, and the question is important, for not only is Flo a consummate mimic, but Rose's career is that of an actress, for which she has rehearsed long before she approaches the stages and studios where the reader rarely sees her. Rose's acting is her story; narrative discourse, her stage.

It should be clear, then, that the relation between Rose and Flo is layered with far more significance than that between Del and her mother.[9] It is a relationship whose meaning is played out in various modes throughout the whole text and links them almost as doubles. Both their names suggest "flower," and what the relationship lacks in consanguinity is compensated for by congruity. Both are superb mimics, but Flo's tendency is toward the satirical, while Rose is more subtle, more apt to assume the reality of the part she plays. Thus Flo exposes, and Rose poses with a curious combination of awareness and credibility. Both roles are inaugurated in "Royal Beatings." Here we find Flo reveling in her travesties of small-town social stereotypes: "Monsters she made them seem; of foolishness, and showiness, and self-approbation" (10). Flo "liked to see people brought down to earth" (23–24). Rose is the nearest and easiest object to satisfy this desire, and her response is at once heroic and theatrical. She is, naturally, the object of "royal beatings," and her childhood considerations of what they were, besides beatings, are fantasies of a ceremonial order. What she wants to know is how they become royal: "She came up with a tree-lined avenue, a crowd of formal spectators, some white horses and black slaves. Someone knelt, and the blood came leaping out like banners" (1). The beatings themselves never "approach such dignity," except for Flo, who invests them "with some high air of necessity and regret" (1). As a consequence, "beatings," which belong to "real life," are opposed as black to white with "royal," and for Rose, despite the narrator's denial, the play of fantasy and the stimulation of language always form another world alongside, "a troubling distorted reflection" informing the real.[10]

The world as distorted elsewhere—the scene that always implies something upon which it is based—is never kept exclusively apart. Nor can the narrator, analogously, prevent herself from distinguishing Rose as participant and perceiver, separating them only to recompose them on another level. Thus, as the father is called in to administer the beating, Rose observes him, "his look at first cold and challenging" (15). As it continues, "it fills with pleasure and hatred" (16). The narrator then declares: "Rose sees that and knows it. Is that just a description of anger, should she see his eyes filling up with anger? No. Hatred is right. Pleasure is right" (17). The relation of narrator to character at such a point is almost seamless, suggesting that the mind of the reflecting, older Rose is questioning and correcting, transposing Rose's pain into a narrative drama, in which the narrator assists the character to act out her perceptions more precisely. And just as there is a certain ambivalence between hatred and pleasure, so there is a more significant ambivalence in the role we see the father developing, who is staged as "a bad actor, who turns a part grotesque. As if he must savor and insist on just what is shameful and terrible about this" (16). But such an assertion, which poses exactly the relation of who we are and who we pretend to be, is immediately reconsidered by an emphatic support of a certain kind of ambivalence that fuses ambiguity into a necessary credibility, recalling Bobby Sherriff again: "That is not to say he is pretending, that he is acting, and does not mean it. He is acting, and he means it" (16). So acting is coterminous with meaning, but because of the narrator's insistence, we are reminded that acting may also be an undermining and deferring of meaning. That is, it may take you away from who "you are."

Munro's text runs, therefore, a certain risk, for it suggests that meaning derives from the part one adopts, but the part one adopts may also break down the sense of who one is. The world becomes theater, self becomes persona, relations are fraught with sham and disguise. Thus this novel rewrites *Lives of Girls and Women* through the prism of the collection discussed in the previous chapter. As a consequence, Rose never seems to come together as an integrated character in the way one senses Del Jordan is about to do. One believes, at least, that Del is capable of integration despite the contradiction between the centripetal force of metaphor in the novel and the general act of shedding that the character undergoes. But perhaps the use of metaphor was too simple, and the relations between characters are more complicated than they at first appear. This, at least, appears to be what the formal discontinuites of the later texts seem to insist upon. To close the gaps, then, in *Who Do You Think You Are?* especially between chapters, would be tantamount to violating a certain mystery, to be a declaration on the narrator's part that too much is known about a character that cannot be known. But what Munro cannot abandon without a struggle is the sense of likeness, something that is sufficiently similar to us that it forms a kind of mocking limit not simply to our pretensions, but also to the fullness of our being, of who we are. We may call it a double, but Munro's understanding of it is more supple than that. Whatever it is, we cannot know ourselves, and, hence, character itself cannot be understood, without acquiring a mode of appropriating the world of likeness. Thus the central act of Munro's fourth book is to inquire into a special aspect of mimesis, mimesis itself, rather than the representation of the given world.[11]

We have already witnessed one mimetic method of "Royal Beatings," namely, Rose's penchant for fantasy, to create imaginatively another world to illuminate the one in which she dwells, which the narrator casually calls "real life" (1). The second chapter begins by announcing the problem of mimesis as its general plan: "Rose knew a lot of people who wished they had been poor, and hadn't been. So she would queen it over them, offering various scandals and bits of squalor from her childhood" (23). To "queen it over them" is a metaphor that allows Rose, at least in imagination, to overcome poverty through the richness of narration, as well as to gain a certain mastery over the Rose who will be part of that narration. Furthermore, to offer "various scandals and bits of squalor" is a phrase that declares precisely the manner of the telling, for Rose's audience is never the same; and it becomes the author's task to censor what might often be repetitious, and to follow the lead of Rose's queening.

The story turns, in effect, upon two major performances—those that occur in the school privy and those that occur on the fire escape. The first, furthermore, instructs the reader how to see the second, and it is posed not as "comical" but "as scenes of marvelous shame and outrage" (23). The word "scenes" governs the discourse of the chapter, for it is beside the privy that Rose is invited to watch the scatological and erotic behavior of her fellow students, which goes so far as to include incest. For Flo there is only one word for such activity. This is to *perform,* and for Rose to move from such an act to such a description prompts her to recall in fantasy a story of incest as amateur theater:

. . . Flo said that people had gone dotty, been known to eat boiled hay, and performed with their too-close relations. Before Rose had understood what was meant she used to imagine some makeshift stage, some rickety old barn stage, where members of a family got up and gave silly songs and recitations. (25)

The function of such a recollection is to gather a central use of the word "perform," which connotes "diversions" and "pretensions" (25). Thus incest itself is not raised to condemn it as a moral issue, but to indicate simply that it would become a public act. For the older Rose, however, Franny, the girl so used, is of interest as a still more complicated mimetic problem. She is a figure that for male writers is usually portrayed as "an idiotic, saintly whore."[12] To do as much is morally weak: "They cheated, she thought, when they left out the breathing and the spit and the teeth; they were refusing to take into account the aphrodisiac prickles of disgust, in their hurry to reward themselves with the notion of a soothing blankness, undifferentiating welcome" (26). Such a statement, however, does not return Franny as she is, but shows the reader, rather, a central preoccupation of Rose's thought. How is the other to be most accurately known?

The answer to this question is given in one form by the second section of the chapter, in which Rose is granted the privilege to which the title alludes. She is given at least a brief entry into the magic world of the three older girls, who set the pattern for the other girls. She is permitted to sit with them, particularly Cora, on the fire escape, and from then on she is in love with her. Even before that moment, Rose is so fascinated by her that Cora's behavior becomes a model to follow. When alone, whatever Cora had done, "she would act that out, the whole scene, the boys calling, Rose being Cora" (31). After that moment, "[i]mitation was not enough" (32). Her relationship with Cora is transposed to fantasy in which both would be together in perfect undifferentiated intimacy. The nearest her desire comes to realization is during a kind of spring ritual in which eros and thanatos combine. Each girl must play dead while the girls heap her with flowers and sing hymns. During Cora's death Rose can find no other means of worship than to "pile up details to be thought over later" (33). Thus, performance, a stylized and mimetic act, which does not appear to imitate anything particular in "the real world," is a cue for further mimesis in which Rose would seek its details, "strain to remember them, know them, get them for good" (33).

As a sequel to this series of performances and transpositions, Rose steals some candy from Flo's store, which she secretly places in Cora's desk. Cora, however, savoring "respectability and the pleasure of grown-up exchange" (35), returns the candy, thus prompting Flo to tell her version of Cora. Nevertheless, "Flo's imitation was off, for once; it did not sound to Rose at all like Cora's voice" (35). And this should not be surprising, for Cora herself was probably trying to mimic adult behavior. The possibility that Cora and Rose may have been in love seems to Flo to be of the same order as all performances. It requires immediate exposure, for it would lead to nothing but "self-deception" (35). It is even worse that Rose should be in love with Cora, who was not attractive, whose father was unknown, and whose grandfather cleaned privies—in a word, a "honey-dumper." Thus both privy scenes and privy acts not only meet in the pretensions that Cora employs to protect herself, but also are conjoined in the pun on "honey-dumper," with its echoes of affectionate names, candy, and the image of Rose's love for Cora, "like the hard white honey in the pail" (33).

But the metaphorical thread that so neatly gathers "the bits of squalor" of the chapter remains subordinate to the principal issue of pretension, pretending, and imitation. In the first of two epilogues Flo is shown pointing out Cora to Rose, referring to her as " 'your idol.' " In response, "Rose pretended to have no recollection," yet, as the narrator elaborates, "Rose's pretense was not altogether a lie" (36). The reason for this is that the Cora of Rose's younger years is not this Cora, a fact that reminds one immediately of the problem that the collection raises as a whole. The sentence also recalls something Flo is unable to understand, that pretense may also refer to a truth in the process of transformation. This kind of truth belongs to the mimetic act and reflects back upon the chapter, permitting the reader to protect Rose, as Rose does herself, from Flo's role that would see anything beyond her view of the normal as both untrue and dangerous. Thus the chapter's second epilogue, which plays upon the new respectability of the town, allows Flo's view to appear to prevail, but within an ironic light. True transformation does not mean flush toilets and the end of the honey-dumper, but, rather, the process of transposition by which the details of the world are so grasped that we might "get them for good."

It might be said, in fact, that Flo's cautionary role acts more as a stimulus to Rose than as genuine protection. Thus Rose is warned, prior to her first venturing forth from her little town in "Wild Swans," that she must be on the lookout for "White Slavers." The most dangerous are "people dressed up as ministers" (55), which prompts Rose to say that she would be unable to "tell which ones were disguised" (55). This discussion not only establishes the sexual framework of the chapter, but also suggests that there is a threat whose presence cannot always be discerned. Men searching for sexual encounters always pretend they are other than they are, which Flo exemplifies by telling of the retired mortician who drives around the country in his hearse seeking women to seduce, singing of a woman with a brow *"like the snowdrift"* and a throat *"like the swan"* (57). He sings, of course, of women like Rose, intact and pure.

It could be argued that the man who takes a seat beside her on the train and introduces himself as a United Church minister may be too readily foreseen from the initial episode. The fact that his entry is predictable, however, not only lends credence to Flo's warning, but also provides the excuse for Rose to yield to what cannot be avoided.[13] No sooner has he sat down than he remarks upon the winter snows, a word that Rose remarks upon with her mind, thus reminding the reader of another simile from the mortician's song. Both nature and language appear to conspire in Rose's adventure, and this is further emphasized in the minister's telling her briefly of some wild swans he had once seen on a pond. Rose, who expressed such incredulity at Flo's song, does not at all seem to perceive that the minister bears all the signs of Flo's mortician. But in the world of sexual allegory that Flo creates, dangerous men in disguise are everywhere, just as much as untried innocence. They can hardly, therefore, be escaped. The design of the story's discourse is not satisfied merely with the irony of Rose's inability to see herself as part of Flo's advice. What it seeks is the fact that Rose is such that her disbelief barely disguises her desire and curiosity. For when the man, under the cover of his newspaper, begins to caress Rose's leg while pretending to be asleep, it impels Rose to indulge in sexual fantasies of other men's hands and their possible pleasures. Thus, rather than reject him immediately, Rose speculates, seeing herself in dramatic relation to both the minister and all the men he represents. But his hand is only the instrument that stimulates the more intense drama that she wages with herself, driven more by curiosity than desire, trapped by the fascination of the event and what might ensue. The combination of his hand and her interior argument creates between them the true scene of what is going on, which is the persistent metamorphosis of the hand in relation to her body, at once hers and "somebody's object" (61). Thinking of the hand, "[s]he did not feel disgust. She felt a faint, wandering nausea. She thought of flesh: lumps of flesh, pink snouts, fat tongues, blunt fingers, all on their way trotting and creeping and lolling and rubbing, looking for their comfort. She thought of cats in heat . . . " (62).

As the train continues toward Toronto, his hand proceeds toward its object, which Rose is unable to prevent, relying, one might say, upon the inevitable that resides in Flo's cautionary discourse. Thus, despite the fact that "her legs were never going to open" (62), they do, and their opening is transposed to a scene of archaic grandeur. One has the sense that what is happening is "as old as the hills," for their opening is a view down upon "the preglacial valley, the silver-wooded rubble of little hills" of the Niagara Escarpment (63), upon a world, presumably, that existed before frigidity and heavy snows. Entering the suburbs of Toronto, the objects of the world become even more explicit and complicit, where oil refineries are known by their "big pulsating pipes" (63). All adverbial qualification is designed to stress the extent to which analogy governs action:

They glided into suburbs where bedsheets, and towels used to wipe up intimate stains flapped leeringly on the clotheslines, where even the children seemed to be frolicking lewdly in the schoolyards, and the very truckdrivers stopped at the railway crossings must be thrusting their thumbs gleefully into curled hands. (63)

Entering Toronto itself, Rose is in such metaphoric consonance with the world that her inescapable orgasm is not hers alone: "The gates and towers of the Exhibition Grounds . . . the painted domes and pillars floated marvelously against her eyelids' rosy sky" (63). Suddenly these objects of unqualified male and female configuration change shape, becoming one in another guise: "They flew apart in celebration. You could have had such a flock of birds, wild swans, even, wakened under one big dome together, exploding from it, taking to the sky" (63). And the sky is at once "rosy" and Rose's, the natural world and its inscribed inevitability permitting Rose's own acceptance of herself as part of the natural and sexual community.[14]

Yet the use of the expression "wild swans" reminds us of the continual presence of this image and the changes it undergoes in the chapter. It connotes woman in her pristine state in Flo's discourse, merely nature in the minister's reminiscence, and, finally, nature and innocence collaborating in the change of the world. It is a sign of nature as theater, and not simply as backdrop, but as the name for theater's function as a scene of disguise and transformation. So the concluding section of the chapter returns to "Flo's messages," in which Rose ruminates upon "men who were not real ministers pretending to be real but dressed as if they were not" (64). Thus we begin to discover that pretending is more than pretense, for another of Flo's messages turns upon a woman she worked with in Union Station, Rose's symbolically—if inadvertently—named destination. Once the woman traveled to Georgian Bay, dressed to imitate the actress, Frances Farmer. This, then, is no ordinary mimicry, for she impersonates a professional impersonator, reminding us of the problem of who one really is. To add to the subtlety of the problem, the woman, whose real name is Mavis, does not register as Frances Farmer, but, rather, as Florence Farmer for fear of full recognition as the actress. Thus she is partly the actress and partly a further invention.[15] Flo (another Florence) is scandalized, but Rose hopes to find Mavis in the gift shop to see if she can recognize her, whoever she may look like. She then considers how fine it would be "to manage a transformation like that, . . . to enter on preposterous adventures in your own, but newly named, skin" (64). Such a closure emphasizes pretending as transforming disguise, in which one is the same but known as other. It is also daring, thus recalling the swans, signs of transformation, which are also wild.

The following chapter, "The Beggar Maid," forms the central section of the book. Rose is at once a beggar, because of her modest origins, and a maid, because of her being so perceived by her future husband as a damsel in distress. Rose is designed to combine, and the combination is a function of interplaying discourses that reflect the impossibility of her ever rising to the role of courtly maiden. Furthermore, when Patrick designates her as such, his language is ironic and true, yet "[t]he pretended irony would not fool anybody; it was clear that he did wish to operate in a world of knights and ladies; outrages; devotion" (74).[16] This puts Rose in exactly the situation to which all her speculations naturally bring her, for to be such a maid would be a marvelous metamorphosis. But it requires living through the eyes of another, which runs the risk of not only acquiring a new name, but losing a sense of one's self, of who one is. This is the risk of becoming his story, not her own.

Such a risk was established thematically in the initial section of the story when she is taken as a scholarship student by a retired professor, whose role is to encourage Rose to develop a career as a teacher or librarian before becoming a mother. Rose will have none of this "deadly secular piety" (69), desiring, rather, "to perform in public" (69). Thus, just as Professor Henshawe has plans for Rose, so does Patrick, which continues the former's role on a more dangerous level. The risk Rose runs is posed as both a loss of a notion of who she is and a loss of origins. Such a loss is played off in the central section of the chapter in which Rose and Patrick visit their respective homes, dramatizing what has already been broached as a delicate problem of self-alienation. For while it is possible for Rose to remark to Patrick that they live in " 'two different worlds,' " to say as much makes her feel "like a character in a play" (75). Nor is she able, once at his parents' house, to rise to the occasion. What she has to say is fully at odds with their interests and expectations. She fails even more significantly when they visit her family, for there she discovers the distance she has taken from her origins, especially as it affects the local sociolect, and how much her past has become theater: "And the things people said were like lines from the most hackneyed rural comedy. *Wal if a feller took a notion to,* they said. They really said that. Seeing them through Patrick's eyes, hearing them through his ears, Rose too had to be amazed" (87).

The problem of self-recognition, then, is defined and exacerbated in the chapter by a clash of discourse, by her embarrassment about her family's speech and her failure to find a discourse that can be shared with Patrick through which she might see who she is. But to speak as Patrick would have her speak means to destroy herself for the sake of "some obedient image that she herself could not see" (82). Given the ambivalence of her situation, it is not surprising that she breaks off her engagement but not long afterward consents to marry him. The moment she does the narrative perspective changes, and the reader is abruptly shifted from the vivid past of their courtship to an indefinite period closer to the present that begins, after a space in the text, with the clause, "[w]hen Rose afterwards reviewed and talked about this moment in her life" (94). Patrick and the younger Rose have themselves become figures of a discourse whose significance continually changes with time and according to the audience it seeks. The themes of her narration are normally pity, greed, cowardice, or vanity, but the true point that is always covered over is "the possibility of happiness" (95), and this is projected as a vision of other selves enacting other roles: "Then it was as if they were in different though identical-seeming skins, as if there existed a radiantly kind and innocent Rose and Patrick, hardly ever visible, in the shadow of their usual selves" (95). It is a vision, however, and very reminiscent of Munro's adjacent worlds, which does not correspond to those people who they think they are.

The epilogue to the chapter is designed to lead the reader to such an understanding of the problem, to understand that it is impossible to become the role to which one is by nature unsuited. It depicts Rose, some time after her marriage is over, meeting Patrick by chance in the Toronto airport. He sees her, and his face is overcome with all the hate he can muster. This recalls to Rose her job as a television interviewer, in which she has often felt that her subjects—"skillful politicians and witty liberal bishops and honored humanitarians" (97)—"were longing to sabotage themselves, to make a face or say a dirty word" (97). To do as much would reveal what civilized intercourse requires they keep hidden. It is also reserved for "the sudden, hallucinatory appearance of your true enemy" (97), and it is precisely this self that Patrick, having masked it so long as protector of the innocent, exhibits to Rose. It is unquestionably a public performance, which thus relates him to Rose and her aspirations to act, and it also reaches the true significance of her meaning for him, at least for that moment. Even dropping a disguise, then, is a kind of acting, and it invests performance with a justifying truth.

The following three chapters—"Mischief," "Providence," and "Simon's Luck"—all form a thematic unity in themselves and address the problem of finding and losing love. Because the first takes place during Rose's marriage and with a married man, and because the second occurs after her marriage and with another married man, they are both characterized by subterfuge and masking. In the third chapter both Rose and Simon are unmarried, and acting is a gesture that they employ for each other. All three chapters, however, raise another issue to prominence in the book by examining the problem of acting at a crucial point. They want to discover whether there is any self behind the projected self at all, and it is this desire that enters persuasively into the form of Munro's work that appears to be so random, especially in its abrupt alterations of perspective.[17] As a consequence, one often has the sense while reading her text that at any moment it may fall apart. Transitions, as I have already indicated, are not always clear, and spaces on the page are designed to underline the discontinuous character of the narrative. Formal discontinuity reflects, one might say, the space between selves or roles that masking does in theater, and the skill of the writer lies precisely in her ability to make us believe that things will not fall apart as she moves back and forth in time, to other aspects of a putative self. But the effort "to get it for good" is one that forces Munro's narrators to approach the lost past of the story over and over, by starting almost in medias res, by moving back in time to recover an important aspect of character, by resuming elsewhere. This effort, which is always raised to the level of form, inscribes loss into both the text and its discourse, and the loss, often of an aspect of self, is poignant indeed.[18] Part of what I am saying is summed up by the comment in "Providence" that "she could remember something between a curse and an apology, the slippery edge of failure. This made her especially eager to try again, to succeed" (146). The success, of course, is the text that emerges against that edge, but it is a success that necessarily underlines the losses and efforts of recovery that her protagonists suffer.

The mischief of "Mischief" appears to be Rose's "affair" with her friend Jocelyn's husband. Not only is it marked by subterfuge, but Rose herself, after their first lustful kiss, discovers that "[d]eceitfulness, concealment, seemed to come marvelously easy to her." In fact, it is of such a character that it "might almost be a pleasure in itself" (110). This Rose is not far from the Rose of "Wild Swans," a Rose for whom a man is pretext, a possibility that permits a certain role. When the narrator questions what she wants of Clifford, the reply is "tricks, a glittering secret" (112). And so after a long period of furtive meetings in the city, they agree upon a rendezvous in a small town where Clifford is on tour with an orchestra. Such an occasion requires a costume other than her usual attire, one that calls for "dramatic sexually advertising clothes" (119). It is not surprising, however, that when she is seen in the town where she is to meet her lover, no one, despite her story, believes she is waiting for her husband. Costumes reveal. They also prepare for revelations, which are not always of an expected kind.

The first revelation of "Mischief" is that Clifford's feelings have appreciably cooled, and even Rose's unintentional imitation of Barbara Stanwyck has little effect. Her mischief has, indeed, apparently been with herself, and the mischief that she seeks through Clifford is of no avail. The story does not, however, conclude so simply. The reader is moved to a later moment in time, after Clifford and Jocelyn have moved from Vancouver to Toronto. There the three meet again, after

Rose's marriage. Here a new Jocelyn is presented, who has renounced her antiestablishment pose, and a new Clifford, about whom Rose perceives "something theatrical" (129). On one of her visits with them in their new life, the three make love before the fire in the livingroom, and this is the mischief toward which the story seems to be heading. In her awakened desire of which she thought she was free, she suddenly grows angry with the couple: "She felt they had made a fool of her, cheated her, shown her a glaring lack, that otherwise she could not have been aware of" (132). It is a mischief that is in accord with her own failure to see the other as anything but instrumental, as subordinate to her own maneuvers. She then writes a letter to them, commenting upon their "selfishness" and "obtuseness," but does not send it, content with the expression alone. Their friendship, in fact, continues, "because she needed such friends occasionally, at that stage of her life" (132).

It would be tempting to underline the word "stage" that forms the cliché of the chapter's closure, but that might be demanding more than the text can provide.[19] It is hard not to notice, however, that the principal loss of the story is a part of Rose. Clifford is no more than a sign of her desire and need for mischief. The loss, then, is a function of the elaborate game that Clifford is drawn into, and where he finally refuses to act. Nor can one fail to notice the random character of the conclusion focused in the word "occasionally," suggesting that in becoming the object of sex for Jocelyn and Clifford, she has lost a self through her own mischief. "Providence," as the title suggests, appears to restore some of that loss. The restoration, however, is ambiguous, for the story turns upon another relationship with a man who suggests a little what Patrick may have become had he not returned from graduate studies to his father's business. Tom "was a courtly man, a historian" (135), and much of their relationship is conducted by mail. Because he is married, most of their letters consist in finding ways to meet, usually at conferences, and their meetings, with one exception, never take place. Action, then, is speculation, the world in which Rose thrives. When she first arrives in the town she moves to after she leaves Patrick, it seems "almost as if some people . . . got together and said, 'Let's play Town.' You think that nobody could die there" (136). No one, however, plays town; they play what Rose plays, for the only other characters of any substance are two women like Rose, separated from men they are somehow involved with.

In contrast to her escapade with Clifford in the previous chapter, Rose's efforts to see Tom are thwarted in each instance, this time by a snowstorm, and Tom seizes the occasion to terminate the relationship. That it is a providential act is symbolized by Rose's daughter's finding a broken public telephone that pours all its change into her hands. As they gaze at the money in Rose's kitchen, the narrator remarks that it is "[b]ounty where you'd never look for it; streaks of loss and luck" (150). This is a kind of providence, one of the rare occasions "when Rose could truly say she was not at the mercy of past or future, or love, or anybody" (150). She is released, the money is the sign of her release, but the plot of the story bids the reader inquire into the nature of what providence has produced. The catalyst of Rose's bounty is her daughter Anna, who frames the story. At the beginning of the chapter Rose dreams of Anna, to whom she poses the question whether she wants to stay with her father or come with her. The dream drifts uncannily into reality, allowing the narrator to give final indications of Rose's life before she leaves Patrick. She pauses long enough to mention Patrick, whom Rose once finds taping over old photographs, laconically referred to as "true lies" (133). How, then, is the photo of Anna and Rose to be understood? How is any relationship to be understood? For Anna her parents represent "the true web of life" (134); for Rose it is a fraudulent relationship. The story is posed as a situation in which Anna must choose between parents, and in the end she returns to her father and his new wife. Thus her role in the story imitates that of her mother, who makes the initial decision, but choosing her father is to leave her mother alone with little more than a fish in a fishbowl and letters from Anna to her father, "never finished, never mailed" (51). The final words are given, then, to Anna, and their childish simplicity resonates through the story, undercutting the wasted passion of the correspondence between Rose and Tom, a relationship that has no apparent substance. Tom, in fact, never enters the text except as he is spoken of, and his absence is the true sign of his relationship with Rose, for whom providence is the chance that moves her from absence to a release from time, which is itself another kind of absence.

By the time of the following chapter, "Simon's Luck," Rose's ambitions have been fulfilled: she "is an actress; she can fit in anywhere" (152). She is, in fact, a sign of the scene; and it is this ability, which one may observe from the first chapter, that makes one question whether Rose exists in any sense at all. Her ability to yield to a word, an atmosphere, a situation suggests that Rose is the name for a certain shifting focus through which the story's discourse is organized, and this becomes increasingly apparent from "The Beggar Maid" on. The title itself of "Simon's Luck" is designed, it would appear, to enhance her role as scene, the place where Simon, not Rose, enters and disappears. Even his entry is prepared so as to make Rose an almost secondary character. The setting is a party whose hostess is dressed in a "theatrical" fashion (153), yet this is a sufficient cue to provide Rose with a small forum in which she can exercise her gift for entertaining and dramatic monologue, and within the genuinely period decor of her hostess's livingroom she regales everyone with an anecdote about how she inadvertently killed her cat in her dryer. At the conclusion of her story she is verbally assaulted by a former student, without warning and provocation. Enter Simon, unnamed, who neatly ushers the boy out of the house. From this moment on Rose's thoughts are turned toward Simon. When he enters again, Rose is in the kitchen talking with a woman who is planning an article on female suicide. The first episode ends with the woman following Rose's interest and remarking, " 'Look, do you come to a party just to meet men?' " (159). Abruptly, following a gap in the text, the narrative resumes, telling the story of Simon's lucky escape from occupied France. It is a kind of false flashback, for it serves as a transition to Simon and Rose in bed after the party. A story of Simon's past and subsequent life, which we may have expected, is suppressed in favor of getting Simon in front of Rose, where he can perform his other lives of which one is "The Humble Workman" and others are "[t]he Old Philosopher, who bowed low to her, Japanese style, as he came out of the bathroom, murmuring *memento mori, memento mori*; and, when appropriate, The Mad Satyr, nuzzling and leaping, making triumphant smacking noises against her navel" (161).

Simon would not seem to exist without Rose, nor does Rose appear to have any role other than as something for Simon to play against. In his absence he lives in her mind, "[a] short, thick man, hairy, warm, with a crumpled comedian's face," who, when he "got home . . . would say, 'I hope I done it to your satisfaction, mum,' and yank a forelock" (164). At another moment she speculates upon his later arrival "with his hands together, praying, mocking, apologizing. *Memento mori*" (168). Simon, like Garnet French, does not, as one might expect, come, despite her elaborate preparations, no matter how much Rose "turned [him] into the peg on which her hopes were hung" (166), and the waiting becomes melodramatic. Instead of Simon, the woman from the store down the road comes, and at that moment "the commotion of [Rose's] heart turned from merriment to dismay, like the sound of a tower full of bells turned comically (but not for Rose) into a rusty foghorn'' (166). The narrator does not resist the parenthetical, ironic intrusion, and the effect of the irony is to enhance not only the distance of Rose from Simon, but also her distance from the narrator through whom all of Rose's efforts to become a theater for Simon are reduced to the vanity contained in the repeated injunction of memento mori. And, as if we had not already understood, the narrator underscores this central aspect of Rose's character: ''this was a situation she had created, she had done it all herself, it seemed she never learned any lessons at all'' (166).

Is there, then, a ''real'' Simon, other than the man with a past, and the man of several guises? If the question may be posed for Simon, surely it may be posed as well for Rose, who decides that her best escape is literally to abandon the scene of her trouble by driving from Ontario to Vancouver. Part of her decision to depart, to find a way out of the labyrinth of love, is her awareness that ''[n]ever since Patrick had she been the free person, the one with . . . power; maybe she had used it all up, all that was coming to her'' (169). The power to which she refers is the power to determine the moves of other people, a power against which she herself has become powerless. It appears to derive from her love for whatever man is for the moment important in her life, and it requires an early morning on the Saskatchewan prairie to clarify this for her: ''she thought how love removes the world for you, and just as surely when it's going well as when it's going badly'' (170). Suddenly she is surprised by her desire for the world, the substance of the world that is sought in Del Jordan's crisis of faith, ''thick and plain as ice-cream dishes'' (170). Then she is able to discover that she is running neither from ''the disappointments, the losses, the dissolution,'' nor from ''the celebration or shock of love'' (170). What she calls ''the world'' has been abandoned, part of which is the place of her origin, to which the concluding chapters return, as if in an effort to recapture that loss. But such a return is possible, if at all, only after another turn is taken in Rose's understanding of her absence from the world.

Finally she reaches Vancouver, and, to emphasize Rose rather than Simon, while at the same time recalling him, the narrator remarks, ''[l]uck was with her'' (171). Her luck is to find employment as an actress, and one day on the scene she encounters the theatrical hostess who gave the party where she met Simon. She informs Rose that Simon had died of cancer, neatly recalling Simon's chant, memento mori. The chapter's closure is played superbly along two lines, one following the television script, and the other Rose's own response. Rose's role is to pursue a young girl around the ferries to protect her (a word that recurs in this chapter and often in the book) from suicide. After hearing of Simon's death, Rose returns "to the scene" (172). The narrator observes that the girl does not commit suicide and the reason is simple: viewers know they will "be protected from predictable disasters, also from those shifts of emphasis that throw the story line open to question, the disarrangements which demand new judgments and solutions, and throw the windows open on inappropriate unforgettable scenery" (172–73). But for Rose the story of Simon's death is "that kind of disarrangement" (172). It leaves her, to use another of Munro's phrases, "at the mercy" not only of other lives, but also of other discourses and other scenes. The moment of her discovery, furthermore, finds her in the position of being analogous to the viewer, unprotected from disaster, as well as the actress whose role is to prevent such disasters. The irony is increased by what she finally discovers about herself, that "[i]t was preposterous, it was unfair, that such a chunk of information should have been left out, and that Rose even at this late date could have thought herself the only person who could seriously lack power" (173).[20]

The narrative distance and poise at this moment are exquisite, and recall with admirable economy all the narrator's indications of other kinds of hard luck endured by other characters in the story. Thus Rose is permitted self-pity, but with a minimum of fuss because it also recalls the narrator's summary of Rose's insights gained on the prairie. Speaking of "the dazzling alteration of love," the narrator continues in Rose's mind: "Either way you were robbed of something—a private balance spring, a little kernel of probity." And the narrator concludes by dryly declaring: "So she thought" (170). We are to infer, then, that for Rose love signifies dissolution and loss, and for the narrator loss may lie elsewhere. I would argue that the narrator has been suggesting not only on this occasion, but all along, that the ease with which Rose moves into another, more protective world of fantasy, theater, and disguise may explain in a certain measure her notion of the world's removal. In either case, at the meeting of those two perspectives are both a sense of loss and powerlessness. Providence has become Simon's luck, and nothing is redeemed.

It is at this state that Rose returns in the final chapters to Flo and West Hanratty; and certainly "Spelling" must be considered a chapter, for it would be difficult to imagine its full effect published separately.

Nor, despite the discontinuous gap between it and the preceding chapter, could it find a better place in this text, as a transition to the conclusion. It takes its title from a scene in the old age home where Rose plans to take Flo. There she is "entertained" by an old blind woman in a crib whose only mode of relating to the world is by spelling words. The scene is at once a parody of a dramatic presentation and a poignant echo of infancy. It focuses Rose's return by giving it a grotesque cyclical character, by drawing an analogy that does not quite fit. It also marks Rose's function as spectator, while at the same time hinting at a kind of vain power since she is allowed to offer some of the words. Nor can Rose help but imagine, recalling the pattern of "Royal Beatings," the words as possessing a certain life of their own beyond literal meaning: "This one limp and clear, like a jelly fish, that one hard and mean and secretive, like a horned snail. They could be austere and comical as top hats, or smooth and lively and flattering as ribbons. A parade of private visitors, not over yet" (184).[21] Nothing in the novel more painfully symbolizes the removal of the world, and now Rose must witness, as well as encourage it, by taking Flo to the same place.

To get her there, Flo must be approached from a variety of angles, each angle proceeding from a different moment in time. The initial scene is set "in the old days" (174), narratively projecting Flo in a scene in which she draws out stories of some woman "going off the track" (174) and who must be taken to the County Home. Flo has now by a metamorphic process become one of the women of drama and story, suggesting how one becomes victim of one's own discourse. Furthermore, her old taunt of asking "Who do you think you are?" has now turned upon her, and in what appears to be a case of Alzheimer's disease, she is unable to recognize Rose upon her return home after several years. The scene shifts again to fill in rapidly a period of two years while Rose has been on tour. Upon her return she finds a letter from her brother Brian and his wife suggesting that Flo be looked after more regularly. This prompts a brief visit to them and a return to Flo. The linearity of the story's plot is only interrupted once more by two moments in which Flo critically reacts to Rose's appearing with one breast revealed in a television play and in which Flo arrives at a reception where Rose is receiving an award. Her appearance is ghastly: "a mauve and purple checked pants suit, and beads like white and yellow popcorn" (186). She also has put on a wig, "pulled low on her forehead like a woollen cap" (187). This is in sharp contrast to her normal attire, and not only does it make her entry dramatic, but it also bids us wonder what has become of her. Flo is no longer who she was, nor can we be sure exactly who she is.

We are led to such perplexity in two ways. The first is Flo as she is contrastively presented. The second derives from the form of the chapter, which itself could be called dramatic because of the rapidity with which the scenes change, moving back and forth in time, and because of the swiftness with which each scene is presented. The plotting prevents the reader from forming a clear picture of Flo, who becomes an image of change, decay, and parodic reversion to the past. Part of this is caught in the final scene when Rose visits Flo, now herself in a crib, and performs for her, wearing Flo's old wig. Flo thinks, however, that she is in the hospital to have her gallstones removed, an event that took place long before Rose's entry with the wig. The scene raises, then, a significant problem. We are, in a sense, who we are according to the narrative we compose of our lives. The narrative depends profoundly upon how we arrange it according to time, and this is a matter of form to which Munro gives acute attention. Flo's loss of her sense of self is clearly dramatized here in its confusion of time.

Part of the wholeness of the novel is the anticipation of Flo in her crib that is given at the conclusion of the first chapter. The beginning anticipates the conclusion, but because of Rose's development the return of the image permits the notion of analogy and metaphor, of which her earlier texts made much use, to be examined from a new and critical perspective. It may be, in fact, that likeness destroys the possibility of being who one is, and it is this central issue of the novel as a whole that the final chapter, "Who Do You Think You Are?", inevitably addresses. It begins with an assumption of knowledge acquired about the relationship between Rose and her brother in the previous chapter. Only certain memories can be agreed upon between them as the same, and one is the role of Milton Homer, the village idiot, in the lives of their childhood. The character, the name, and his possibilities for transformation form the core of the story.

Being an idiot, Milton Homer represents the world removed. Nothing can touch him, and inasmuch as he is the scion of the family who established the local flax mill, he is never institutionalized. He is permitted two roles in life: to bless newly born children and to play a carnivalesque role in the annual Orange Walk.[22] He is, then, the consummate mimic, a figure who seems to be nothing other than what he imitates. He is, one might say, an example of the worst pitfall of the actor's profession, and thus the focus upon him at the novel's conclusion is designed to suggest the worst possibility of Rose's life. What is even more suggestive is the fact that she hardly knew him, and her best examples of him, as she tells an acquaintance early in the story, come from seeing an old school friend, Ralph Gillespie, " '*doing* Milton Homer' " (191). Thus the mimic is mimicked, producing through acting and parody a kind of *mise en abyme* of representation and its transposition to other registers.[23] In the process something is lost, and she speculates whether this is an inhibition imposed by society or something else, something "that ordinary people lose when they are drunk, Milton Homer never had, or might have chosen not to have—and this is what interests Rose—at some point early in life" (194). The interjection connects Rose to Milton Homer at a crucial point, and it reminds one of the theme of loss that governs the second half of the novel. Nor is the ambiguity to be resolved. At some point, however, inhibition is lost, and in some instances it is never recovered.

One of the results of Milton Homer's achievement is that he becomes the subject of various stories, true and false, the subject of legendary discourse at a point where the real and legendary blur. At such a point self-knowledge disappears, either into the discourse of the other or into the other whose role is assumed. This is illustrated in brief anecdotes and even more significantly in a discovery that Ralph Gillespie makes by changing the title of Keats's sonnet, "On First Looking into Chapman's Homer," to make the final words read "*Milton Homer*" (194). It is a metamorphic gesture at one with Rose's own propensity to fantasize about language and to modify stories to fit changes of perspective and audience. Once such a discovery is made, the "real" Milton Homer is no longer necessary. He has been transposed to the core of myth where change is continually possible.

Milton Homer also runs the risk of merely courting pretention, thus drawing in the other level of the novel's central preoccupation. This is illustrated in the efforts of his sisters to have a petition signed in church to ask the Canadian Broadcasting Corporation to remove certain American comedies from the air on Sunday evenings. Milton helps by sitting at the table with whiskers drawn in ink and drooling on the paper. It is perceived "as a comedy" (198) of a particularly embarrassing kind. For Flo it is a defeat, but Rose cannot tell whether it is a defeat "of religion or pretension" (198). Into this defeat of his sisters Milton Homer is drawn. This scene is preceded by another that similarly castigates Rose for pretension. Rose's defeat springs from her talent to

memorize rapidly, an actor's talent, and this prompts her teacher, Miss
Homer, to fling at her the question of the novel's title.

The analogy, then, between Rose and Milton Homer is implicit, and
it ranges through all the problems of acting from pretension to mimicry
and finally self-loss. Nothing more vividly excites in her the falseness
of her position than when she is at home in Hanratty, where the
slightest inquiry about her appearances on television excites feelings of
inadequacy. Although she reserves a special place for acting, she senses
that her role as a television interviewer is a sham, and certain things
she remains ashamed of. While revealing a breast is not one of these,
she senses "a failure she couldn't seize upon or explain" (203). This
particular discussion takes place at the Legion Hall, where she meets
Ralph Gillespie again, at the time when she is putting Flo in the
County Home. He has returned from the Navy with a pension for an
injury, and he is now seen through the eyes of those who never knew
him as a boy, for whom he is now known as "old Ralph" (203), an
expression that echoes earlier ones used for Milton Homer. Indeed, for
newer people in town, it cannot be said whether he is imitating Milton
Homer or, because they never knew the latter, whether he is an idiot
himself; and so we are reminded that analogy may destroy the possibility
of analogy as one term is absorbed by the other, in which being is
only the imitation of being.

Their meeting again is too brief to lead to the insight Rose appears
to desire, for Ralph seems unable to reveal himself beneath his surface,
despite all her television interviewer's charm. In recalling their conversation, however, Rose is brought directly to her problem with herself
and its bearing upon her acting. Her sense of shame arises from the
fact that she may be, like Milton Homer and Ralph Gillespie, only a
mimic, "reporting antics, when there was always something further, a
tone, a depth, a light, that she couldn't get and wouldn't get" (205).
Not only is this true for acting, it is true for her whole life.[24] Upon
reconsideration, she feels that she did not make any mistakes in her
conversation with Ralph, that perhaps her difficulty arises from sexual
desire for him. Such a thought immediately raises the problem of
transposition in a new guise, which she calls translation. She feels that
there are "feelings which can only be spoken of in translation; perhaps
they could only be acted on in translation; not speaking on them and
not acting on them is the right course to take because translation is
dubious. Dangerous, as well" (204–5). Such an insight reflects on her,

as well as on the two other central characters in the chapter, fixing them in the melodramatic, perhaps tragic, situation of their lives.[25]

What she discovers in never penetrating Ralph's mask is that she must protect him from translation into other discourse. The narrator then poses a final question that transposes the title question: "What could she say about herself and Ralph Gillespie, except that she felt his life, close, closer than the lives of men she'd loved, one slot over from her own" (206). The question is not simply rhetorical, for Rose has chosen silence, but the question reverberates through all the seeming madmen of whom Munro is so fond, and of whom Bobby Sherriff is such a seminal representative as actor and creator. These are the figures who make the real and the legendary meet and, thus, provide Munro with the means of transcending the real for a more encompassing mode of vision. But Rose's refusal to speak at the novel's conclusion differs from the desire for endless transposition into other modes of discourse that seems to reach a climax in the previous text. Thus *Who Do You Think You Are?* marks an important and profound change in the development of Munro's thinking because of its desire not to yield to the possibilities of metaphor and analogy, but to probe their limits. We are made to know that translation—the Latin word for metaphor—possesses danger, particularly as it makes possible the interchange of lives and the loss of self that is part of the transaction. Translation is also a trope, a method of transposing texts, which constantly turns upon the same core of material. As the exchange between Ralph and Rose exemplifies, the turning may illuminate the absence of a core, that point where the real is lost in the acting and speaking, in the discourse by which it is hoped to be recaptured. Rose, too, is a translation, a character who is also a vehicle for Munro to meditate on the problems of her craft. By bringing her to her moral triumph at the novel's conclusion, Munro raises triumph to the edge of failure, for Rose's refusal to speak is a refusal to make the kind of discourse that comes so naturally to Munro's hand.[26]

Chapter Six
The Syntax of Absence
The Moons of Jupiter

If I had been making a proper story out of this . . .[1]

If analogy and metaphor lead naturally, if deceptively, to relationships that may be only illusory, the writer is forced to proceed without the support of conventional economies. Such a discovery would be crucial to a writer like Munro, whose fundamental structure depends upon the interplay of the continuous, which is illustrated by analogy and metaphor, and the discontinuous, which is part of the formal design of her narrative. The repression of the similar leads to a further problem, for one of Munro's central preoccupations from her earliest stories is the role of the narrator, the figure who organizes the material and establishes the relationships. This is especially manifest in Munro's fondness for particular words that in their repetitions orchestrate the plot, encouraging a theme or attitude to resonate through the narrative so as to overcome any tendency that might pull the story apart. In consort with metaphor and analogy, this overcomes the centrifugal pull of the discontinuous. As Munro's craft and thinking has developed, however, it has become increasingly evident that the demands of story could not be accommodated by the clarity and tidiness of its discourse. This is particularly marked in *Who Do You Think You Are?*, a collection of which the title itself poses such a searching question about the relation of self to being that, as I argued in the previous chapter, to avoid its implications would be tantamount to a moral failure on the writer's part. Munro responded by examining how fragile and illusory this relationship is. For if we know ourselves in relation to the other, rather than in a hypothetically pure state, what do we know? Our life in the Mirror Stage, as it has been called,[2] in which we abide in perfect reflection with the mother, is of very short duration. Soon we acquire the use of language, and no sooner is that acquired than we are faced with the problems of syntax, tense, attribution, subject, object: that is, the grammatical convention within which "you" begins to "think."

The significance of Munro's second novel is its questioning of the ordering premises of the first, particularly in respect of character. In grammatical and psychological terms it seeks the subject in the sentence. In its interest to preserve the subject in the midst of its many defining relationships it gradually refuses easy similarities, and finally it refuses to speak at all when a fundamental analogy is intuited. This casts an inevitable feeling of solitude over the book into which, in the end, Rose hermetically withdraws. Like her namesake, she becomes a mystery unto herself. This poses a problem because, as I have indicated, part of the power of Munro's writing resides in the marvelous intimacy that may be seen between narrator and protagonist or between early and later aspects of the narrator with her narrated self. It means, then, a loss of the narrator's presence, that sense of reliability that a narrator provides as a sign of the continuous. Munro's solution to the problems of character and narrator has been to yield to what appear to be the configurations of the discontinuous, allowing the shaping hand of the implied author to dominate as the figure who mediates events, rather than simply giving them voice. This author is someone who endows events with their curious syntax in the manner of Prue, a character from the story of the same name: "She presents her life in anecdotes, and . . . it is the point of most of her anecdotes that hopes are dashed, dreams ridiculed, things never turn out as expected, everything is altered in a bizarre way and there is no explanation ever."[3] The emphasis in this description falls upon the matter not told, as distinguished from the teller. Prue has a talent of distancing herself as teller from the self in the story. As a consequence, her auditors are relieved "to meet somebody who doesn't take herself seriously" (129). The dominant is the syntax, not the subject or self.

It is characteristic of Munro's technique, however, that she draws our attention to the problem of order as the central issue of her collection in the first story of *The Moons of Jupiter.* It is in two parts, playing off the two sides of the narrator's family, suggesting their differences within the order of the family. The first part is entitled "Connection," asking the reader immediately to reflect upon filiation, continuity, and likeness. It is only half of the story, and, within that half, connection itself is the art of not telling all. The word is initially used to probe the meaning of family connection, particularly the meaning of her mother's maiden name. The context for the inquiry is a visit by four of the narrator's cousins, which prompts her to recall her mother's conjectures that the family might be related to British aristocracy. There

is, however, no agreement on the mother's proposal. As the narrator
later discovers, her mother's notion of family connection with the upper
class is a fiction, despite their recollections of the presumptuous behavior
of the narrator's great-grandfather. But there are other kinds of significance to be attached to the family connection: the cousins, besides
being "a show in themselves," "provided a connection . . . with the
real, and prodigal, and dangerous, world" (6). They serve, then, the
same function as Uncle Benny in *Lives of Girls and Women,* relating
the familiar to the strange. As the discourse of the story argues, however,
the validity of connections lies in their significance, not in their mere
existence, and their significance belongs to change in time. And time's
surprise is what alters the syntax, for it is only by chance that the true
family connection is discovered (the great-grandfather was a butcher's
apprentice before coming to Canada), and that one of the cousins later
arrives to visit the narrator as an adult. The cousin's presence is difficult
because the narrator's husband has persistently tried to separate her
from her country past.

The two halves of the story permit a reflection upon this connection
with her childhood and the extent to which it is now an embarrassment
for her. The narrator must, in fact, correct herself, while reviewing her
own version of the visit: "I was dishonest when I said that I wish we
had met elsewhere, that I wished I had appreciated her, when I implied
that Richard's judgements were all that stood in the way" (16). The
visit clearly places the present and past of the narrated self in difficult
connection, and no effort is made to reconcile them. It is perhaps fatal
to their marriage that the husband immediately starts to criticize the
shortcomings of the cousin on her departure, for the narrator finally
throws a plateful of pie at him, making a kind of "verdict" on *their*
connection (18). Then, with no transition, the narrator presents herself
as a child in bed, hearing the cousins repeat the round sung earlier in
the story, ending in the line, *"Life is but a dream."* And there the
story ends, marking connection as a meaning not to be wholly grasped,
as the narrator hears "[o]ne voice in which there is an unexpected note
of entreaty, of warning, as it hangs the five separate words on the air.
Life is. Wait. *But a.* Now, wait. *Dream"* (18). The syntax of the
sentence is punctuated by separation, the interruption of connection.

The second part of the story is entitled "The Stone in the Field"
and draws attention to the farm formerly owned by the narrator's
father's family (a connection broken), where there is a stone marking
the grave of an old man of unknown background who was buried in

the field. The relation that is made between the narrator's immediate family and her father's is through her mother's fellow antique dealer, Poppy Cullender, a connection that is already an embarrassment for the narrator. Seeing one of her father's sisters by chance in town prompts her to comment that "she was as strange a sight, in her way, as Poppy Cullender was in his" (22). She then adds: "I couldn't really think of her as my aunt; the connection seemed impossible." Just as the connection with Poppy Cullender is weakened by the phrase "in her way," the connection with the father's family is further attenuated by the narrator's refusal to see it. Contrasts, rather than connections, are implicit between the two families—her mother's possession of a love of theatricality and play,[4] her father's appearing completely moribund, unable to respond to the narrator's mother's vision of life "as change and possibility" (29). The connections, then, between the two are purely fortuitous, despite similarities the narrator may have with her mother and father.

The conclusion of the story, and thus both stories, is dominated by the figure of Mr. Black, who was buried beneath a boulder in one of the family's fields. He is the subject of pieces of information that recall the treatment of the great-grandfather in the first half. By chance, while doing some work "in connection with a documentary script" (32), the narrator discovers a newspaper story of Mr. Black, which urges her to return to see if the stone is still there. The rock, the visible sign of the narrator's relation with her father's family's former connection with the field, is gone. The narrator then confesses that this might have required a story, had she been younger. The story would have turned upon a secret love between him and one of her father's sisters. The love would never have been expressed, and she "would have made a horrible, plausible connection between that silence of his, and the manner of his death" (35). The connection, however, is not drawn, for she no longer believes "that people's secrets are defined and communicable, or their feelings full-blown and easy to recognize" (35). What is significant about her refusal is not only the explicit reflection made upon the narrator's role and the degree to which she may intrude upon the character, but also that connections that narrators make run the risk of being not simply plausible, but also horrible, thus in some way violating observed events. "Now," she observes, "I can only say, my father's sisters scrubbed the floor with lye, they stooked the oats and milked the cows by hand" (35). Of course she says, and has said, more, but the desire is to abdicate a function, the ordering function that narrators possess that inscribes meaning, for another, suggesting that meaning is subordinate to event, and events are subject to change and possibility. Thus the narrator who seeks sense must give way to the teller as arranger of events, a teller who appears more as an author implicit in the text.

The special role that authors may possess is explicitly raised in "Dulse," the following story. The idea of the author is focused in the figure of Willa Cather, the long-dead American writer who is the object of a quest by one of the characters. Although it is a subplot, the implications of the quest are of importance for Lydia, the main character, who is in the process of trying to come to terms with a broken relationship. She spends a night on an island off the coast of New Brunswick, dines with Mr. Stanley, who is under Cather's spell, and passes the evening with three men playing cards. As the focalizer of the story, her thoughts carry a freedom that breaks the temporal linearity of conventional time, for she is living not only in the present, but also in the several fragments of the past that bear upon her being on the island. No small part of her being there is her lack of explicit motivation. She seems to have drifted onto the island in the same way that her past drifts into the present. Thus the points of contact with Mr. Stanley, as well as with the three telephone workers, are constantly interrupted by recollections of her former relationship and her sense that "she could not make the connection between herself and things outside herself" (41). While this sense is applied specifically to the moment that she is aware of the loss of her lover, it accords equally with the Lydia with whom the reader is presented. She is unconnected, and no effort is made by the implied author to arrange the story with easy transitions. Sometimes the text is clearly punctuated with spaces to make interruptions clear. At others, Lydia is simply allowed to drift in and out, as she does in the following exchange with Mr. Stanley:

He smiled, and said in a confidential way, "Willa could be imperious. Oh, yes. She was not perfect. All people of great abilities are apt to be a bit impatient in daily matters."

Rubbish, Lydia wanted to say, she sounds a proper bitch.

Sometimes waking up was all right, and sometimes it was very bad. This morning she had wakened with the cold conviction of a mistake—something avoidable and irreparable. (56–57)

Mr. Stanley continues with how Willa arose in the morning, and we are permitted to see a parallel between the two women, at least in their rising, but also to see Lydia's powerlessness posed against Willa's overbearing personality. At the same time, Lydia's absence from the conversation is underscored.

It might be said, then, that Lydia's sense of herself corresponds to the description given of her lover's apartment: "No attempt has been made to arrange things to make a setting; nothing was in relation to anything else" (53). Nevertheless, the arranger's hand is present to the extent that "[a]ll disorder was actually order, carefully thought out and not to be interfered with" (53–54). How suggestive this is, however, of Cather, whose temper is described as "imperious," and it summons the reader to inquire whether Munro is not ironically raising questions about authorial skill and control. She is assisted in this enterprise through the same exchange between Mr. Stanley and Lydia, the former remarking, " 'She knew things as an artist knows them. Not necessarily by experience' " (57). Lydia is prompted then to ask: " 'But what if they don't know them?' " and she is so concerned she repeats the question. We have already seen this concern with the epistemological problem of self and character, and now Munro has carried the implication of the problem to its logical term. If the knowledge of character is mysterious and perhaps, finally, beyond knowing, we cannot very well put faith in the author, who is required to possess this knowledge. Thus the poignancy with which Lydia is endowed begins with the teller and her awareness of her ability "to get it right." As the conclusion of their exchange makes clear, the author is no more privileged than anyone else. For no matter how sure Mr. Stanley may be of Cather's knowledge and providential fortune, the facts of her behavior may be otherwise. Furthermore, the reports he has received of her may have been colored by various interests, not permitting any knowledge other than conjecture. But Mr. Stanley inhabits, as the narrator indicates through Lydia's focalization, "a lovely, durable shelter" (59), suggesting a notion of Cather's art that is hermetically sealed.[5]

It is precisely this notion of art, I would argue, that Munro finds wanting. For if fiction is knowledge, what knowledge can it lay claim to? It is easy, perhaps wrong, to speculate about the hidden life of the character, and the hesitations that we have observed about Mr. Black in the previous story are proof of this. It could be argued that this is simply a strategy to obtain another effect of the real. The same technique, for example, is employed in "The Turkey Season," in which the narrator, speaking in the first person, tries to come to terms with an event that occurred in her adolescence while working in a turkey slaughterhouse.

The climax concerns Gladys, Herb, and Brian, who are caught in a sexual triangle in which the two men have a homosexual relationship, and into which the girl unwittingly enters. She is then humiliated by Brian, who is chased from the turkey barn. The speaker, as a consequence, goes through two stages of reflection, one immediate, and another at a sexually more advanced stage. This first is marked by a series of questions concerning Herb's shame. Later she understands the problem as involved with Herb's efforts to humiliate Gladys. At a third stage she decides to refuse explanations of what she does not know. She is content "to think of Herb's face with that peculiar, stricken look; to think of Brian monkeying in the shade of Herb's dignity; to think of my own mystified concentration on Herb, my need to catch him out, if I could ever get the chance, and then move in and stay close to him" (74). What she wants is "to know things. Never mind facts. Never mind theories, either" (74). Such a desire is of a purely phenomenological character that would carry the speaker past the empirically real, as well as the theoretically possible, into a space of intimacy that would permit a special knowledge of the character.

To speak so naturally makes the character appear referential, as if the speaker were describing someone perceived, whose true motivations escaped her powers of understanding. This is a valid argument to a certain point, and it suggests the degree to which Munro is a realist. To use such a term would obscure, however, many of the other aspects of her work that break the allure of realism. We have already noted Munro's early fondness for, and refusal of, fantasy, and such apparently metafictional interventions as occur in "The Turkey Season" and elsewhere are in accord with this strategy. Furthermore, the desire to eschew the effects of metaphor, and her effort to attain a plainer style, are in accord with such a refusal. To use the narrator as a means, however, of discussing what should be done, and particularly, as in this instance, to privilege the observer with respect to the observed, and implying, as the quantum physicist Werner Heisenberg does in his uncertainty principle, that knowledge is dependent upon the observer and therefore valid only under certain circumstances, is not a role the realist-narrator need employ. Indeed, the persistent questioning the implied author urges upon the narrator and the characters leads the reader to doubt whether a clear contract is possible between author and reader. That doubt wears away the foundations of the conventions of realism, and by expressing the intent to achieve an intimate kind of knowledge, distinct from the limiting reflections of language, places narrator and character frequently at a tragic disadvantage. For no one with Munro's sensitivity to the way language fabricates a world can make the reader believe that there is a pure knowledge, unaffected by language. Thus her strategy is one that not only makes one wary of realism, but also heightens one's awareness of how fragile our sense of self and the other is, so utterly dependent as it is upon language and consequent conflict of meanings. It is sufficient to distance oneself by raising the problem. This would also account for another peculiarity of Munro's sense of character, which is at once so intimate and so removed that it makes the character emblematic of the narrative problem. So Lydia, at the conclusion of "Dulse," finds a gift of dulse left by the one man for whom she had any intimate feeling, and it was a present that "slyly warmed her, from a distance" (59). Connections appear to be made only to suggest how dependent they are upon how we construe them. In themselves they may possess no meaning at all, for they are only facts, not knowledge.

The quest for knowledge, then, is coterminous with the quest for form, for both serve to draw character and narrator into a temporal situation that at once fragments them and makes them appear to have no other possible reality. So it is that Munro's characters always seem to be searching for a knowledge whose perception does not seem to depend upon their efforts, if it occurs at all, but comes by chance or providence. Thus the life of the protagonist of the following story, "Accident," appears to her as arranged, as the title remarks, by accident. What nags Munro, however, is the fact that accidents may not be as random as they appear, and this is the line of reasoning that the protagonist takes up when, as a result of a fatal accident, her future husband decides to change his life and marry her: "It was a long chain of things, many of them hidden from her, that brought him here to propose to her" (106–7). She then considers that "it was quite useless to think, would anyone else have done as well, would it have happened if the chain had not been linked exactly as it was?" This question is sufficient for her to acquiesce in a belief in some destiny that is powerful enough to overcome the role of chance. But her belief is curiously supported by the idea that the accident is a part of fate, for "she had always believed something was going to happen to her, some clearly dividing moment would come, and she would be presented with her future" (107). This is an ambiguous destiny in which the links in the chain are inexplicably separated to permit a new juncture. It does not resolve the contradiction between fate and chance but, rather, finds a satisfactory way of accommodating each to the other. Thus at the end of the story she continues to remain troubled by the problem of chance, and perceives her life as dependent upon a series of hypotheses that grammatically correspond to the inescapable role of chance.

The formal consequence of such thinking dominates the rest of the collection, continually demonstrating that because character is process, any firm knowledge that is sought will always escape the reader. Hence, form becomes the dominant knowledge, a form that displays the character always in pieces, and always vainly trying to fit them to a fiction that will satisfy. Unlike her usual practice of spacing, Munro's strategy in "Bardon Bus," one of the major pieces of the collection, is to number the sections in order to assist the reader and also to call attention to the problem of fragmentation. To respond in advance to the problem her protagonist confronts, the first section begins with a meditation on "being an old maid" (110) that is designed to serve as an ironic introduction to the theme of "perfect mastery" (111), as if a life lived completely within oneself were possible as a means of overcoming the irrational fragmentation of daily life. The test of the fantasy is the persistent return "to the moment when you give yourself up, give yourself over, to the assault which is guaranteed to finish off everything you've been before" (111). The stakes are high: self-loss and a disconnection with origin, a theme that haunts Munro's text. Thus the section ends, announcing the problem on the levels of both character and, by implication, form.

Section 2 provides a setting. She is writing a book in her friend Kay's apartment, and "in connection with this book, [she] had to spend some time in Australia" (111). There she meets X (or *ex,* a sign of disconnection) who, as the ending makes clear, must remain anonymous. One might overlook the fact that she uses the phrase "in connection with" (so naturally does it slip into her discourse) just as it was used in an earlier story in which the almost-anonymous Mr. Black was discovered. Connections provide links, but they do so, as we observed in "Accident," by chance. Connections, then, are ambiguous; they are fatal chances, thus appearing to give a life a necessity, while removing necessity simultaneously. Knowledge and form must be satisfied with that sober fact, and so sections 2 and 3 are given over to a brief account of her relationship with X, allowing the linearity of its description to provide an order that seems destined, one thing naturally following another. The flow is immediately broken by section 4, which calls the reader back to Kay's apartment. It begins with the narrator describing a dream about a letter she had received from X. The new setting, which allows a clear break in the temporal, sequencing order of her life, also permits a description of Kay and the crucial differences that may be established between her personality and that of the narrator. Kay, it appears, possesses a certain center in her life that the narrator lacks. As a result, Kay "never tires of a life of risk and improvisation. . . . She doesn't feel the threat that [the narrator] would feel, she never sees herself slipping under" (115). Kay, then, need not strive for "perfect mastery"; she has already the support of a certain class and family. Thus Kay seems to have a sustaining force the narrator lacks, particularly in surviving love relationships. When they are dying out, she has the power to see that love is perhaps only self-love. As she remarks to the narrator in respect of a comment made by Victor Hugo's daughter, who, after years of loving a certain man, meets him by chance, "but she can't connect the real man any more with the person she loves, in her head" (117). Thus she and Kay survive disconnections by seeing all connection as illusory.

Both the narrator and Munro are aware that such a resolution of the problem is superficial, and the section ends on that statement without comment. The following section begins at a point earlier in time than her affair with X, when she first met him in Vancouver. She now seeks a connection between his former "Lutheran" self, and the later personality marked by a "courtesy" "that did connect with his attention to women later" (118). Such a memory prepares the way for the following two sections that shed light on X's way with women through the special knowledge of his friend Dennis. What appears to be a discourse of admiration for X's philandering suddenly turns, at the end of these sections, with Dennis's remark that women are happier than men because they can more organically experience the benefits of "renunciation" and "deprivation" (122). So we are reminded again of the motif of the old maid, but the narrator is left explicitly without comment. What appears to Dennis as self-completion runs the risk of self-loss for the narrator, unaware that both the life of self-giving and self-mastery turn upon the same edge: both are lives of "risk and improvisation."

As if to announce her refusal to face the dilemma of her situation, the next section begins with the narrator meditating on a line of verse. This takes her back to her farewell from X, whose final word, echoing hers (which she avers to be a lie) is " '[p]erfect' " (123), thereby recalling the dream of "perfect mastery." The memory then prompts another, a scene of violent lovemaking, after which X comments, " '[w]e almost finished each other off' " (125), ironically echoing the image of the old maid in the same section. At no time is she safe from some sort of annihilation, and at no time, being no more than process, can she achieve a state of perfection in which everything reaches an enduring moment of equilibrium and poise. In this respect the narrator/protagonist is in exact accord with the syntax of the story's discourse.

Toward the end of the story she dreams that the "innocent, athletic underwear" (127) she and X are wearing is transformed into "gauzy bright white clothes, and these turned out to be not just clothes but our substances, our flesh and bones and in a sense our souls" (127). She then remarks that "because of the lightness and sweetness of our substances," their "[e]mbraces . . . were transformed . . . into a rare state of content" (127). So in dream, at least, process reaches a certain, heightened perfection. In the subsequent section, however, as part of the story's closure, she realizes that there is something wrong with the dream, that it, like love, forces upon us an illusory sense of order. This occurs at the moment of "letting go," which imparts "an uncalled-for pleasure in seeing how the design wouldn't fit and the structure wouldn't stand" (127–28). It is a discovery of "everything that is contradictory and persistent and unaccommodating about life" (128). Thus the dream belongs to the fantasy of "permanent vistas" that are not life, and what are they if not a "misplacement . . . the clue, in love, the heart of the problem" (128)? And as she implies in the following paragraph, such insights belong to "definitions of luck" (128).

The final section presents a closure at once rueful and comic, with Kay arriving to describe the beginnings of a new affair with a man so suggestive of X that one is forced to wonder whether Kay was the unnamed narrator's alter ego, created for the nonce. If this is so, one can only wonder at the extent to which she is prepared to surrender to the implications of her new insights on the contradictions of life and love. But the comic repetition that the ending generates suggests that the narrator may have insights, yet there is no reason that these insights are conclusive. Furthermore, the design from which they emerge suggests that, no matter how much the narrator might meditate, her story still leaves her "at the mercy," always open to contradiction, whether it be attributed to life or love. Even if she will no longer oscillate between the illusory poles of self-loss and self-mastery that are the risks of love, nothing guarantees freedom from contradiction, accident, and the abrupt transformations that inhere in process. The meaning of her life that she seeks lies here, always just beyond reach, and always inscribed into a discourse that is moved by discontinuity.

Her fate, then, is highly suggestive of Prue, the protagonist of the brief story of the same title. Prue's story, too, has "no explanation" (129), and consists in little more than a sketch of her character and the information that she lived awhile with the man with whom she is now having dinner. She spends the night with him, and in the morning she takes one of his cuff links and later puts it in a tobacco tin containing other small mementos. The final observation of the narrator is that "[s]he just takes something, every now and then, and puts it away in the dark of the old tobacco tin, and more or less forgets about it" (133). The only hint of any depth in Prue's life is the "dark" of the tin. Otherwise it appears an aimless existence, despite the narrator's comments on how Prue fictionalizes her life for others. Like the narrator of "Bardon Bus," Prue seems to marginalize herself, unable to find a center of sense. Nor does she try, unlike the other narrator, who is offered and occasionally creates her own ways of understanding. Neither world, with or without sense, is of use, for both characters cannot find the connection that would provide a frame of order. The narrator of "Bardon Bus" sees the problem, but her life never seems to acquire sufficient equilibrium to retain a central core of meaning. She knows, as some of her insights suggest, that an unapparent sense is sometimes to hand. Speaking of a line of verse that randomly runs through her mind, she observes: "I can usually see that the poem, or the bit of it I've got a hold of, has some relation to what is going on in my life. And that may not be what seems to be going on" (122).

Thus the discourse of the story composes two levels, and a rapport may be made from time to time. The finesse of the stories in this collection is that Munro provides both narrator and protagonist with fewer central clues to understand the level beneath the surface. The result is that the form appears more accidental, making the principal perceivers seem more powerless and vulnerable than formerly. Because the plot has less of a structured design, protagonist and narrator are subordinate to its whims, unable to talk their way into the clarity, apart from the story's discourse, that they desire. This is precisely the point of a later story in the collection, "Hard-Luck Stories," in which two old friends meet in the presence of Douglas, a friend of the narrator, and exchange stories. The setting of the story occurs later than these exchanges and is designed as a brief introduction of the two friends; it also permits the implied author to use the two friends to provide a clue to how fictions are created. Seeing the narrator, Julie is reminded of once-popular stories that have unexpected endings and wonders why they have lost their savor. The narrator speculates that " 'people thought, that isn't the way things happen. Or they thought, who cares the way things happen?' " (182). The stories that are told, however, have very explicit intents, and all three have to do with the use men make of women. It is a use that places them clearly on a margin, outside a core of sense. The more relations are made, the less claim that women seem to have upon such connections. Julia, for example, tells two stories directed toward a theme developed in the narrator's tale, in which she remarks there are two kinds of love, one sensible, the other irrational. Julia's fictions are designed to suggest that she herself has missed both kinds. The narrator's story argues that in one instance she was only the object of a sensible love, while her partner was irrationally in love with another woman. Certain things, however, are deliberately missing in the story as a whole that suggest that the implied author does not wish us to know all that we might about the narrator. By contrast, Julia is so persuasively drawn that we do not feel the need to know more, for we have been given something essential about the limits of her life. The portrayal of the narrator is different. We know that the narrator has taken risks in her life, and this implies in Munro that she may have experienced an irrational love. We are not permitted to know this with any certainty, nor are we permitted to know the character of the narrator's broodings toward the end of the story when the three are visiting an old church. She withdraws from Julia and Douglas to remark that "I felt that I had been overtaken—stumped by a truth about myself, or at least a fact, that I couldn't do anything about" (197). Only a hint of what this truth or fact might be is given, and it occurs when she is meditating on the dead in the graveyard, a memento mori that recalls "Simon's Luck." There she is overcome by "a shadow, a chastening" at the thought of the dead—"disintegrating dark leaves"—in contrast with them, "three middle-aged people still stirred up about love, or sex" (196).

What she thinks about this contrast is not articulated other than by an awareness of difference and of life as passage. Likeness is an illusion, and time continuously moves things apart, hence she observes: "Something unresolved could become permanent. I could be always bent on knowing, and always in the dark" (197). We know that her brooding on the surface is directed toward Douglas who, it is implied, is her former lover, and how he would receive her story; but it is prompted by her sense of her own mortality and the consequent insignificance of "the way things happen." So the narrator is left in the dark because of the ambiguity of being at once the teller and the told. Nor will the design of the story allow her to go further, for when she suddenly perceives some trillium in a stained-glass window, they become the discovery that she wishes to convey to Douglas and Julia. And almost for the fun of it the implied author changes the tone of the story, drawing them from melancholy to a kind of gaiety at the end in which they speculate on changing their lives in a fantasy of escaping to Nova Scotia. As a consequence, the narrator herself is marginalized from possible meaning, for she is not given enough clues to know.

It is precisely because of these dead ends, where narrators especially no longer understand, that one is urged to read Munro as one bent on using fiction as a method for understanding what the limits of fiction are. Such a use of fiction minimalizes its referential function, for it is designed to privilege the character as problem and not as mimesis.[6] The character is problem simply because of the frequent confessions of inadequacy of depictive power that form a leitmotiv in Munro's text, her characters being continually lost in the web of disclosure that persistently tells, alludes, trails off, and tries again, relating only to demonstrate the illusion of the relation. Thus the little story "Visitors," with its curious cast of characters—Mildred and Wilfred, his brother Albert, and his wife and sister-in-law, Grace and Vera—is one in which people in a family visit and part, and one wonders what happened. What happens, of course, is the fiction made of them, and the fictions they tell, reminiscing. The relationships are deliberately designed as a comic puzzle, the names of the central couple rhyming to stress an aspect of their union, and Grace and Vera being used to suggest their allegorical ethereality. Albert stands oddly out, and Mildred observes this, especially the lack of "a thread of connection" (212) between the two brothers, while, contrastively, the two sisters speak "like two mouths out of the same head" (212). The connection of family remains "a mystery to her [Mildred]" (212), for it is by nature random. Their difference is, furthermore, emphasized in how they narrate stories; and no matter how unobtrusively this observation enters the story itself, it reminds the reader once again of Munro's preoccupation with the world as only a function of how it enters fictional space. The difference reminds one also of Munro's own practice in various modes. For if Wilfred had been the narrator, the story "would have gone some place, there would have been some kind of ending to it" (215). Albert's stories, which require frequent interruptions for more significant information, simply end in suspension, and this is because, as Albert remarks, " '[i]t's not

a story. It's something that happened' " (215). The story "that happened," is, of course, no truer than any other, but its telling is so
designed, wittingly or not, that it comes closer to the real than Wilfred's
kind, which has a more perceptible design. Both techniques are, however,
merely strategies for the demonstration of truths specific to their respective
modes. This reminder in the midst of the larger story is sufficient to
distance the characters from the reader, and yet uncannily to permit
the poignancy of their lives to assume a new dimension. Because their
reality is diminished by our awareness of their being creatures of fiction,
we tend to be moved in an almost compensatory fashion. Their frailty
becomes even more manifest; and when Wilfred cries after his brother's
departure, uncertain of ever seeing him again, the reader is aroused to
find a way to protect him from his grief. This is especially so as
Wilfred's normal manner is not to put an unhappy color upon events,
and he usually gives reasons for his crying that are "only distantly
connected with the real reason" (216). This time Mildred is given a
reason that connects, which, paradoxically, sheds light upon a severed
connection.

Such illumination is rare indeed in this text. To underscore the
problem of the degree to which knowledge of the other is unattainable,
Munro portrays a character in "Mrs. Cross and Mrs. Kidd" who can
communicate only by grunting. The setting of the story is an old-age
home. The title characters are childhood friends who resume their
relationship in the home. The relationship is interrupted by the arrival
of Jack, a former newspaper editor from Red Deer, who lost his voice
from overwork. Mrs. Cross uses on him "her old managing, watching
power, her capacity for strategy" (168), and it is she who discovers
where he is from and a little about his outside relations. Beyond these
details, however, Jack must remain a mystery, a symbol of the frustration
from which the principal figures in *The Moons of Jupiter* suffer. He is
also a sign of the discontinuity in himself and between others, unable
to achieve even the minimum of expression that would relate him, that
would permit discourse to establish relation. This is particularly ironic
inasmuch as he was formerly a writer, and one might expect such a
figure of pathos to take a tragic turn. Munro, however, avoids the
temptation of tragedy here and elsewhere because of her faith in process
and continual variation. She seems to have little faith in the finality of
absolute and tragic closure, always preferring the kind of turn that
figures like Prue and Wilfred can give their discourse. As a consequence,
it comes as no surprise that Jack, in a fit of frustration and rage, turns

against the domination of Mrs. Cross and takes up with a meek friend that Mrs. Kidd has made in the meantime. This allows the old relationship between the title characters to resume, which is a comic closure, despite the fact that Mrs. Kidd, in giving all for Mrs. Cross, may die of heart failure. It is a noble gesture, and Mrs. Kidd is prompted to make it because of her fear of Mrs. Cross's being "at the mercy" (179) of emotions too strong for her to bear. This is a world in which everyone is drawn in by the implied author's skill at presenting the unknown and its attendant fears and eliciting, consequently, efforts of protection and masking.

As I have argued, part of the reason for such a response to Munro's characters is not entirely due to their substantive presence in the text, but rather because of their always appearing to slip away, either through self-loss—their fragmentation in the broken temporality of the narration—or because of their palpable fictionality. In one of her most achieved stories, "Labor Day Dinner," these qualities are present, but marvelously held in suspension by the polyphonic character of the discourse. The story is what it announces itself to be: a long holiday dinner shared by Roberta and her family and Valerie and hers. The central family is Roberta's, consisting of the man she lives with and her two children, Angela and Eva. It is evident from the outset, however, that they are less a family than four people living together, "costumed," as they are, "in a way that would suggest that they were going to different dinner parties" (135). It is this very difference that allows them to emerge as distinct figures immediately, but within an intimacy that allows their stories to interpenetrate, each colored by the other. Furthermore, so distinct do they become that their individual existences begin to assume a precariousness that living together cannot protect them from. Indeed, it accentuates it, for the first episode is designed to indicate how strained relations are between Roberta and George. Thus on the drive over to Valerie's they are "[s]hut up together, driving over the hot gravel roads at an almost funereal pace, . . . pinned down by a murderous silence" (136). Roberta is depicted as "[o]n the edge of it," and one senses her marginality as mortal. Thus a leitmotiv of the dinner is Roberta's meditation over the sense of her relationship with George. Unlike Munro's more characteristic approach to such a problem, such as that in "Bardon Bus," her thinking is almost drowned by the conversation around her. Discourses compete, as if the survival of the character depended upon how it would relate.

Their arrival at Valerie's provides the narrator with the occasion not
only for introducing the hostess, her daughter Ruth, as well as her son
and his fiancée, but also to establish other connections that provide
links between Valerie and her cousin, Roberta's former husband, and
George, a former colleague of Valerie. Thus more detail is provided
about these figures as they assume discursive variety depending on the
focalizer. We learn, for example, through Valerie that George " 'drops
women rather hard' " (140), a piece of information that can only
increase the sense of Roberta's precariousness. Also, as they move through
the house, the narrator is allowed to move in time, providing backgrounds
from other moments, but nothing of Roberta's plight is allowed to slip
from notice. Thus when Valerie comments on the blooming of love
between George and Roberta, Roberta thinks that "love is really
something Valerie could do without being reminded of" (140). No
reason is given for this, but such a comment puts Valerie into a
paradigm of other characters in Munro, who have been victims of love.
Later, when thought is given to George's restoration of his house, and
the harvest that is being put up, the sense of Roberta's being "on the
edge" returns as the narrator observes: "Sometimes she looks into the
freezer and wonders who will eat all this—George and who else? She
can feel her own claims shrinking" (142).

George is not entirely filtered through Valerie and Roberta. He is
also presented through the narrator, interrupting in a certain measure
the conversation of the two women. Thus the centrality of the focus
on Roberta is shifted, permitting her to be judged through less sympathetic eyes, not quite the person Roberta would want us to see. She
becomes a woman whose life is directed by her children, and, worse,
neither she nor they seem to do anything, leaving him to bear all the
work of the family. Nor is George the only focalizer, for Angela too
remarks in her journal that her mother is " 'on the verge of being a
nervous wreck' " (147) because of her relationship with George. Thus
we see Roberta through more than one register, as an object of discourse
for lover and daughter. By so shifting the focus, the narrator prevents
the scrupulous reader from generating a new discourse in the form of
a descriptive paraphrase that would gather Roberta once for all. Roberta
must be the creature of more than one voice, and to find a pattern
that would unify her would transgress the narrative intent. We are
assisted in making such an assessment by one of Roberta's own comments
while she is trying to reckon with her guilt over leaving her husband.
When Valerie remarks that punishment for guilt is never symmetrical,

Roberta agrees, saying: " 'I don't think you get your punishment in such a simple way. Isn't it funny how you're attracted—I am—to the idea of a pattern like that? I mean the idea is attractive, of there being that balance. But not the experience. I'd like to avoid them' " (149). Thus Roberta must be as she appears, a composite of the feelings of those observing her, possessing no more of a symmetry and pattern than the discourses that produce her.

To emphasize this fact, much of the story is given in the true polyphony of conversation of a group with divergent interests, allowing several layers of talk to continue almost simultaneously. Through it, Roberta gradually achieves a kind of transcendent state that permits not only self-acceptance, but also an indifference, finally, to George that "flows past him; it's generous; it touches everybody" (156). Such a bounty of indifference is sufficient to translate her sense of her own superfluity into something she can appear to control, if not escape. As if to echo her awareness, the conversation gradually shifts to a discussion of how to live with reports of disaster everywhere in the world while enjoying such an idyllic dinner. Valerie's son remarks that life now is like " '[t]he Incas eating off gold plates while Pizarro was landing off the coast' " (157). His fiancée cannot accept such despair, and Ruth, one of Munro's most beautifully realized minor characters, observes: " 'I think maybe we're destroyed already. . . . I think maybe we're anachonisms. No, that's not what I mean. I mean relics. In some way we are already. Relics' " (157). So in this splendid moment the dinner reaches its climax, pauses, and allows Eva, the younger daughter, to refuse to consider herself a relic, inciting laughter and Valerie's agreement. The dinner concludes with Valerie's calling everyone's attention to the smell of the river, speaking in a voice that "sounds forlorn and tender, in the dark" (158).

The dinner concludes, then, in a kind of aporia, everything suspended "in the dark," as Ruth's word "relics" firmly seizes on the sense of the whole and the characters' relation to it. The apparent lack of formal design within which the characters intermittently appear only to lapse into silence and dark make them seem as figures left behind with no reason given. At this moment there is a gap in the text followed by the words " 'A gibbous moon' " (158). We do not know immediately that they are spoken by George as "an offering," and so they seem to imitate the moon by being ambiguously suspended in the text. The image itself, furthermore, of the moon not yet full, yet moving in that direction, both sides convex, propose a figure at once in equipoise and process, a figure that marks precisely the discourse at this moment. The story is turning toward its conclusion, George is offering an armistice to Roberta, and she is still "on the edge," but now "on the edge of caring and not caring" (158). This is the perfect equipoise of process. At this moment a car at a crossroad suddenly arrives in front of them, bearing the dark down upon them, "a huge, dark flash, without lights" (159). It is both light and dark, a kind of grotesque inversion of the moment that George and Roberta share. They survive to sense the meaning of the event, to "feel as strange, as flattened out and borne aloft, as unconnected with previous and future events as the ghost car was, the black fish" (59). As the metaphor of the fish suggests, they have been removed from their natural element, especially the sense of time that orders their lives. The near accident is a sign for the discontinuities that cross the text, forcing meaning to enter where the gaps are. A wonderful sense of how the opening is made perceptible is dramatized in the story's closure through a remark of Eva's, who has already refused to be a relic and has slept on the trip home: " 'Are you guys dead?' " Eva says, rousing them. " 'Aren't we home?' " (159). And home, as we have discovered, is where "the moonlight comes clear on the hesitant grass of their new lawn." The dark of the story has been illuminated in an order of oppositions that makes it difficult to distinguish accident from fate, the random from the carefully veiled design, recalling the room of Lydia's friend in "Dulse": "All disorder was actually order, carefully thought out and not to be interfered with" (53–54).

The art of Munro is an art of accommodating contradictions, and this is what her principal figures, narrators or not, must be brought to learn. Their gradually acquired habit, which comes to fruition in "The Moons of Jupiter," is to learn how to be "at the mercy" without asking for much more. Something of the design within which they are figures must always be beyond their grasp. Thus the title of the whole collection is perfectly apt, putting a shade of remoteness over the stories that recalls the wonder and awe of such thinkers as Pascal as he contemplated the vast order of the cosmos as it reflected upon his own insignificance. It is fitting, then, that the collection ends with the title story, following the poignancy of old age as dramatized in "Visitors." The theme of the story is human mortality, and it consists in a series of meditations of a woman awaiting the possible death of her father. From certain references it is evident that it belongs to the cycle collected under the title of *Who Do You Think You Are?* but its inclusion there have been out of place. None of the themes of performance and pretension are present, no sense that one can outwit what is beyond one by self-evasion. No evasion is possible, least of all from the necessity of mortality, and so the narrator accepts ultimate vulnerability in a manner suggestive of Roberta in "Labor Day Dinner." Meditating on the possibility of her daughter Nichola's once having leukemia, she remembers how she had acquired a kind of "care—not a withdrawal exactly but a care—not to feel anything much" (229–30). What she acquires is a "love in fact measured and disciplined, because you have to survive" (230).

The frame and pretext for these insights is the impending heart operation that her father has decided to undergo. Once having established this as a context of thought, the narrator is free to allow her meditation to turn continually upon issues of the human condition. She seems like so many of Munro's most fully realized characters, less a character than a medium of reflection, and her apparent high degree of mimetic presence is more attributable to the obsessive and paradigmatic structure of her thinking than to the kind of spatiotemporal detail that might make her more real, if less palpable. Yet the very character of her meditation, which makes her so substantive, is paradoxically designed, particularly by its allusions to fiction and change, to remind us how frail she, in fact, is. One afternoon, while waiting for her father to have some preparatory tests, she goes to a planetarium to watch a show on the latest discoveries in the solar system. She learns of "[m]oonless Mercury rotating three times while circling the sun twice" (231). This she terms an "odd arrangement, not as satisfying as what they used to tell us" (231). Then it rotated once, which is aesthetically more symmetrical. Munro's world, however, in which one learns to accommodate the asymmetrical, to learn that Mercury is not in "perpetual darkness after all" (231), impels her to wonder: "Why did they give out such confident information, only to announce later that it was quite wrong?" (231). This is because certain aspects of scientific thinking may, in their change of the paradigm, require looking upon its past as an error, a kind of fiction. Such information is brought forward within the context of the universe and its galaxies, which are "[i]nnumerable repetitions, innumerable variations" (a Pascalian consideration) (231). The difference between the two images of galaxies and solar system is marked as the difference between "realism" and "familiar artifice" (231), a distinction that makes the reader wonder in turn about the kind of world the narrator perceives herself in. It is one that transcends both, at least in respect of her role as perceiver, equally remote and present, without the supports of either the real or the familiar.

Her father exemplifies her dilemma, as well as that of several other characters, particularly during the scene in which the narrator arrives while he is trying to recall a poem whose first words heard are " '*Shore-less seas*' " (225). It is said with some emphasis because after a night of failed efforts at recollection it not only comes again to mind, but it also underscores the ambiguity of the father's position between knowing and unknowing, life and death. His comments on his problem may be also read as a gloss on the book as a whole and what besets its characters:

"I ask my mind a question. The answer's there, but I can't see all the connections my mind's making to get it. Like a computer. Nothing out of the way. You know, in my situation there's a great temptation to—well, to make a mystery out of it. There's a great temptation to believe in—You know." (225–26)

The narrator completes his sentence with the word "soul," which he more or less accepts. What is significant, however, is that connections are made, usually by chance (in this instance by the narrator's entering the room), and in a manner that escapes the conscious knowing of the character. "Soul" is a makeshift solution to the problem the mystery evoked, that dimension that is always beyond our knowing that clarifies only to suggest a farther dark beyond the light.

This is the darkness—an aspect of the faith Munro appears to seek— that must limit and qualify any light that the narrator might share with her father. Like the narrator of "The Turkey Season," they would both "like to know things" (74), and nothing more touchingly suggests how powerfully knowledge is at once a connection and a sign of limits as their final conversation in which the narrator pursues her father's knowledge of the moons of Jupiter, gradually turning observed, scientific phenomena into myth. His final words are: " 'Ganymede wasn't any shepherd. He was Jove's cupbearer' " (233). It is a fiction that sustains him in his mortality, despite their both knowing that this is only a sign of how perceptions of the world change from belief to fact, and finally, possibly, transcending into fiction. The final word, then, is on the story and on the discourse that will give it its significance. Both narrator and her father must give way to it, content with the limit of their discoveries, prepared to yield to the necessity of a new fiction as well as the satisfaction of an old truth. What connections that are there, as the father's simile of the computer insists upon, are not of our making. Mystery—where the author implicitly dwells in dark—must be allowed for.

Chapter Seven
Fiction as Destiny
The Progress of Love

"—but Mama was another story."[1]

The title of Munro's recent book, *The Progress of Love,* appears to gather in two words all the thematic and formal concerns of her other texts. Love in its various manifestations clearly abounds in Munro, which is why one is from time to time reminded in a curious manner of Dante. The use of "progress" in the title, however, is evidently designed to give the seasoned reader of Munro pause. It is not possible to speak of progress in the formal structure of the majority of her stories, for they exist suspended in a kind of archeology of temporal zones, each zone possessing a significance, and the function of climax and closure is not to eclipse such significance, but to harmonize it. And closure does even more, that is, to place the reader upon a threshold of a mystery that the story prepares but cannot always elucidate. Indeed, the discourse and structure of the story seem to argue against the possibility of clarification, crossed as it is by the discontinuities of its meditation. Thus "progress" should be understood in an ironic sense, for the connotation of amelioration is subdued by structure. In fact, it may often be taken inversely, for formal progress is most frequently analeptic; that is, discourse is constantly returning in the somewhat vain hope that meaning lies near the source. Meaning is, rather, inscribed in process for Munro, and the gesture of return, the trope of analepsis, the dance that informs the title of her first collection and captures the imagination of Del Jordan at the conclusion of *Lives of Girls and Women,* is where we are to behold progress in Munro's sense.

As we have also seen from the first collection, part of the turn resides in the effort to reach what she calls the "other country," as if the self would remain sealed in its own opacity if it could not draw the other somehow into its own signifying space. That moment, and the gathering preparations for that moment, is a kind of progress, for in that moment the kind of transcience that Munro sees everywhere becomes the burden of the self's destiny, the subject becoming the sign of things slipping away, not quite understood. So Dorothy, at the end of "Marrakesh," not only sees the lovers in their helplessness, but the two remain inscribed forever "[o]n the underside of her eyelids,"[2] at once a part and not a part of her life, the lovers' lives "endangered as people on a raft pulled out on the current."[3] Their story and the meaning that she gives it is now a part—and for the moment the core—of hers. Such an event raises a crucial question: if the self is realized through the other, is it possible to speak of the subject as something all by itself? For Munro this is problematic, and it bids us ask, as a consequence, where the character begins and ends. As we have seen, character begins in discourse, as a function of the discourse that produces the subject. To be reminded of this is to be awakened to the fragility not only that characters possess, but also that we possess, coming and going in the exchange of discourses.

This is why perhaps—and more so in this collection than in the previous ones—characters often seem so small and far away. Part of this may be attributed to Munro's fondness for temporal settings in the 1930s and '40s. Everyone is in a certain measure diminished by nostalgia and the sense that the past is irrevocable. But it is also possible for the past to so encroach upon the present that the latter has little significance by comparison. Thus one is never sure whether a character appears small by being telescoped into the past, or because the present makes the character appear lost. Such is the effect of "The Moon in the Orange Street Skating Rink," a story which leads the reader so gently into its past that one tends to forget its frame in the present. It is the story of two cousins, Sam and Edgar, and their friend Callie. Sam has returned to the town where he passed a year with his cousin in the 1930s while attending business college. Callie runs a "variety and confectionary store" (132). We then observe Sam walking through the town, which only for the moment is a town contemporary with the reader. He sees the old boardinghouse, and then the narrator remarks: "The house used to be light tan, and the trim was brown" (133). Not until we reach the framing conclusion of the story does the present tense return, but the transition is almost seamless, the narrator refusing, unlike Munro's usual practice, to draw attention to the change of perspective. The dominant time is the past, their meeting and eventual mating with Callie, their escapades in the skating rink, and their marvelous departure together for Toronto, where Edgar and Callie marry. It is as if the meaning of life resided in the escapes of youth, all sanctioned by Callie's cleverness and androgyny that permit her, as a girl, to be joined to the boys in a curious, asexual camaraderie that frees the three of them from the responsibilities of adult life. That freedom is emphasized in the moment on the train, sign as it is for adventure and detachment from the "real world" (156), which for a moment "was flooded—with power, it seemed, and with possibility" (156–57). This sense of power is immediately qualified by the narrator who remarks: "But this was just happiness. It was really just happiness" (157). And so in melancholy anaphora the moment fades, as if happiness were such a limited good that its presence and evanescence can only evoke sadness.

Yet happiness is the point around which Sam's story turns because it is at once a sign of culmination and ending. After relating his story, Sam is inclined to state that its aftermath " 'was a little more complicated than we expected' " (157). That is, "Edgar became a person he didn't know. Callie drew back, into her sorry female state" (160). Such a turn prompts the narrator to wonder whether "such moments really mean that we have a life of happiness with which we only occasionally intersect? Do they shed such light before and after that all that has happened to us in our lives—or that we've made happen—can be dismissed?" (160). The question suddenly reinvokes the past, irrevocably lost, at the expense of the present, reminding us that such moments, whose meaning also escapes us, do not occur in what the narrator calls "real life," but at a level of what is elsewhere qualified as "legendary," a zone of discourse where meaning is riddled with mystery. And Callie's final word, asserting that Edgar is " 'happy,' " cannot resolve the mystery, but only make it somewhat sadder.

Memory, then, does not necessarily clarify; and the more Munro becomes familiar with an art that depends so heavily upon the evocations of memory, the less able she appears to understand it. As a consequence, she appears to have allowed memory to do what it will, without attempting conclusions. And what memory wills is often, as we have seen elsewhere, to prompt uncanny similarity between past and present, suggesting that in the recurrence of the similar something transcends what is really before us now. The problem for Munro, however, is not how to lead the reader to such knowledge (for she is not primarily a rhetorical writer), but whether the light of such knowledge is valid. This is why she loves to play with fantasy, to make us believe that fantasy is only fantasy, then to suggest that there may be meaning in fantasy, and then to throw the whole thing over to speculation. The line, of course, between memory and fantasy is easily blurred, both serving as guides to the other (country) that perforce leads the subject to itself. Nor is common sense sufficient immunity from the enticements of fantasy, as Mary Jo discovers in "Eskimo." Mary Jo is being sent to Tahiti for a winter holiday by her boss and lover. While on the plane, her imagination is taken up by a couple across the aisle from her. Unable to determine their racial origin, she begins to speculate upon a television program. She sees a likeness between the man on the plane and the Khan on television, immediately hypothesizing: "If you travel the world in great airliners, aren't you bound to see, sooner or later, somebody you have seen on television?" (197–98). So with the ease that Sam slips into his past, Mary Jo is able to remark: "The woman must be one of his wives" (198). The indeterminacy of "his" allows her and the reader to accept the possibility that he is the Khan. She is jolted out of the fantasy only when the woman later informs her that she is Eskimo. Such knowledge, accompanied by her confession that she is sixteen, serves, however, to excite new fantasies of abduction, but these begin to fade as Mary Jo witnesses the girl paying homage to him: "She licks him all over his face, then takes a breath and resumes her kissing" (204). Clearly the girl across the aisle and the one in Mary Jo's imagination are not quite the same, the former only acting as a catalyst of Mary Jo's narrative desire, for her one thought turns on how to explain all this to her lover, Dr. Streeter. This is how her fantasies began—as something for a letter to him—and as they unfold, he is drawn in as well. But narrative desire is also interwoven with sexual desire as she looks at the couple, a desire which Dr. Streeter clinically disposes of. As he does so, her desire modulates to "shame and aversion" (205), but with the perfect awareness that Dr. Streeter is almost a delusion, something "she manufactured . . . herself" (204), which permits her to retain a certain self-possession, at the same time "purely hating him" (205). Having reached a state of emotional equilibrium, "[s]he starts telling herself a story in which things work out better" (205). The first word of the story is "Suppose" (205), marking the similarity of fiction and fantasy. This time she sees herself in the ladies' washroom of the Honolulu airport, where she is urging upon the girl some method of escape. At this moment we are told that her narration has moved from fantasy to dream, suggesting that she is no longer in conscious control of her discourse and reminding us that Mary Jo is indeed subordinate to her narrator, putting her "at the mercy" of the other as both fantasy and narrator. As a result Mary Jo is as much an object of her observation as the Eskimo girl, and what she sees is herself turning to find the girl "lying on the floor. She has shrunk, and has a rubbery look, a crude face like a doll's. But the real shock is that her head has come loose from her body, though it is still attached by an internal elastic band" (206). Her dream then shifts to Dr. Streeter's office, where she senses "lapses in time she hasn't noted" (207). A third woman from the washroom asks whether " '[t]he court is in the garden' " (207). This permits the narrator to speculate on the possible meanings of "court" in a manner suggestive of dream psychology. What is important is the privileging of the narrator as focalizer, replacing Mary Jo, who is within her dream.

The story concludes with Mary Jo waking and trying to recover the moment in the dream when she "was telling the girl how she could save herself" (207). The use of the dream as another level of fantasy raises the problem of similarity in the story to an unmistakable prominence, transposing to the level of narration the suggested similarity between the devotion of the two women—Mary Jo and the Eskimo girl—to the two men, both of whom possess characteristics that are disgusting to Mary Jo. The play of Mary Jo's imagination and its yielding to the narrator's discourse remind the reader how problematic, finally, fiction is. For if Dr. Streeter's voice is manufactured by Mary Jo, who appears so real to us in her efforts to understand the couple across the aisle, so her dream is not "hers" but the creation of the narrator. All characters in fiction are, needless to say, of such a nature, but for Munro this is the problem that seeks examination. It also lends a special poignancy to Mary Jo in the final sentences of the story:

The man and the girl across the aisle are asleep with their mouths open, and Mary Jo is lifted to the surface by their duet of eloquent and innocent snores.
     This is the beginning of her holiday. (207)

The adjective "innocent" is sufficient to remind one of the difference between Mary Jo's Eskimo and the story's, and the final sentence, brisk in its dispatch, suddenly projects Mary Jo into a kind of helplessness we cannot reach. And how well we think we know the protagonist, witnessing her projection into the Eskimo girl, but permitted as well to see the play of narrator, protagonist, and Eskimo as a kind of elaborate teasing designed to expose what we think we know.

With the exception of "Jesse and Meribeth," however, a story that depends upon playing out an elaborate fantasy that is narrated by Jesse

to her friend Meribeth, the collusion of memories is the more common
mode in this text of suggesting significance within events.[4] And yet the
degree to which imagination shapes both memory and observation is
difficult to measure. The narrator in "Miles City, Montana," for example,
begins by telling the story of a boy who drowned at some time in her
childhood. The initial two paragraphs appear to be designed to stress
as factually as possible what took place from the time the body was
discovered. Each sentence suggests the simplicity of the actions involved:
"My father came across . . . ," "There were several men together
. . . ," "The men were muddy . . . ," "Even the dogs were dispirited
. . . ," and so forth (84). This is the kind of syntax that surely must
inspire faith in the narrator, but this faith is immediately eroded at the
beginning of the third paragraph when the narrator remarks: "I don't
think I really saw all this" (84). It is more likely, as she says, that "I
must have heard someone talking about that and imagined that I saw
it" (84). By being so candid, the narrator gains in reliability, but the
reader now knows that no event occurs without depending upon an
observer for its existence, and in this instance the observer is observing
through a filter of narration, which is both hers and that of eyewitnesses.
What she calls "imagination" is the gesture that includes her in the
event. But is it only hindsight that permits us to say this? As the story
suggests, the relation between event and observer is in fact so intimate
that to say "include" is not precise enough to describe the character
of their relationship.

The boy's drowning serves as prologue to the main story, that occurs
some twenty years later, itself a reminiscence. The protagonist is returning
to Ontario with her husband and children to visit their respective
families. The narrator reveals some of her attitude toward her husband
and much more of their mutual relationship with the two children.
The trip is uneventful until they decide to stop at Miles City so the
girls can take a swim. Leaving them in the care of a lifeguard and her
boyfriend, she goes for a walk. Suddenly, in the midst of a revery, she
wonders where the children are. Returning to the pool, she sees only
her older daughter and moments later "just within [her] view, a cluster
of pink ruffles appeared, a bouquet, beneath the surface of the water"
(100). The girl nearly drowns, and the reader is urged to perceive this
event in relation to the prologue, as if the drowning of the boy were
a palimpsest of the girl's near drowning. The two texts are irrevocably
inscribed in each other. To remind us of their significance to each other,
the only notable sight along the way before reaching Miles City is a

dead deer being carried by a pickup truck, which later forms part of a guessing game. So that we do not fail to perceive the connections between prologue and the girl's near-drowning, the narrator's meditation draws the two without transition into one order of thought. Following a lengthy passage of speculation of what it would have been like had she drowned, a paragraph begins: "When I stood apart from my parents at Steve Cauley's funeral and watched them, and had this new, unpleasant feeling about them, I thought that I was understanding something about them for the first time" (103). What she understands is that the giving of life is the conferring of mortality, thus conjoining "sex and funerals" (104). Thus the two complementary themes of *Lives of Girls and Women* are brought together in one act, the act that, we discover, is the crucial event of the story. And what the narrator discovers is how well merged her younger and older selves are. For, released from the earlier memory, she is returned to the later moment of her life, now adult, but bearing the burden of her younger insight, "trusting to be forgiven in time what first had to be seen and condemned by those children: whatever was flippant, arbitrary, careless, callous—all our natural, and particular, mistakes" (105).

We are to believe, if only for a moment, that this is an ethical statement that endeavors to embrace the errors adults commit simply by creating children. But these are "natural . . . mistakes" for which we cannot exactly be held accountable. We are "at the mercy" of our nature, as much as our children are of us. And just as the two events of drowning and near-drowning blur into one, we begin to notice that the blurring occurs only as the narrator's discourse. She realizes each event, and by doing so we are summoned to understand that they are events subordinate to that event that shows us, no matter how partially, who the speaker is. This is tantamount to saying that we are our particular fictions and, as a consequence, our fictions are our destinies. Thus fiction is burdened, as Del Jordan glimpses toward the end of *Lives of Girls and Women*, with a necessity for truth and legend. Because these are burdens indeed, they are not easily assumed. That uneasiness is one way of explaining Munro's penchant, as we have already observed, for the discontinuous. Not only does discontinuity reflect the unexpected turns of the narrating mind, but it also displays its hesitancy to be sure of the truth it seeks and to assume it once discovered. Here, I think, is where the moral level of Munro's fiction takes its rise, and why both discontinuity and her developed sense of focalization are more than literary strategies. Thus *différance,* that act by which difference is discerned and delay adopted, is not the kind of metaphysical *divertissement* that it appears to be among such postmodernists as Robert Kroetsch and Hubert Aquin. It is, rather, that gesture that is part of the act of determination.

"Monsieur les Deux Chapeaux" begins with a crucial, demonstrative question: " 'Is that your brother out there?' " (56). We are to know that the words "your brother" contain the kernel of the story's system of signification. Because of the delicacy of the relationship, however, it can be approached only indirectly, urging us to see that there is something peculiar about the brother (Ross) referred to, who has been hired for spring cleanup at the local school and does so wearing two hats. The two hats symbolize Ross's two roles, his public and private ones, and explain in a certain measure the difficulty of his relationship with his brother Colin. To reach this difficulty requires a series of entries into the story, the second of which is a description of the similarities between the two brothers. The third, referring back to the first, introduces the reader to the boys' mother and Colin's wife Glenna. Time, then, is not a problem and its use of a series of reprises as it is, for example, in "Something I've Been Meaning to Tell You." Yet linear as the sequencing is, the discontinuous ordering reminds us how deceptive our sense of linear time can be. No one's recollection is ever fully connected by all the metonymical signs that narrators provide to give the illusion of the way things unfold. Furthermore, it is a method that permits the narrator to focalize in any way desirable, and in some instances treat all characters equally so that no one appears to dominate. This allows the family's tendency to tell stories to emerge gradually. Colin tells his mother of Ross's public behavior, the possibility of Glenna's first meeting with Ross before Colin becomes "a family joke" (61), and this leads almost imperceptibly to the story of Ross's schooldays' infatuation with Wilma Barry, as well as another incident in high school that is a recurrent story. But the one Ross persists in having told is the time, as he says to Colin, when " 'you shot me dead' " (63), but that Glenna refuses to hear again.

In order to suggest that that story is not the main story, the narrator effectively delays it by several sections that describe Ross's passion for "souped-up" cars and his mechanical abilities. It is an interest that Glenna shares, which is gratifying to Colin, "as if from now on Ross could stop being a secret weight on him" (66). What that weight is is revealed by the story Glenna refuses to hear. The occasion for the story is provided by a character who has recently become a friend of the family and who also possesses certain mechanical abilities with cars. She has joined them all for supper, and while she is trying to have it brought to Ross's attention that the engine he is mounting is too powerful for the car he is restoring, the boys' mother begins telling her about the twenty-fifth wedding anniversary party she gave herself in her husband's absence. As the two stories interweave, it is evident that danger to Ross is their common motif. At last it is revealed how Colin as a boy accidentally shot Ross during the party. Believing Ross dead, Colin ran to the river and climbed the girders of the bridge. Eventually, Colin perceives that Ross was faking; he comes down, and their mother's story concludes. The next section returns to Colin and Glenna later discussing Ross and his car and concludes with a commentary on Glenna's ability to deal with Ross, not to speak of any other problem that might present itself.

After a gap in the text, focalization immediately turns to Colin at the moment of the accident as it is recalled by an older Colin. He recalls what might have been expected of him, namely, fear, remorse, and the possibility of even committing suicide. He also recalls how silly all of these things were, and how silly it was to "have a name and [that] it should be Colin, and that people should be shouting it" (82). Equally silly "was to think in these chunks of words" and, finally, "[t]o see it as an action, something sharp and separate, an event, a *difference*" (82). What Colin is brought to understand is the absolute inseparability of word and event that only spectators have the privilege of enjoying. Whom they call Colin he is; what they call the shooting of Ross he is, as well. What he might subsequently do, therefore, is no longer a consideration, for "progress seemed not only unnecessary but impossible. His life had split open, and nothing had to be figured out any more" (82). The event was such as to take Colin to the center of himself where event and what gives it significance become coterminous. The structure of the whole story, however, makes it equally evident that this is the kind of knowledge that is a function of how we narrate our lives, for the dominant rhythm of the story is the urge itself to tell stories. For Colin, this is the story that articulates a destiny: "He knew that to watch out for something like that happening—to Ross— and to himself—was going to be his job in life from then on" (83). Such a statement, forming the closure for the story as a whole, reflects paradoxically upon the use of linear (progressive) time in the narrative discourse, suggesting that it is both a necessity and an illusion, for once the crucial event occurs and becomes translated into significant destiny, time loses its pressure, yielding to truth and legend.

It is for this reason that Munro's fascination with the past is so deceptive, why it seems so real. But its reality is not sui generis, for it exists only in the manner by which it informs the present of the articulating mind. The past, paradoxically, resides in some eternal now of narration. Munro's characters, as the title of the second part of "A Queer Streak" suggests, are in some ineluctable fashion in the possession of the past to which they give assent. As a result, "the past," which always appears so wonderfully recaptured in Munro's prose, is in fact idiosyncratic, and not necessarily consensual. Were it the latter, it would become so representative as to appear less real, if more accurate. Violet's past, including its rural setting, is unique to Violet, the protagonist of the novella, "A Queer Streak." Its two parts address her childhood up to the breakup of her engagement and, after the passage of several years, her maturity and old age. As a novella, the two parts, respectively titled "Anonymous Letter" and "Possession," are not simply sequential. They bear a recursive relation to each other, the second continually folding back upon the first to discover an elusive significance. Violet's childhood is presented as one of strange relationships in which her mother is also known as her aunt, her father is called King Billy after a horse he may have ridden in the annual Orange Walk, and she herself assumes the role of the mother in the house. To underline what the reader cannot miss, the narrator observes that "[c]onfusion abounded in the world as she knew it" (210).

Violet's one hope, it would appear, is to get away. She does so by going to Ottawa to attend normal school. There she meets the man to whom she becomes engaged, a United Church minister. Just before her final exams, she is asked to return home to help her family inasmuch as King Billy has been receiving threatening letters. Within a matter of a few days Violet discovers that their author is her younger sister, Dawn Rose. For incomprehensible reasons Violet sends all the letters to her fiancé, who can do nothing else but break off the engagement on the ground that a minister's wife "must not have anything in her background or connections that would ever give rise to gossip or cause a scandal" (230). In her dilemma Violet prays for help, and her prayer is answered by telling her to look after her family, to "[l]ive for others" (232), a task for which she has always seemed suited. And so she does, apparently giving up the ambition of her childhood. Ironically, Dawn Rose never manifests any "queerness" again (233), and the first part concludes with Violet hearing a voice telling her that her life is tragic. As an image and symbol of her tragic situation, Violet is seen to drive into a ditch, to flee the car at the approach of another car, and to hide in a tangle of berry and hawthorn bushes.

The second part is initially focalized by Dawn Rose's son Dane, allowing us to see Violet not only at a later age, but as if we were becoming acquainted with someone familiar but not well known. This slightly obscures our knowledge of her, and when he notices her intimacy with a married man, he is aware that he has encroached upon a secret life that endows her with a mystery new to him and to the reader. Eventually the man's wife dies, Violet marries him, and then he dies in the space of a few pages. It is at this point that we begin to understand the meaning of "possession" in the title of the second part. Violet begins to have visions, one of which is King Billy riding by on his horse. Next she is visited by a couple of girls who claim to be the daughters of Violet's other sister who had moved to Edmonton. Their interest is in women's theater, as well as in their family history. What she has done, as she informs her nephew Dane, is to give them the history of her childhood, which they have referred to in a note as *"a classic story of anti-patriarchal rage"* (248). Through the girls she has relived her past, but in such a way as to suggest that her identity has been with Dawn Rose in opposition to her father.

By allowing Violet's story to be mediated only by Dane, Munro never permits us to perceive how Violet herself is coming to terms with it. He remains the principal focalizer, and she appears only in conversation. Thus, while the two girls may indeed be real and not visions, Violet is perceived as in possession of her childhood. We are to infer this from Dane's watching some Americans on television, for the most part women "who believe themselves to be invaded and possessed, from time to time and in special circumstances, by spirits" (244). Violet looks like them, even though she does not, like them, actively seek possession. She is "at the mercy," and it is sufficient for Dane to feel again the presence "of something concealed from him—all around him, but concealed—a tiresome, silly, malicious sort of secret" (247). We know, in some way, the secret, for it turns upon the anonymous letters that fatefully determine the direction of Violet's life. Their abiding and recursive power throughout the story confirms its genre as a novella, which in turn is used to demonstrate how fiction appears to be a kind of fate. Yet not all is known about Violet's suffering because, while time is allowed to move on for the reader keeping pace with it, time for Violet remains in the past to which she alone, not having been permitted to move on, has access. Part of this immobility is played upon by the closures of both sections, one enacting, the other recalling Violet's entanglement in the bush, the sign of her tragic life. She recalls it, for just before she dies, she is trying to burn the letters that have shaped her life over the gas flames in her kitchen. Dane arrives, sends her outside, and puts out the fire. Outside, she stumbles into some rosebushes, the same clump where Dane first notices her intimacy with her future husband, the man who had also disentangled her from the bushes beside the road. The bushes compose, then, a central paradigm for the story as a whole, holding her mercilessly within the pattern of her life, the place that gathers past, writing (e.g., the letters), and her futile attempts to hide from all that, to acquire the concealment that Dane always sees her abiding in. It is a place, finally, that returns us to the initial image of the story. Violet's mother's first children were all boys, and she had "lost them" (208). Violet knew they had died, but she imagines her mother actually losing them in "the waste ground" along "the edge of the barnyard" (208). There "[s]he would stand hidden by the red-stemmed alder and nameless thornbushes" on occasion and "contemplate getting lost" (208). This place, real as it may be, possesses all the weight the unhappiness that her life can give, merging with the other thorny places, all symbolically the same place, of her lost freedom.

This place, it could be argued, is where most of the characters in *The Progress of Love* arrive. Sam never recovers again the happiness of the flight to Toronto, Mary Jo longs for "the clear part" (207) that illuminates her understanding of the Eskimo girl, the protagonist of "Miles City, Montana" remains profoundly preoccupied by the inevitable conjunction of birth and mortality, and Colin's life enters the presence of its significance the night he thought he killed his brother. As the protagonist remarks at the end of "Jesse and Meribeth," believing she had changed since the period of her great fantasy, "I didn't see that I was the same one, embracing, repudiating. I thought I could turn myself inside out, over and over again, and tumble through the world scot free" (188). Freedom is precisely what is discovered as lost in these stories, and the discovery, as Munro delicately suggests, resides in how the separate fictions are shaped by the narrations of memory, fantasy, and imagination. We have already mentioned the increased bleakness of *Who Do You Think You Are?* in respect of the earlier books. *The Progress of Love,* after the occasionally extraordinary moments of brightness to be found in *The Moons of Jupiter*, evokes that bleakness, but with a profound generosity of spirit.

Nothing could impress more firmly upon the reader the notion of destiny as a matter of fiction than the intertextual closure of the final story, entitled "White Dump." One of the characters reads:

> Seinat er at segia;
> svá er nu rádit.
> (It is too late to talk of this now; it has been decided.) (309)

The lines come from the poetic *Edda,* stories of old Norse mythology. It is a wonderfully gnomic statement that tersely inscribes the sense of an irrevocable past, one that can only be endured and not fully understood. It figures in a story whose focusing is shared among three women, Denise, the daughter of Isabel, who is in turn the daughter-in-law of Sophie. The initial part addresses a visit that Denise pays to her father and stepmother at the lake. Typically the story plays off two times, namely, the present and a moment from Denise's childhood in which they planned the father's fortieth birthday celebration. The event is brought up in present time, but, as the story develops, it is given separate status, allowing Denise to return in memory to the context of the party. This gives way to further recessions in time that include her father's meeting Isabel, as well as their relationship with Sophie. For Denise, her parents keep "something hidden," a secrecy that is only hinted at as she recalls the preparations for the party, part of which consists of an airplane flight over the lake and collecting a cake made by the pilot's wife. The first half of the story concludes with two sections, one in which the pilot's wife has a secret talk with Denise's father a year after the party, and one in present time in which Denise herself wonders why she continues to return on such a regular basis.

The second part is initially focalized by Sophie the morning of the birthday party. It recalls a curious scene in which she is swimming nude, as she usually does, in the lake. There she is abused by some teenagers who tear up her bathrobe and throw it and her cigarette lighter into the lake. This scene is juxtaposed with another that Sophie recalls from her past of visiting another family down the lake while getting the milk. By the conclusion of the memory it has become linked with an affair with her German teacher, the outcome of which is her illegitimate son, Laurence, whose birthday is now to be celebrated. The section concludes with her flight over the lake. The final part begins with Isabel later on the day of the birthday recalling its unfolding, which is punctuated by Sophie's naked return from the lake and the flight from which Isabel is excluded. The end of the flight, however, is illuminated by a look from the pilot, which contains a "promise" that split her like "lightening" (305), a phrase that recalls the moment of Colin's *prise de conscience*. As one might surmise, Isabel has an affair with the pilot, and part of it is mediated in conversation with her daughter Denise.

The comment from the *Edda* occurs at the end of the birthday, when all that will occur has already been determined. By organizing the story as Munro has through a complicated method of layering memories through the three women who participated in the birthday, it becomes apparent that something resides in the story's discourse that draws all the women together in a shared destiny that seems to transcend their individual parts. This use of multiple focalization enables the event to acquire a shape that is dramatically distinct from the characters, but as the same event becomes the obsessive object of their discourse we sense a somewhat greater degree of importance in it than if the event had been simply focalized by a single character. Yet the party serves the same role as the recurring thornbushes in "A Queer Streak": it is the sign of some unshakable decision, and the discursive return creates the event as it seems it must be.

Another aspect of what acquires the effect of destiny resides in how little we are given of the characters. The sense of something concealed is repeatedly brought out in "A Queer Streak," and, indeed, we are permitted to know only enough in the other stories that will make an event become crucial, causing a kind of end to time. Thus we are told that Peg in "Fits" is "self-contained" (109), and this is one of the few clues given to her character. It is, however, insufficient explanation for her version of how she describes a murder-suicide. Her version is neat; the police version emphasizes its violence. Her husband cannot fully understand this difference, and his efforts to do so become the substance of a long meditative walk in the snow in which he reviews his life and his relationship with Peg. In the course of it he recalls the end of his last affair which concluded in "the excitement of saying what could never be retracted" (128). It is a moment of "urgent truths" of a kind similar to other climaxes we have witnessed. But his story is secondary to Peg's, which is never clearly revealed. Nor is it made clear whether he returns from the walk during which he observes strange things that he thinks of "telling Peg about" (131). The story of the murder has gone on long enough, a story she barely recounts: "They needed some new things to talk about" (131). It is only faintly suggested that he could have frozen to death in the snow, but even this is withheld from the reader, wrapping the story of their relationship in even greater mystery.

Within the narrative utterance the character dwells, at once mysterious and determined. A curious example of this occurs in "Lichen," a story that probes the relationship of a separated couple, who visit annually on the wife's father's birthday. The husband, David, has brought along his current friend, whom he is on the point of leaving for another, younger woman. At one point he shows a nude photograph of the new woman to his wife. From her perspective, the girl appears to be huge and part of nature. One breast is out on the horizon, the legs reaching "into the foreground." They are "spread wide—smooth, golden, monumental: fallen columns. Between them is the dark blot she called moss, or lichen. But it's really like the dark pelt of an animal, with the head and tail and feet chopped off" (42). In this elaborate, hybrid image the wife captures some of the violence David does to women in the ease with which he reduces them to natural objects of his desire. Following his intention, David leaves the picture behind in a rather spiteful manner, and she discovers it a few weeks later. Since it is a Polariod picture, it has faded in the light, and she remembers saying that the girl's pubic hair "looked like lichen" (55). Seeing it again,

She said "Lichen." And now, look, her words have come true. The outlines of the breast have disappeared. You would never know that the legs were legs. The black has turned to grey, to the soft, dry color of a plant mysteriously nourished on the rocks. (55)

The truth of her assertion is repeated in the final paragraph in such a way as to call attention to the wife's pain. But the repetition also reminds the reader how much our lives dwell within our words, shaping us as we think we are.

Never far from the surface of Munro's narrative, however, is the sense that fiction may be only fiction, no matter with how much truth it may be invested, nor how much we make it legend through its repetition. Thus, playing against the presence of destiny, that is everywhere felt in these stories as crucial to the utterance of self, is the possibility that the narrator might be wrong in the remembrance of things past and that, like Rose in "Privilege," she may never "get them for good."[5] This is precisely the dilemma of the title story; and since it is the initial story of the collection, the reader is urged to bear it continually in mind. The story, simply by the way it is begun, suggests the narrator is hesitant to take the reader to the core of a matter whose truth she herself appears somehow unsure of. It takes some six starts in four and a half pages to begin a sustained narrative. Taken together, the sequence of starts aptly reflects the narrative as an act of meditation, apparently trying to reckon with the death of the speaker's mother. First she receives a call from her father, announcing it. Then she discusses his tone of voice and the circumstances of finding his wife. In the next section she recalls her mother's religious habits and her father's integrity. Then, in a paragraph, she recalls their house and its poor state of repair. The following section moves forward in time from the initial episode to a period when her father is in an old-age home. The next section recalls a conversation with her mother on the color of her hair before it turned white. Finally, in a summary section, the narrator observes: "All these things I remember. All the things I know, or have been told, about people I never even saw" (7). To whom does this admission refer, and what is it supposed to signify? She has made only brief mention of her grandparents, and all that she has recounted are things she has witnessed or heard about people she knows. As the story makes clear, the statement is to be understood proleptically, reflecting a mind coming to terms with unknown figures, their stories as they are handed down by various speakers, and how, as a consequence, the shift of focalization within the single focalizing mind skews the narration of self, prompting perplexity and doubt about the self in its process of articulation.

The first sustained entry into story begins with the visit of the narrator's Aunt Beryl when the narrator is twelve. This is the first of a series of recessive moves, the next of which goes back to her mother's childhood, such that the two childhoods are placed in tandem. The shift, furthermore, in focalization from narrator to mother weakens the narrator's dominance in the narrative, making it difficult to see the narrator as a clearly defined character, containing as she does so many voices, so many superimposed planes of vision. Characters in turn are not all self-contained. For example, the narrator's mother Marietta, "in [the narrator's] mind, was separate, not swallowed up in [her] mother's grownup body" (9). Such an assertion is designed to guarantee the discontinuous in Munro, permitting the reader to perceive the self as existing in distinct moments of time, each aspect of the self no more necessarily related than moments of time. The narrative act, dependent upon its use of time, is therefore intimately related to the making of the self, conjoining those aspects that have a signifying function. The temptation, as we have seen, is to succumb to an elegant solution. Once, however, one is aware of how fiction seeks division, rifts in thought and memory cannot be glossed over.

The story that the narrator tells of Marietta, her mother who is not (yet) mother, recounts Marietta seeing her own mother in the barn about to hang herself. Her mother tells Marietta to fetch her father, whom she wants to stop from flirting with a girl at work. In the time it takes her to find him, her mother has been discovered by a neighbor. When Marietta returns, her mother is sitting in her neighbor's kitchen, laughing. Here Marietta's reported story ends with the statement, "[h]er heart was broken" (13). For the narrator some things are never sufficiently explained by the story, and she "always had a feeling, with my mother's talk and stories, of something swelling behind" (13). It is described as "a cloud, a poison, that had touched my mother's life" (13). This is the kind of story we have seen elsewhere in this text, and it is of a kind that in its concealments utters an essential self. It is in fact so powerful that when the narrator grieves for her mother, she becomes part of the poison it carries. Or does she—the sentence is ambiguous— become part of her mother's life, that is, the story that utters it? The blurring is important, for what does occur is an exchange that allows us to see how stories "about people I never saw" become a text within the narrator's own text.

What appears only a minor episode is quickly passed over in the resumption of the story of Beryl's visit to the narrator as a child. Yet toward the end of the section Beryl's version of the mother's faked suicide is brought up. In this version motivation is given (her husband " 'was supposed to be interested in some girl that kept coming around to the works' " [21]), and it is suggested that the father was fully aware of his wife's possible suicide while Marietta was looking for him. Beryl, moreover, was the one who noticed that the rope was not tied to a rafter, but just thrown over it. Later Beryl's story becomes a problem for the narrator, and her first response is to rationalize it. "Beryl was strange" (23) is the explanation, and this is sufficient for the mother's version to dominate for a time. How that domination erodes is only indirectly suggested and by means of another story.

A similar framing method is employed to dramatize her gradual understanding of how stories are structured as much by our desire for a certain truth as by truth itself. The narrator recalls visiting her family home after it had been sold. There she remarks to a friend that her mother had once burned up the three thousand dollars inherited from her father in the kitchen stove. The friend remarks that she must have hated her father a great deal. The narrator asserts that the true point of the story is that her husband permitted her to do it, and then comments that this is an act of love. The following section is a recollection of the time when she heard Beryl's version of the near-suicide. She overhears a conversation between Beryl and her mother over the inheritance in which the mother admits to the burning and asserting that her father was not there. The final section returns to a time closer to the present in which the narrator puzzles over why she had told her friend the other version. Nevertheless, she continues to "see the scene so clearly" (29), and her father present, "not just to be permitting her to do this but to be protecting her" (30). She then remarks that it is difficult for her to believe the story was simply made up. Indeed, "[i]t seems so much the truth, it is the truth" (30).

How much this appears to follow the thinking of Luigi Pirandello, who captures what Munro is saying in the title of his play, "It *Is* So, (If You Think So)" (*Così è, se vi pare!*). Certainly her view is apt for this particular story, for the version she gives to her friend is meant to reflect not only upon her parents' marriage, but also on that of her grandparents. She sees her comment to her friend as a moment "of kindness and reconciliation" (30), which is "more valued, and deliberately gone after, in the setups some people like myself have now than in those old marriages, where love and grudges could be growing underground, so confused and stubborn it must have seemed they had forever" (31). No matter how fitting this comment is as closure for this story, it does not permit us to forget the relation the narrator establishes between narration, truth, and self, and the degree to which narration determines a truth of self, even if its truth is at variance with "facts." The truth is perhaps all the more compelling simply because it includes belief, awareness of illusion, and the necessity to narrate one self at the expense of another. It is here that the grandeur of Munro's writing resides, and this story is a particularly stunning instance of how finely tuned Munro's moral habit of mind is, refusing to find moral presence in the drawing of conclusions, but rather in the continuous adjustment of narrations of the self as they are intertextually layered by other such narrations. In this sense, Munro is a consummate writer of *auto*biography in which, paradoxically, the self is at once self and other, acquiring itself in the endless elaboration of *differance*.

It is within this context that one of the most exquisite stories in the collection, "Circle of Prayer," should be addressed. Although the story is principally focalized by Trudy, her story is mediated—indeed, it is an unremittent dialogue—by those of her daughter and estranged husband as they impinge upon hers. As a consequence, the events of two or three days expand to include glimpses of Trudy's meeting her husband, their honeymoon, the end of their marriage, as well as episodes that take place at the Home for Mentally Handicapped Adults where Trudy works. The event around which everything apparently turns is the funeral of a school acquaintance of Trudy's daughter Robin. Typically, Trudy does not witness the funeral, so that it becomes a story within the story. The climax of the funeral occurs when the girls file past the coffin and drop jewelry on the dead girl. Robin drops a necklace that had been given to her by her father's mother, which was being saved for her until she grew up. This act impels the initial sequence of the story in which Trudy, discovering the necklace gone from the jug where it is kept, throws the jug across Robin's room. The story proceeds analeptically from this point.

The incident itself is somewhat trivial, but it is only a pretext for a meditation on the significance of a human life. What emerges is that Trudy is not the woman whose physical characteristics are given only through her husband's desire—"her skinny bones, her curly hair, her roughening skin, her way of coming into a room with a stride that shook the windows" (264). Trudy does not end in what we may physically see. She is, rather, a composition of relationships as they extend to daughter, husband, friend, and patients at the Home. Hence, when her friend suggests sending a prayer through the friend's Circle of Prayer in an effort to recover the buried necklace, it is made metaphorically evident that the most appropriate figure for defining the character in Munro is the circle that includes all those who touch upon the protagonist's life. The usefulness of the metaphor lies in the fact that faith is required to bring it to life. We may feel that Trudy's skepticism in respect of the Circle of Prayer marks her lack of faith. But this is only one aspect of faith, and the most superficial one; for Trudy moves in her own circle, and the circle continually moves in signifying curves.

The crucial curve, one might say, are the moments that connect her memories of her husband, especially the breakup of their marriage, and the funeral. Clearly a metaphorical connection is established between one as a figurative, the other as a literal, death. Yet, the connection the narrator intends is not that of death, but one of love, suggesting that Trudy's turns are creating a progress of love. The most obvious link occurs at the end of the description of the funeral, which concludes with the dead girl's sister crying. There follows a gap in the text. Then her husband remarks, referring to their separation: " 'This is a test of love' " (264), transposing death and dying to an act of giving. A reversal of the same collocation occurs later when the husband leaves definitively. The section ends with the word "[g]oodbye" (267). The next section of only one paragraph begins with the sentence: " 'All I want is to know why you did it?' " (267). The sentence may, of course, be read as referring to the departure of the husband, and certainly the interweaving of the two levels of Trudy's thinking would permit such a reading. But Trudy is addressing her daughter. Nevertheless, the power of the paragraph lies in the next two sentences, when she asks: " 'Did you do it just for show? Like your father—for show?' " (267). With these two sentences we witness Munro's unshakable preoccupation with likeness, with metaphorical thinking. Yet metaphor is only a gesture toward a gathering vision that would go beyond the deceptions of similarity.

Near the conclusion of the story Trudy recalls a moment from her honeymoon. She remembers "her young self" (273) standing at the cottage window gazing at her mother-in-law playing the piano. She recalls standing "outside her own body," indeed, "outside her own happiness in a tide of sadness" (273). She then recalls her husband's leaving, when "she stood outside her own unhappiness in a tide of what seemed unreasonably like love" (273). Then she observes that once outside there are no oppositions—"it was the same thing" (273). They are, however, the same thing only as they are something else, and she asks: "What are those times that stand out, clear patches in your life—what do they have to do with it?" She then answers: "They aren't exactly promises. Breathing spaces. Is that all?" (273). How ethereal this moment is in Munro's writing, for it begins with the older self separate from the younger, outside the window, then recalling the younger self standing outside herself, only to change the denotation of the verb so that standing out in space comes to mean conspicuous in time. For the younger Munro (another, younger self) such a sequence could easily have completed the story, and without the final question. But for this Munro, it is not all, and the next section begins with the sentence: "She goes into the front hall and listens for any noise from upstairs" (273). She is at the Home, within another zone of her circle. The section indicates a reconciliation with Robin. Then after the briefest recollection of throwing the jug, returning us as in a circle to the moment of the beginning of the story, the final section begins with Trudy asking one of the patients whether he ever prays. His answer is that if he were smart enough to know what to pray for, there would be no need to pray. He would have acquired the knowledge, then, that would have answered Trudy's questions. Thus he is intimately a part of her circle, and to convey the sense of his answer, "[h]e smiles at her" (274). The smile or the answer—for the referent is unclear— is "not meant as comfort, particularly. Yet it radiates—what he said, the way he said it, just the fact that he's there again, radiates, expands the way some silliness can, when you're very tired" (274). And his radiance is so knowing on Munro's part, for it gathers the moments Trudy has just recalled, "clear patches in your life," allowing his text to give meaning to hers, and not only to hers, for as the final sentence observes: "In this way, when she was young, and high, a person or a moment could become a lily floating on the cloudy riverwater, perfect and familiar" (274). What is important is that she is not floating, but someone else or a fragment of time, transposed to metaphor within an image that combines the elements of earth and air, making it unclear whether the image is to be seen up among the clouds or down on the surface of the river. But in this image there is no opposition: "it was the same thing, really."

Since it is the same thing, we should recall Munro's preoccupation with the past, with transience, with the significance of the subject within that world of loss and doubtful recovery, and with the discourse appropriate to the summoning of the problem. I have already suggested one response, and it is one that is more apparent in this text than the others, and yet may be seen edging out of the others, particularly *The Moons of Jupiter*. This story especially recalls the wonderful evanescence and cohesion of that volume. One of the expressions that critics of Munro are fond of indicating as characteristic of her style is the phrase "clear jelly" from "Material." Ironic as I think that phrase is, for it refers to a style that the narrator is critical of, the sense of illumination that it contains may be found everywhere in Munro's work. While I hesitate to use the word mystical because of its religious connotations, Munro's luminosity seems to have such a character, radiating, as it does, the things of the earth. Since the objects of its radiance are earthly, they are fraught with the burden of time passing. But were Munro merely the recorder of surfaces as some would have us believe, how could we explain her relentless urge to show us how surfaces cohere in unexpected, yet believable, ways? Because they so cohere, no linearity of exposition, no order of lists that naturalists must depend upon, will make us believe in her vision. And yet we have no difficulty in echoing her words, perceiving ourselves within the "perfect and familiar." The phrase is apt, for it points to the classical in Munro's work, something more enduring than the apparent accuracy of her memory. For we know that the memory of her narrators is fallible, and correctly so. These are memories that are as much, if not more, preoccupied, like Del Jordan's, with truth at the expense, if necessary, of the real. As we have seen, it is here that the legendary in some ineluctable manner issues forth, bearing with it the recurrent, the "perfect and familiar." The problem, however, is to convince us, skeptic as we are, and so illusion, fantasy, discontinuity are continually and increasingly employed.

But what are we asked to believe? Not, I think, that lives are to be understood as hopelessly fragmented, scattered through moments in time and, therefore, recoverable only as *bricolage,* as odds and ends that may arbitrarily cohere. What this volume affirms, rather, and that should affect in some way our consideration of the previous texts, is that lives retain possibilities of an archetypal coherence. That they do, without appearing to, requires an attentiveness to the turns of narrative discourse that would gradually allow such possibilities to stand forth in whatever radiance they can gather into themselves. To take this as the primary gift of her art marks Munro as a writer of unassailable moral integrity. Earlier I suggested with Isaiah Berlin that Munro dwelt among the hedgehogs of literature, knowing one thing well, and it is this that she knows so well, continually adumbrating the character as within a discourse that becomes a *habitus,* a movement of spirit that is its own and other, and known only through its continual exchange with the other.

Yet this is not the final story. The book ends with "White Dump," whose closure is two lines from the *Edda,* reminding us of the function of the text as an act of destiny. Destiny is not in Munro, however, as grim as it is often portrayed in Old Norse with whose texts, emphasizing the oral, the legendary, and the true, Munro has many affinities. Destiny is often a moment of illumination that raises certain essential truths about the self in such a way as to remove it for a moment from time. In this way, the transient and temporal, for all their palpable texture, become illusory, giving way to the real within that makes the self what it is. For what happens on the surface is so often something that does not happen at all: Colin does not shoot his brother, Peg does not relate how her neighbors died, Meg does not drown, Jesse has no affair, the husband in "Progress of Love" does not protect his wife as she burns her father's money. What happens is the endless reckoning with what does not happen, and here, between what is and is not, caring and not caring, as it is put elsewhere, the discourse of Munro's stories takes its rise, mysteriously, poignantly, and abounding with love.

Chapter Eight
Conclusion

". . . to make this structure which encloses the soul of my story . . ."[1]

Although Canada is rarely perceived from the outside as more than a few acres of snow, Munro, though Canadian, rarely takes notice of the weather and what it brings. Such notices that one finds are mentioned in passing; they are, nevertheless, rarely ornamental. At the opening of the chapter entitled "Lives of Girls and Women" from the novel of the same name, as an introduction to the theme of heroism, we read: "The snowbanks along the main street got to be so high that an archway was cut in one of them, between the street and the sidewalk, in front of the Post Office."[2] The landscape, after Mr. Chamberlain masturbates in front of Del Jordan, becomes "post-coital, distant and meaningless."[3] The night she meets Garnet French, "the weather had suddenly turned warm."[4] The season of the novel she is planning—a novel of Gothic passion—is "always the height of summer—white, brutal heat."[5] The winter wind that occasionally blows through the story of the same name is a blizzard that lasts for a week, but for the narrator "[a] blizzard in town hardly seemed like a blizzard,"[6] and thus it is not the snow itself that is important. The roads that Roberta and her family travel over in "Labor Day Dinner" are "hot gravel roads," and their pace is "funereal."[7] Finally, one of the most memorable moments occurs in "Fits" when Robert walks across the snow, meditating on his life. The scene is described for the length of a paragraph, and the narrator remarks upon the peculiar light the snow leaves on the trees. It is then qualified: "It wasn't like the casing around twigs and delicate branches that an ice storm leaves. It was as if the wood itself had altered and begun to sparkle."[8]

What these passages attest to is that the weather as scene in Munro is functional only as it bears upon character. There is no scene in Munro in the conventional sense, for the scene is the character and the discourse by which it is composed. Although this should not appear surprising, the paucity of references to the weather reminds us that Munro fails

to make use of one of the most frequent markers of transience, as well
as a common sign of the real. And yet a sense of the transient is never
far from the surface of her fiction, and a striking example occurs in
"Marrakesh" in which Dorothy takes note of the loss of the elm trees
to disease. No matter how sensitive she is to loss, she is prepared to
be the witness of change "because there was in everything something
to be discovered."[9] But the elms are only signs, among many others,
of change. They have no other function than their relation to Dorothy,
who composes them within the range of perception and memory. And
acquiescent as she may appear now, as a child "she *hated* change."[10]
The change and the changing, then, are not within the landscape, but
within the character. Andrew Stubbs, commenting on this section of
the story, argues that the landscape for Dorothy is no more than a
kind of cue from whose brooding "the elegiac note is entirely absent."[11]
He then remarks that "awareness of the tentative, momentary nature
of things represents a kind of wish fulfillment, occasions a great
concentration of imaginative energy." The value of what is perceived
depends upon its uncanny ability to gesture "beyond itself to what is
'not there.' " Thus discourse talks around a center of something unsaid,
some central core that persists beyond both the immediately perceptible
and the loss that is always attendant upon the immediate.

It could be argued, especially from some of the early stories, that
characters exist apart from weather, and that this constitutes one of
Munro's distinctive means of realizing the character.[12] Although I have
already cited the following sentence, it is worth a further consideration.
It occurs at the end of "Walker Brothers Cowboy":

. . . I feel my father's life flowing back from our car in the last of the
afternoon, darkening and turning strange, like a landscape that has an
enchantment upon it, making it kindly, ordinary and familiar while you are
looking at it, but changing it, once your back is turned, into something you
will never know, with all kinds of weathers, and distances you cannot
imagine.[13]

This is clearly weather, but just as clearly it is a weather that does not
belong to nature. It is, rather, possessed by the father. Nor is it a
landscape, but "like a landscape." How wonderfully "it" is repeated
in the sentence, so easily referring to "landscape," making us believe
that what we perceive is what is "there." The referent, however, is
"my father's life"; the rest is all analogy, and no real weather at all.

Yet this is the power of desire in reading, to believe that tropes are constitutive of the real rather than figurative of thought. And Munro is so persuasive in leading her readers to perceive what they take the real to be that she finally had to reckon with her writing as something other than fiction in a brief statement entitled "What Is Real?" She begins by composing a kind of narrative:

Whenever people get an opportunity to ask me questions about my writing, I can be sure that some of the questions asked will be these:
"Do you write about real people?"
"Did these things really happen?"[14]

She then glosses both narrative and implied dialogue by suggesting responses, all of which is summarized by the comment that "[i]t would seem quite true that they don't know what fiction is" (223). So to speak of the real she must speak of fiction. Her answer to the central question, however, is not so dissatisfying as it would at first appear, content as she is to remark after some four pages that there is a reality outside the story, which we would call the referent, and, posed against this reality, the reality of the story. "I use bits of the real," she remarks, "in the sense of being really there and really happening, in the world, as most people see it, and I transform it into something that is really there and really happening, in the story" (226). The problem with her answer is its syntax. Despite transformation, the phrase "really there and really happening" is repeated to suggest analogy, likeness, and a parallel order. As if to avoid such a charge, she concludes that she is "not concerned with using the real to make any sort of record or prove any sort of point," thus limiting her role as a documentary writer.

Of fundamental value in her response, however, is her description of what happens in the writing of a story. This she begins by reflecting upon how she reads, which is not to follow the pages in a consecutive manner, but to read in any direction desired. Her movement within the story is then compared to moving and residing in a house. "House," then, becomes the metaphor for story, and "[e]verybody knows what a house does, how it encloses space and makes connections between one enclosed space and another and presents what is outside in a new way" (224). What distinguishes houses from stories, of course, is that the former are not paginated, and it is precisely the tyranny of the numbered page that Munro wants her reader to be delivered from. Thus the random movement that she enjoys as a reader she wishes to inscribe into the structure of her house. The real of the story, then, depends, for its articulation, upon the kinds of movement that I have endeavored to describe. These are not the movements of the world "outside," but are those most frequently of a mind that must "move back and forth and settle here and there, and stay . . . for a while" (224). It is mind, one might say, that at once creates and enters its own discourse. As a consequence, we cannot help but sense the presence of writing that is discovering itself in the act of writing, prepared, therefore, for dead ends, for spaces in its text that require adjustments to the new moment of awareness. It is not, then, toward a conclusion that the writer is intent. It is toward a "feeling . . . [that comes] from being inside the structure" (224). This feeling is understood to be "the soul of the story" around which everything has to be built up, "to fit." The story's soul is its formative principle. Whatever is drawn upon in the referential world is put "together to make the shape I need." How easily the governing metaphor of the house as structure slides from the feeling within it to the feeling as the soul of the story. This is virtually the text of Aristotle, who speaks himself of plot as the soul of tragedy.[15] The coincidence is perhaps not remarkable, for, as I have argued, Munro's primary concern is the arranging, the effort to get it right; and one novel, *Who Do You Think You Are?* expressly addresses the problem of mimesis. Mimesis, however, in Aristotle's sense is not the reflection of the real. It is the poet's task, rather, to use an optative discourse, to speak of what would happen in all likelihood or, even, according to necessity.[16] Thus the decisions of the poet (and Aristotle does not distinguish the poet because of the use of verse) require a discourse that differs from the historian whose matter is the event as it occurred, no matter how improbable.

My overture to Aristotle is not primarily, however, to argue that Munro is mimetic in a particular way, but to suggest an even more curious sequence of similarities. For Aristotle the model tragedy is *Oedipus Tyrannus,* a play that not only encourages us to understand that the mimetic is a function of plot to which character is subordinate, but also urges upon us the problems of truth and legend. In many respects Oedipus is at the mercy of a discourse that he cannot escape, a discourse that is at once legendary and true. His tragedy is not simply, as Aristotle asserts, that it involves a change of fortune, but that it carries with it the burden of discovery.[17] A truth is found, whether Oedipus desires it or not. The process of discovery is a series of analepses, each episode of the play taking the spectator farther back, and each

time from a different perspective, until the truth blinds. The past is
our burden, and what we have done with it puts us, willy-nilly, into
the time of who we are. Furthermore, it is a burden that is at once
a destiny and a deferral of destiny, something that the character
continually approaches but that also prevents immediate access.

So it is that the real of the story is continually jostled by other
problems besides the real that beset Munro's imagination. The real is
always transformed by fiction—the act by which it acquires soul—and
it is somehow bound ineluctably to the discourse of legend, as much
as it is obsessed by the need for truth. Each in a certain measure
corrects the other, for Munro is perfectly aware of how fiction can
obscure truth, just as legend can alter the real. What is even more
important, finally, is that these are not always referential terms, as one
might speak of "the truth" or "the real." They are designations of
kinds of discourse, each one affecting our perception of event and
character. What holds them together is a certain feeling, the soul of
the story. Later in her statement Munro returns to this phrase, only to
use it in a way that deviates somewhat from Aristotle. In order to
answer the hypothetical question, " 'Why do you put in something true
and then go on and tell lies?' " she replies: " 'I do it for the sake of
my art and to make this structure which encloses the soul of my story,
that I've been telling you about' " (225). Hence we find that within
the structure is the soul. They are coterminous, if not the same. She
differs from Aristotle on this point inasmuch as she is speaking as a
writer, not as a theorist, and it is this awareness of a feeling—*her*
feeling—that draws our attention to the intimacy of her prose. It also
reminds us that the necessity to get it right is related to getting the
character right according to the discourses that compose the story. This
is perhaps why, as her most recent collection makes emphatically clear,
we are not only the discourse of which we are composed, but we are
also that discourse and no other. The feeling gives access, then, to what
I have referred to as the archetypal in Munro or, to modify her usage
of the word somewhat, to the soul, which is at once the beginning
and end of her fiction's meditation.

Munro once remarked that one must not expect a writer to progress
in the elaboration of her work.[18] Although a writer's maturity may
deepen, as well as the skill with which the craft is developed, there is
a certain sense in which Munro is unassailably correct. For the story in
its essence is neither its polish nor the writer's wisdom. It is more
elusive, "happening somewhere, not just in [the writer's] head, and in

its own way, not [the writer's]" (225). And the story that is finally written "is still only an attempt, an approach, to the story" (225). It keeps, then, some part of itself, its soul, that must escape the grasp of the writer, and toward which, in the end, the critic can but gesture. What is called "soul" may only be perceived in the story's discourse, that continually summons into the text a surface that reflects a hidden depth. In conversation with John Metcalf she denies that this surface is able to evoke "a religious feeling," but its intensity seems to be akin.[19] It is toward that center, that radiant core of energy, that Munro's stories have continually endeavored to reach. It is to that place that it has been the burden of this essay to endeavor, in corresponding fashion, to move.

Notes and References

Preface

1. Alan Twigg, "What Is: Alice Munro," *For Openers: Conversations with 24 Canadian Writers* (Madiera Park, B.C.: Harbour Publishing), 16.

Chapter One

1. *Something I've Been Meaning to Tell You* (Toronto: McGraw-Hill Ryerson, 1974), 201.
2. See Joyce Wayne, "Huron County Blues," *Books in Canada* 11, no. 8 (October 1982):9. It might be noted that referring to the newspaper in the novel as the *Herald-Advance* might have been imprudent.
3. Ibid., 10.
4. Ibid.
5. "Women in the Wilderness" in *A Mazing Space: Writing Canadian Women Writing,* ed. Shirley Neuman and Smaro Kamboureli (Edmonton: Longspoon & NeWest, 1987).
6. See Martin Knelman, "The Past, the Present and Alice Munro," *Saturday Night* 94, no. 9 (November 1979):18.
7. Wayne, "Huron County Blues," 11.
8. Cf. ibid.
9. Cf. J.R. (Tim) Struthers, "The Real Material: An Interview with Alice Munro" in *Probable Fictions: Alice Munro's Narrative Acts,* ed. Louis K. MacKendrick (Downsview, Ont.: ECW Press, 1983), in which a chronology of these texts is provided.
10. See Knelman, "The Past," 18.
11. Wayne, "Huron County Blues," 12.
12. See Struthers, Interview, 17.
13. *The Progress of Love* (Toronto: McClelland & Stewart, 1986), 274.
14. *Morningside,* CBC Radio, 2 June 1987.
15. W. J. Keith, *Canadian Literature in English* (London and New York: Longman, 1985), 162. In fairness to Keith, it ought to be remarked that the statement is qualification, but even with the qualification, the statement remains.
16. *Something I've Been Meaning to Tell You* (Toronto, Montreal, New York: McGraw-Hill Ryerson, 1974), 43. A further page reference to this work is cited in parentheses in the text.
17. Roland Barthes, *S/Z,* trans. Richard Miller (New York: Hill & Wang, 1974), 19.

18. Ibid., 84.

19. Ibid., 75.

20. Ibid.

21. Ibid., 76.

22. Ibid.

23. John Llewelen, *Derrida: On the Threshold of Sense* (London: Macmillan, 1986), 51.

24. Jacques Derrida, *Positions,* trans. Alan Bass (Chicago: Chicago University Press, 1981), 29.

25. Ibid.

26. *Something I've Been Meaning to Tell You,* 246.

27. Cf. Llewelen, *Derrida,* 102–3.

28. For a full discussion of the matter, see Sholomith Rimmon-Kennan, *Narrative Fiction: Contemporary Poetics* (London and New York: Methuen, 1983), chap. 6.

Chapter Two

1. Alan Twigg, "What Is," 16.

2. Cf. Struthers, "The Real Material: An Interview," 28–29.

3. See, for example, Hugh Garner's Foreword to *Dance of the Happy Shades* (Toronto: Ryerson Press, 1968); hereafter page references to this work are cited in parentheses in the text. See also B. Pfaus, *Alice Munro* (Ottawa: Golden Dog, 1948), 48.

4. Cf. Eileen Dombrowski, " 'Down to Death': Alice Munro and Transcience [*sic*]," *University of Windsor Review* 14, no. 1 (Fall-Winter 1975): 21–29, and John Orange, "Alice Munro and A Maze of Time," in *Probable Fictions,* 83–98.

5. The presence of Joyce has been frequently observed, notably by J. R. Struthers, "Reality and Ordering: The Growth of a Young Artist in *Lives of Girls & Women,*" *Essays on Canadian Writing* no. 3 (1975): 32–46; W. R. Martin, "Alice Munro and James Joyce," *Journal of Canadian Fiction* no. 24 (1979): 120–26; and Barbara Godard, " 'Heirs of the Living Body': Alice Munro and the Question of a Female Esthetic," in *The Art of Alice Munro: Saying the Unsayable,* ed. Judith Miller (Waterloo, Ont.: University of Waterloo Press, 1984), 65–66. The latter argues that *Lives of Girls and Women* is "a *Bildungsroman* written *against* Joyce," 65.

6. John Metcalf, *Kicking against the Pricks* (Downsview, Ont.: ECW Press, 1982), 151–52.

7. Whenever I am not using "story" to refer to a genre category but distinguishing it from its discourse, I follow Seymour Chatman, *Story and Discourse: Narrative Structure in Fiction and Film* (Ithaca, N.Y.: Cornell University Press, 1978).

8. See Munro's second thoughts on this practice in her interview with Struthers, "The Real Material," 9.

9. It is, for example, expressly forbidden in "The Peace of Utrecht," 191. On various ways in which the narrator relates to narrating, see Margaret Gail Osachoff, " 'Treacheries of the Heart': Memoir, Confession, and Meditation in the Stories of Alice Munro," in *Probable Fictions*, 61–82.

10. Cf. Joseph Frank's seminal essay, "Spatial Form in Modern Literature," in *The Widening Gyre: Crisis and Mastery in Modern Literature* (New Brunswick, N.J.: Rutgers University Press, 1963).

11. See Rae McCarthy Macdonald, "A Madman Loose in the World: The Vision of Alice Munro," *Modern Fiction Studies* 22, no. 3 (Autumn 1976): 369.

12. See Walter J. Ong, *Orality and Literature: The Technologizing of the Word* (London and New York: Methuen, 1982), 41.

13. Cf. Robert Thacker, " 'Clear Jelly': Alice Munro's Narrative Dialectics," in *Probable Fictions*, 37–60.

14. Cf. Orange, "Alice Munro and A Maze of Time," 86, and Brandon Conron, "Munro's Wonderland," *Canadian Literature* no. 78 (Autumn 1978):115.

15. Cf. Bronwen Wallace, "Women's Lives: Alice Munro," in *The Human Elements*, ed. David Helwig (Ottawa: Oberon, 1978), 52–67, and Lorna Irvine, "Changing Is the Word I Want," in *Probable Fictions*, 99–111.

16. Cf. Catherine Sheldrick Ross, " 'At least part legend': The Fiction of Alice Munro," in *Probable Fictions*, 114.

17. The same gesture of shedding may be observed at the conclusion of "The Ottawa Valley," *Something I've Been Meaning to Tell You* (Toronto, Montreal, New York: McGraw-Hill Ryerson, 1974), 246.

18. See Thacker's excellent discussion of the story " 'Clear Jelly,' " 43–49.

19. Cf. Michael Taylor, "The Unimaginable Vancouvers: Alice Munro's Worlds," in *Probable Fictions*, 127–43.

20. Cf. Beverly J. Rasporich, "Child-Women and Primitives in the Fiction of Alice Munro," *Atlantis* 1, no. 2 (Spring 1976):10.

Chapter Three

1. *Lives of Girls and Women* (Toronto, Montreal, London: McGraw-Hill Ryerson, 1971), 79; hereafter page references cited in parentheses in the text.

2. Mari Stainsby, "Alice Munro Talks with Mari Stainsby," *British Columbia Library Quarterly* 35, no. 1 (July 1971):30.

3. Struthers, "Reality and Ordering," 33; cf. Martin, "Alice Munro," 125.

4. Cf. Susan Warwick, "Growing Up: The Novels of Alice Munro," *Essays on Canadian Writing* 29 (Summer 1984):205–6, and Miriam Packer, "*Lives of Girls and Women*: A Creative Search for Completion," in *The Canadian Novel Here and Now,* ed. John Moss, vol. 1 (Toronto: NC Press, 1978), 143.

5. Cf. Irvine, "Changing," in *Probable Fictions,* 107–8.

6. Graeme Gibson, *Eleven Canadian Novelists* (Toronto: Anansi, 1973), 241.

7. Ibid., 258.

8. It is evident that the form of *Lives* and *Who Do You Think You Are?* differ markedly from Munro's collections. Each contains a central figure and, while the chapters may be read separately as short stories, they relate serially and by cross reference. Munro herself is ambivalent about *Lives.* She doubts it is properly a novel (Gibson, *Eleven Canadian Novelists,* 258). But cf. Metcalf, "A Conversation," in which she calls them "organically linked" (60). In the same interview she also refers to it as "an autobiographical novel" (58). Struthers refers to it as an " 'open-form novel,' " a form in the main derived from Eudora Welty's *The Golden Apples.* See "Alice Munro and the American South," in *The Canadian Novel: Here and Now,* ed. John Moss, I (Toronto: NC Press, 1978), 122–23. I prefer to see it as a discontinuous novel. Cf. Sherrill E. Grace, who argues that this novel follows a "serial pattern," "Duality and Series: Forms of the Canadian Imagination," *Canadian Review of Comparative Literature* (Winter 1980):447.

9. Cf. James Carscallen, "Three Jokers: The Shape of Alice Munro's Stories," in *Centre and Labyrinth: Essays in Honour of Northrop Frye,* ed. Eleanor Cook, Chaviva Hosek, Jay Macpherson, Patricia Parker, and Julian Parker (Toronto, Buffalo, London: University of Toronto Press, 1983), 132–35, who argues that the subtext for this opposition is the Bible.

10. On metonymy, see David Lodge, *The Modes of Modern Writing: Metaphor, Metonymy, and the Typology of Modern Literature* (London: Arnold, 1977).

11. Cf. Irvine, "Changing," in *Probable Fictions,* 87.

12. Cf. Anthony B. Dawson, "Coming of Age in Canada," *Mosaic* 11, no. 3 (Spring 1978):55–56.

13. Cf. Rasporitch, "Child-Women," 11.

14. See Struthers, "The Real Material," in *Probable Fictions,* 14.

15. For an excellent introduction to the narratological function of the protagonist as potential artist, see André Belleau, *Le Romancier fictif: essai sur la représentation de l'écrivain dans le roman québécois* (Québec: Les Presses de l'Université du Québec, 1980), 39–56. On Munro and the *Künstlerroman,* see Struthers, "Reality and Ordering," and Phyllis Sternberg Perrakis, "Portrait

of the Artist as a Young Girl: Alice Munro's *Lives of Girls and Women,"* *Atlantis* 7, no. 2 (Spring 1982).

16. I have discussed this at greater length in "Prisms and Arcs: Structures in Hébert and Munro," in *Configuration: Essays in the Canadian Literatures* (Downsview, Ont.: ECW Press, 1982). Cf. Irvine, "Changing," in *Probable Fictions,* 99.

17. Gibson, *Eleven Canadian Novelists,* 258. Cf. Struthers, "The Real Material," 14–15.

18. Cf. Rae McCarthy Macdonald, "Structure and Detail in *Lives of Girls and Women,"* *Studies in Canadian Literature* 3, no. 2 (Summer 1978).

19. On the sterility of the aunts, see Nancy I. Bailey, "The Masculine Image in *Lives of Girls and Women,"* *Canadian Literature* no. 80 (Spring 1979):114. Godard, " 'Heirs,' " in *The Art of Alice Munro,* 55, argues more positively that the aunts are the source of oral storytelling and "radical scepticism."

20. On the feminist role of Tennyson, see Godard, in *The Art of Alice Munro,* 64–65.

21. Cf. Macdonald, "Madman," 367.

22. Thus it seems to me that Carscallen's argument in "Three Jokers" would have greater validity if he had indicated that the Bible is a subtext only to be subverted.

23. Despite Godard's comment that this novel belongs to a "tradition of historical writing," this is clearly not its dominant function as an intertextual discourse. See Godard, in *The Art of Alice Munro,* 57.

24. Cf. the concluding paragraph of the preceding chapter.

25. Cf. James Carscallen, "Alice Munro," in *Profiles in Canadian Literature,* ed. Jeffrey M. Heath (Toronto: Dundern, 1980), 2:76.

26. Godard, in *The Art of Alice Munro,* argues that the loss of language and kinship with the animal world is characteristic of "many women writers," and that Del's experience brings her to a "wordless plenitude of meaning" (67). Many mystics of both sexes have reached such a state, not to speak of such poets as T. S. Eliot and Wallace Stevens. Munro's point, however, would seem to be that this is a rite of passage that prepares for meaning in language.

27. An excellent examination of the nonmimetic character of this passage is made by Smaro Kamboureli, "The Body as Audience and Performance in the Writing of Alice Munro," in *A Mazing Space,* 37.

28. For Juliann E. Fleenor, the true significance of this passage lies in the fact that it is a rape fantasy that serves as a female initiation rite. See "Rape Fantasies as Initiation Rite: Female Imagination in 'Lives of Girls and Women,' " *Room of One's Own* 4, no. 4 (1979).

29. A loss whose importance is tellingly underlined by Wallace, "Women's Lives," in *The Human Elements,* 57.

30. See Eva-Marie Kröller, "The Eye in the Text: Timothy Findley's *The Last of the Crazy People* and Alice Munro's *Lives of Girls and Women,*" *World Literature Written in English* 23, no. 2 (Spring 1984):370.

31. As I have indicated in the first chapter, this word is a coinage by Jacques Derrida in order to describe a function of writing which at once defers and enunciates difference. *Différence* is particularly developed as the distance between the narrated and narrating self is opened. For a lucid discussion of the problem, see Jonathan Culler, *On Deconstruction: Theory and Criticism after Structuralism* (Ithaca, N.Y.: Cornell University Press, 1982), 95–110.

32. Cf. Mary Agnes, who almost died of suffocation in the "birth canal," 39.

33. Bailey, "The Masculine Image," 116, happily avoids the common temptation to relate the photographer to Munro's "documentary" impulse.

34. Cf. W. R. Martin, "The Strange and the Familiar in Alice Munro," *Studies in Canadian Literature* 7, no. 2 (1982):219–20; and Irvine, "Changing," in *Probable Fictions,* 100. Godard, in *The Art of Alice Munro,* argues that Del's passion for lists is androgynous, involving "a union of fathers and mothers" (54).

35. Cf. Bailey, "The Masculine Image," 117.

36. Struthers, "Reality and Ordering," notes the echo of Joyces's *Ulysses* as one that "emphasizes the dignity of daily life" (46). Godard, in *The Art of Alice Munro,* sees the word as not only subverting its use in Joyce and part of Del's refusal to be an Earth Mother, but also, because of the refusal to express gratitude, a mark of her desire to assert "her own being." According to Godard, an expression of gratitude would signal "the humility and submissiveness of the stereotyped female role from which Del is escaping" (69–70). Despite the validity of Harold Bloom's argument in *The Anxiety of Influence: A Theory of Poetry* (New York: Oxford University Press, 1973) that requires the emerging younger writer to overcome the father, this is a dialectical process, which also requires a long communion with the older writer that issues in a sublation through which the former is somehow transcended. This does not occur between Bobby and Del, who simply takes Bobby's great gift without struggle, as if it were her "due."

Chapter Four

1. *Something I've Been Meaning to Tell You* (Toronto: McGraw-Hill Ryerson, 1974), 124; hereafter page references cited in parentheses in the text.

2. On narratee, see Rimmon-Kenan, *Narrative Fiction,* 86–89.

3. *Lives of Girls and Women,* 100.

4. Cf. Struthers, "Alice Munro's Fictive Imagination," in *The Art of Alice Munro*. This is one of the rare articles that address this issue so cogently.

5. Cf. W. H. New's perspicacious analysis, "Pronouns and Propositions: Alice Munro's Stories, *Open Letter*, 3d ser., no. 5 (Summer 1976):40.

6. Cf. Margaret Anne Fitzpatrick, " 'Projection' in Alice Munro's *Something I've Been Meaning to Tell You*," in *The Art of Alice Munro*, 18.

7. An excellent examination of such division as an issue in women's writing is developed in Part 1, "Toward a Feminist Poetics," of Sandra M. Gilbert and Susan Gubar, *The Madwoman in the Attic: The Woman Writer and the Nineteenth-Century Imagination* (New Haven: Yale University Press, 1979).

8. Kildare Dobbs's review of *Something* set a kind of pattern in Munro studies by suggesting that "clear jelly" was the aim of Munro's art. See "New Direction for Alice Munro," *Saturday Night* 89, no. 7 (July 1974):28.

9. Cf. Wallace, "Women's Lives," 61.

10. Although control is a flaw to which Munro confessed at the time of writing this collection (Gibson, *Eleven Canadian Novelists*, 257), it was one that she was also gradually overcoming.

11. Cf. Irvine, "Changing," in *Probable Fictions*, 106.

12. See New, "Pronouns," 49.

13. Cf. Gerald Noonan, "The Structure of Style in Alice Munro's Fiction," in *Probable Fictions*, 174.

14. On metafiction, see Linda Hutcheon, *Narcissistic Narrative: The Metafictional Paradox* (Waterloo, Ont.: Wilfrid Laurier Press, 1980). Cf. Struthers, "Alice Munro's Fictive Imagination," 106.

15. See Gibson, *Eleven Canadian Novelists*, 243–44.

16. This is characteristic of what Osachoff, " 'Treacheries of the Heart,' " calls a meditation, in *Probable Fictions*, 64.

17. Cf. Dombrowski, " 'Down to Death.' "

18. Cf. the conclusions of "Memorial" and "Day of the Butterfly."

19. Cf. Orange, "Alice Munro and A Maze of Time," in *Probable Fictions*, 93.

20. Cf. the grandmother's anonymous friend in "Winter Wind," 201. New's analysis of this paragraph in "Pronouns" is admirable (42–43).

21. Despite Munro's comment in Gibson, *Eleven Canadian Novelists*, that what she admires in the painting of Edward Hopper, Andrew Wyeth, and Jack Chambers is "a kind of superrealism," 256, which has served as a guide for many critics, Munro's preoccupation with the past is never so static. It is most frequently an exchange between past and present—in fact there may be many moments of the past arranged in anachronic order—that at once creates the real, while at the same time questioning the character of the reality created. One of the problems with photography, furthermore, as she mentioned in her interview with Struthers, "The Real Material," in

Probable Fictions, 5, is that "photographs are too explicit to relate to stories. Thus the reference to "snapshots" at the conclusion of "The Ottawa Valley," 246, ought to be considered metaphorical, in the same way as what is considered to be the "documentary" character of her fiction. The document, whether photograph or documented detail, is a textual register.

22. Fitzpatrick, " 'Projection,' " in *The Art of Alice Munro,* 17.

23. Cf. the conclusion of "How I Met My Husband."

24. Although Irvine, "Changing," considers this passage as central, she reads the phrase "Women's bodies" as one that suggests the merging of "these bodies with the figure of the mother and with the act of writing," in *Probable Fictions,* 105. The merging, I think, is more subtle and mediated by both the husband and the mirror at the end that contains the sisters.

Chapter Five

1. *Something I've Been Meaning to Tell You,* 221.

2. Warwick, "Growing Up," 207.

3. Cf. Hallvard Dahlie, "Alice Munro," in *Canadian Writers and Their Works,* Fiction Series, ed. Robert Lecker, Jack David, Ellen Quigley, (Toronto: ECW Press, 1985), 7: 252–53.

4. Isaiah Berlin, *The Hedgehog and the Fox: An Essay on Tolstoy's View of History* (1953; reprint, New York: Mentor Books, 1957), 7.

5. Ibid., 8.

6. The American publication of this collection bears the title *The Beggar Girl.*

7. *Who Do You Think You Are?* (Toronto: Macmillan of Canada, 1978), 41; hereafter page references cited in parentheses in the text.

8. Cf. Godard, " 'Heirs,' " in *The Art of Alice Munro,* 46; Warwick, "Growing Up," 210–13; and Orange, "Alice Munro and A Maze of Time," in *Probable Fictions,* 96.

9. Cf. Dahlie, "Alice Munro," 248.

10. Cf. Taylor, "The Unimaginable Vancouvers," in *Probable Fictions,* 130.

11. On mimesis as representation of the given world, see Erich Auerbach, *Mimesis: The Representation of Reality in Western Literature,* trans. Willard Trask (Princeton: Princeton University Press, 1953).

12. Cf. Lawrence Mathews, *"Who Do You Think You Are?* Alice Munro's Art of Disarrangement," in *Probable Fictions,* 181.

13. Cf. Warwick, "Growing Up," 209.

14. For an interpretation of the comic aspects of this scene, see Joseph Gold, "Our Feeling Exactly: The Writing of Alice Munro," in *The Art of Alice Munro,* 8–10.

15. See Stephen Scobie's useful commentary on the function of Frances Farmer in "Amelia or: Who Do You Think You Are? Documentary and

Identity in Canadian Literature," *Canadian Writers in 1984,* ed. W. H. New (Vancouver: University of British Columbia Press, 1984):264–66.

16. On this play of nouns, see Helen Hoy, " 'Dull, Simple, Amazing and Unfathomable': Paradox and Double Vision in Alice Munro's Fiction," *Studies in Canadian Literature* 5 (Spring 1980):100–15. Cf. Lorraine McMullen, " 'Shameless, Marvellous, Shattering Absurdity': The Humour of Paradox in Alice Munro," in *Probable Fictions,* 144–62.

17. Cf. Warwick, "Growing Up," 207–9.

18. By coincidence both Warwick, "Growing Up," 209, and Dahlie, "Alice Munro," 247, concur in designating this novel as "bleaker" than *Lives.*

19. Cf. Mathews, "Disarrangement," in *Probable Fictions,* 188–89, who also almost yields to such a temptation.

20. Cf. Mathews's fine analysis of this problem, ibid., 183–84.

21. See Taylor, "The Unimaginable Vancouvers," in *Probable Fictions,* 134. Godard's argument that the spelling performances of the old woman are an example of what Mary Daly calls "croneology" (" 'Heirs,' " in *The Art of Alice Munro,* 46) strikes me as dubious.

22. On the carnivalesque, see Mikhail Bakhtine, *Rabelais and His World,* trans. Helene Iswolsky (Cambridge: M.I.T. Press, 1968).

23. A curious echo, furthermore, of the story "Providence" occurs on p. 207, in which Tom tells her of an anonymous woman with whom he is having an affair, and one wonders if Rose herself is not transposed to anonymity when he is talking of her to the other woman.

24. Cf. Warwick, "Growing Up," 219.

25. Cf. Mathews, "Disarrangement," in *Probable Fictions,* 190–92.

26. Warwick, "Growing Up," also considers Rose's refusal "crucial." See the whole discussion, 223–24.

Chapter Six

1. *Something I've Been Meaning to Tell You,* 246.

2. Jacques Lacan, "The Mirror Stage as Formative of the Function of the I," in *Ecrits: A Selection,* trans. Alan Sheridan (New York and London: W. W. Norton & Co., 1977).

3. *The Moons of Jupiter* (Toronto: Macmillan, 1982), 129; hereafter page references cited in parentheses in the text.

4. Cf. Kamboureli, "The Body as Audience," in *A Mazing Space,* 34.

5. As Professor Frances Kaye of the University of Nebraska once remarked to me, "Willa Cather was a man!" It is evident, I think, that there is a correspondence between Munro's Cather and Hugo in "Material."

6. A clue to the problem as an awareness and dismantling of mimesis may be glimpsed in the picture on the cover of the dust jacket of the hardbound edition. The disparities between the girl and her reflection are

striking: the former's hair is wavy, while the latter's is straight. Moreover, it appears the girl is looking at an angle, while her reflection is looking down in another direction, eyes closed. What is the girl looking at? One might say the girl is gazing inward at a reflection of herself as truth, rather than as reality.

Chapter Seven

1. *The Progress of Love* (Toronto and New York: McClelland & Stewart and Knopf, 1986), 21; hereafter page references cited in parentheses in the text.

2. *Something I've Been Meaning to Tell You,* 174.

3. Ibid., 173.

4. The two stories are also paired according to a shared motif. While Mary Jo is having an affair with her employer, Jesse is having a fantasy of an affair. Similar pairing may also be observed in "Monsieur les Deux Chapeux" and "Miles City, Montana," each sharing the motif of someone who nearly dies. The mutual enhancement that this kind of arrangement can achieve has been examined in *Something I've Been Meaning to Tell You* by W. R. Martin, "Hanging Pictures Together," in *The Art of Alice Munro.*

5. *Who Do You Think You Are?,* 33.

Chapter Eight

1. Alice Munro, "What Is Real?" in *Making It New: Contemporary Canadian Stories,* ed. John Metcalf (Toronto: Methuen, 1982), 225.

2. *Lives of Girls and Women,* 143.

3. Ibid., 171.

4. Ibid., 209.

5. Ibid., 247.

6. *Something I've Been Meaning to Tell You,* 197.

7. *The Moons of Jupiter,* 136.

8. *The Progress of Love,* 130.

9. *Something I've Been Meaning to Tell You,* 163.

10. Ibid., 162.

11. Andrew Stubbs, "Fictional Landscape: Mythology and Dialectic in the Fiction of Alice Munro," *World Literature Written in English* 22, no. 1 (1984):55.

12. Cf. the concluding paragraph of "The Time of Death," *Dance of the Happy Shades,* 99.

13. Ibid., 18.

14. "What Is Real?" 223; Further references to this work cited in parentheses in the text.

15. Aristotle, *Poetics,* VI. 19.

16. Ibid., IX. 1–2.

17. Ibid., XI. 4. Cf. Munro's comments on the significance of discovery in John Metcalf's "A Conversation with Alice Munro," 61.

18. Struthers, "The Real Material," 12.

19. Metcalf, "A Conversation," 56.

Selected Bibliography

PRIMARY SOURCES

1. Novels

Dance of the Happy Shades. Toronto: Ryerson, 1968.
Lives of Girls and Women. Toronto: McGraw-Hill Ryerson, 1971.
Something I've Been Meaning to Tell You: Thirteen Stories. New York: McGraw-Hill; Toronto: McGraw-Hill Ryerson, 1974.
Who Do You Think You Are? Toronto: Macmillan, 1978.
The Moons of Jupiter. Toronto: Macmillan, 1982.
The Progress of Love. New York: Knopf; Toronto: McClelland and Stewart, 1986.

2. Memoirs

"Working for a Living." *Grand Street* 1, no. 1 (Autumn 1981):9–37.

3. Articles

"The Colonel's Hash Resettled." In *The Narrative Voice: Stories and Reflections by Canadian Authors.* Edited by John Metcalf, 181–83. Toronto: McGraw-Hill Ryerson, 1972. Reprinted (excerpts—"The Authors on Their Writing") in *Personal Fictions: Stories by Munro, Wiebe, Thomas, and Blaise.* Edited by Michael Ondaatje, 224–25. Toronto: Oxford University Press, 1977.
"What Is Real?" *The Canadian Forum* 62 (September 1982):5, 36. Reprinted in *Making It New: Contemporary Canadian Stories.* Edited by John Metcalf, 223–26. Toronto: Methuen, 1982.

4. Interviews

Gibson, Graeme. "Alice Munro." In *Eleven Canadian Novelists*, 239–64. Toronto: House of Anansi, 1973. Broadcast ("Interview with Alice Munro") *Anthology.* CBC Radio, 10 March 1973 (29 min.). Reprinted (excerpts—"The Authors on Their Writing") in *Personal Fictions: Stories by Munro, Wiebe, Thomas, and Blaise.* Edited by Michael Ondaatje, 241, 243, 246, 248. Toronto: Oxford University Press, 1977.
Gzowski, Peter. "Interview with Alice Munro." *Morningside.* CBC Radio, 2 June 1987.

Hancock, Geoff. "An Interview with Alice Munro." *Canadian Fiction Magazine* no. 43 (1983): 74–114.

Horwood, Harold. "Interview with Alice Munro." In *The Art of Alice Munro: Saying the Unsayable.* Edited by Judith Miller, 123–34. Waterloo, Ont.: University of Waterloo Press, 1984.

Metcalf, John. "A Conversation with Alice Munro." *Journal of Canadian Fiction* 1, no. 4 (Fall 1972): 54–62.

Stainsby, Mari. "Alice Munro Talks with Mari Stainsby." *British Columbia Library Quarterly* 35, no. 1 (July 1971): 27–30.

Struthers, J. R. (Tim). "The Real Material: An Interview with Alice Munro." In *Probable Fictions: Alice Munro's Narrative Acts.* Edited by Louis K. MacKendrick, 5–36. Downsview, Ont.: ECW Press, 1983.

Twigg, Alan. "What Is: Alice Munro." In *For Openers: Conversations with 24 Canadian Writers,* 13–20. Madeira Park, B.C.: Harbour, 1981.

SECONDARY SOURCES

1. Bibliography

Thacker, Robert. "Alice Munro: An Annotated Bibliography." In *The Annotated Bibliography of Canada's Major Authors.* Edited by Robert Lecker and Jack David. Vol.5, 354–414. Downsview, Ont.: ECW Press, 1984. Lists Munro's books, audiovisual material, manuscripts, and contributions to periodicals and books. Secondary materials are provided with lengthy commentary.

2. Books and Articles

Bailey, Nancy J. "The Masculine Image in *Lives of Girls and Women.*" *Canadian Literature* no. 80 (Spring 1979):113–20. Studies the role of the masculine in the formation of Del Jordan's growth as woman and artist.

Barbour, Douglas. "The Extraordinary Ordinary." *Open Letter* 3d ser., no. 3 (Late Fall 1975):107–10. Comments upon Munro's courage in abandoning traditional narrative form.

Blodgett, E. D. "Prisms and Arcs: Structures in Hébert and Munro." In *Configuration: Essays in the Canadian Literatures,* 53–84. Downsview, Ont.: ECW Press, 1982. Compares Anne Hébert and Alice Munro in respect of the use of metaphor and metonymy.

Carscallen, James. "Alice Munro." In *Profiles in Canadian Literature* 2, edited by Jeffrey M. Heath, 73–80. Toronto and Charlottetown: Dun-

dern, 1980. A general introduction to Munro with special emphasis on
Lives of Girls and Women as a bildungsroman.

————. "Three Jokers: The Shape of Alice Munro's Stories." In *Centre and
Labyrinth: Essays in Honour of Northrop Frye,* edited by Eleanor Cook,
Chaviva Hosek, Jay Macpherson, Patricia Parker, and Julian Parker,
128–46. Toronto, Buffalo, London: University of Toronto Press, 1983.
Argues that Munro's fiction follows various cycles whose pattern is
provided by the Bible.

Conron, Brandon. "Munro's Wonderland." *Canadian Literature* no. 77
(Autumn 1978):109–12, 114–18, 120–23. An overview of Munro's
first four texts, celebrating her attention to surface detail, the complexity
of human relationships, and realism.

Dahlie, Hallvard. "Alice Munro." In *Canadian Writers and Their Works,*
Fiction Series, edited by Robert Lecker, Jack David, and Ellen Quigley,
vol. 7, 215–56. Toronto: ECW Press, 1985. A broad introduction to
Munro, situating her in a critical and literary context.

Dawson, Anthony B. "Coming of Age in Canada." *Mosaic* 11, no. 3
(Spring 1978):47–62. Compares *Lives of Girls and Women* with other
Canadian novels that share the theme of adolescence, and distinguishes
Munro by her emphasis on language.

Dobbs, Kildare. "New Direction for Alice Munro." *Saturday Night* 89,
no. 7 (July 1974):28. A reading of *Something I've Been Meaning to Tell
You*.

Dombrowski, Eileen. " 'Down to Death' ": Alice Munro and Transcience
[sic]." *University of Windsor Review* 14, no. 1 (Fall-Winter 1978):21–29.
Examines themes of death and mutability.

Fitzpatrick, Margaret Anne. " 'Projection' in Alice Munro's *Something I've
Been Meaning to Tell You*." In *The Art of Alice Munro: Saying the
Unsayable,* edited by Judith Miller, 15–20. Waterloo, Ont.: University
of Waterloo Press, 1984. Examines the psychology of projection in
Munro's use of character.

Fleenor, Juliann E. "Rape Fantasies as Initiation Rite: Female Imagination
in 'Lives of Girls and Women.' " *Room of One's Own* 4 no. 4 (Winter
1979):35–49. Examines rape fantasy in Munro's first novel as a structure
beneath the patriarchal linear narrative.

Godard, Barbara. " 'Heirs of the Living Body': Alice Munro and the
Question of a Female Aesthetic." In *The Art of Alice Munro: Saying
the Unsayable,* edited by Judith Miller, 43–72. Waterloo, Ont.: University
of Waterloo Press, 1984. A wide-ranging study of the sexual and textual
body in Munro's writing.

Gold, Joseph. "Our Feeling Exactly: The Writing of Alice Munro." In *The
Art of Alice Munro: Saying the Unsayable,* edited by Judith Miller, 1–14.

Waterloo, Ont.: University of Waterloo Press, 1984. Analyzes the way in which feeling is displayed in language.

Hoy, Helen. " 'Dull, Simple, Amazing and Unfathomable': Paradox and Double Vision in Alice Munro's Fiction." *Studies in Canadian Literature* 5 (Spring 1980):100–15. Studies paradox as it illustrates the theme of doubleness.

Irvine, Lorna. "Changing Is the Word I Want." In *Probable Fictions: Alice Munro's Narrative Acts,* edited by Louis K. MacKendrick, 99–111. Downsview, Ont.: ECW Press, 1983. A study of the role of flux and ambiguity as characteristic of the female in Munro.

Kamboureli, Smaro. "The Body as Audience and Performance in the Writing of Alice Munro." In *A Mazing Space: Writing Canadian Women Writing,* edited by Shirley Neuman and Smaro Kamboureli, 31–38. Edmonton: Longspoon and NeWest, 1986. Examines "Chaddeleys and Flemings" (*The Moons of Jupiter*) and *Lives of Girls and Women,* indicating the use of the feminine body and its textual inscription.

Knelman, Martin. "The Past, the Present and Alice." *Saturday Night* 94, no. 9 (November 1979): 16–22. Biographical sketch of Munro.

Kröller, Eva Marie. "The Eye in the Text: Timothey Findley's *The Last of the Crazy People* and Alice Munro's *Lives of Girls and Women.*" *World Literature Written in English* 23, no. 2 (1984):366–74. Examines the "I/eye" of Del Jordan as an undermining of the mimetic level of the text.

Macdonald, Rae McCarthy. "A Madman Loose in the World: The Vision of Alice Munro." *Modern Fiction Studies* 22, no. 3 (Autumn 1976):365–74. An examination of Munro's vision which is characterized by the tension between the world of survivors and "the other country" of outcasts.

———. "Structure and Detail in *Lives of Girls and Women.*" *Studies in Canadian Literature* 3, no. 2 (Summer 1978):199–210. An analysis of the novel as a series of deepening crises whose role is to rid the protagonist of her illusions about life.

McMullen, Lorraine. " 'Shameless, Marvellous, Shattering Absurdity': The Humour of Paradox in Alice Munro." In *Probable Fictions: Alice Munro's Narrative Acts,* edited by Louis K. MacKendrick, 144–62. Downsview, Ont.: ECW Press, 1983. Studies paradox in Munro as it reveals ambiguities in language and experience.

Martin, W. R. "Alice Munro and James Joyce." *Journal of Canadian Fiction* no. 24 (1979):120–26. Examines the relation between James Joyce's *Dubliners* and *Dance of the Happy Shades,* as well as *Portrait of the Artist as a Young Man* and *Lives of Girls and Women.*

———.*Alice Munro: Paradox and Parallel.* Edmonton: University of Alberta Press, 1987. Analyzes the use of opposition and irony in the patterning of the stories. Discusses the approximately dozen uncollected stories, and also compares versions of stories published in magazines and later in collections.

————. "Hanging Pictures Together: *Something I've Been Meaning to Tell You.*" In *The Art of Alice Munro: Saying the Unsayable,* edited by Judith Miller, 21–36. Waterloo, Ont.: University of Waterloo Press, 1984. Discusses the manner in which the several stories of the collection interrelate.

————. "The Strange and the Familiar in Alice Munro." *Studies in Canadian Literature* 7, no. 2 (1982):214–26. Examines the function of oppositions and their resolutions.

Mathews, Lawrence. "*Who Do You Think You Are?:* Alice Munro's Art of Disarrangement." In *Probable Fictions: Alice Munro's Narrative Acts,* edited by Louis K. MacKendrick, 181–93. Downsview, Ont.: ECW Press, 1983. An analysis of the distrust of fiction in Munro's work.

Murray, Heather. "Women in the Wilderness." In *A Mazing Space: Writing Canadian Women Writing,* edited by Shirley Neuman and Smaro Kamboreli, 74–83. Edmonton: Longspoon and NeWest, 1986. Although Munro is not discussed, the notion of the "pseudo-wilderness" is developed as a sign of female, mediating space.

New, W. H. "Pronouns and Propositions: Alice Munro's Stories." *Open Letter,* 3d ser., no. 5 (Summer 1976):40–49. A close examination of the interplay of theme (the inability to communicate) and symbolic structure and its implied meanings.

Noonan, Gerald. "The Structure of Style in Alice Munro's Fiction." In *Probable Fictions: Alice Munro's Narrative Acts,* edited by Louis K. MacKendrick, 163–80. Downsview, Ont.: ECW Press, 1983. Studies the development in Munro's work of the use of paradox as a narrative strategy that is at once verbal wit and a problem at the heart of the relation between event and structure.

Orange, John. "Alice Munro and A Maze of Time." In *Probable Fictions: Alice Munro's Narrative Acts,* edited by Louis K. MacKendrick, 83–98. Downsview, Ont.: ECW Press, 1983. A study of the function of time in the structure of the story.

Osachoff, Margaret Gail. " 'Treacheries of the Heart': Memoir, Confession, and Meditation in the Stories of Alice Munro." In *Probable Fictions: Alice Munro's Narrative Acts,* edited by Louis K. MacKendrick, 61–82. Downsview, Ont.: ECW Press, 1983. An examination of the kinds of narrative voice employed in Munro's stories.

Packer, Miriam. "*Lives of Girls and Women:* A Creative Search for Completion." In *The Canadian Novel Here and Now: A Critical Anthology.* Vol. 1 of *The Canadian Novel,* edited by John Moss, 134–44. Toronto: NC Press, 1978. A character analysis of Del Jordan, her search for fulfillment, and her endeavor to find a more rewarding life than the other women in the novel.

Perrakis, Phyllis Sternberg. "Portrait of the Artist as a Young Girl: Alice Munro's *Lives of Girls and Women.*" *Atlantis* 7, no. 2 (Spring 1982):61–67. Examines Del Jordan's growth as a woman and artist.

Pfaus, B. *Alice Munro.* Ottawa: Golden Dog Press, 1984. A brief introduction to Munro's work.

Rasporich, Beverly J. "Child-Women and Primitives in the Fiction of Alice Munro." *Atlantis* 1, no. 2 (Spring 1976):4–14. Analyzes the problem of women caught in old ideologies and unable to invest the present and future with significance.

Ross, Catherine Sheldrick. " 'At least part legend': The Fiction of Alice Munro." In *Probable Fictions: Alice Munro's Narrative Acts,* edited by Louis K. MacKendrick, 112–26. Downsview, Ont.: ECW Press, 1983. Studies the legendary that is concealed in the real world.

Scobie, Stephen. "Amelia or: Who Do You Think You Are? Documentary and Identity in Canadian Literature." *Canadian Writers in 1984,* edited by W. H. New, 264–85. Vancouver: University of British Columbia Press, 1984. A brief analysis within a large context of the text of the documentary and its role in play of identity.

Struthers, J. R. (Tim). "Alice Munro and the American South." *Canadian Review of American Studies* 6 (Fall 1975):196–204. Reprint (revised) in *Here and Now: A Critical Anthology.* Vol. 1 of *The Canadian Novel,* edited by John Moss, 121–33. Toronto: NC Press, 1978. Places Munro in the context of writing from the American South with special emphasis on the Scots-Irish ethos of both that region and Southern Ontario.

———. "Alice Munro's Fictive Imagination." *The Art of Alice Munro: Saying the Unsayable,* edited by Judith Miller, 103–12. Waterloo, Ont.: University of Waterloo Press, 1984. A study of Munro's work as metafiction.

———. "Reality and Ordering: The Growth of a Young Artist in *Lives of Girls and Women.*" *Essays on Canadian Writing* 3 (Fall 1975):32–46. Examines Munro's first novel as both bildungsroman and Künstlerroman with an emphasis on the model of James Joyce's *A Portrait of the Artist as a Young Man.*

Stubbs, Andrew. "Fictional Landscape: Mythology and Dialectic in the Fiction of Alice Munro." *World Literature Written in English* 23, no. 1 (1984):53–62. Discusses the relationship between surface and depth in the perceived world.

Taylor, Michael. "The Unimaginable Vancouvers: Alice Munro's Words." In Probable Fictions: Alice Munro's Narrative Acts, edited by Louis K. MacKendrick, 127–43. Downsview, Ont.: ECW Press, 1983. Analyzes the role of wordplay as a functional element in Munro's fiction.

Thacker, Robert. " 'Clear Jelly': Alice Munro's Narrative Dialectics." In *Probable Fictions: Alice Munro's Narrative Acts,* edited by Louis K. MacKendrick, 37–60. Downsview, Ont.: ECW Press, 1983. Detailed study of early stories (both collected and uncollected) that examines the interplay of past and present, as well as experience and its understanding.

Wallace, Bronwen. "Women's Lives: Alice Munro." In *The Human Elements,* edited by David Helwig, 52–67. Ottawa: Oberon, 1978. A personal and feminist reading of the various roles Munro's characters are given.

Warwick, Susan. "Growing Up: The Novels of Alice Munro." *Essays on Canadian Writing* 29 (Summer 1984):204–25. An examination of the theme of growing up in *Lives of Girls and Women* and *Who Do You Think You Are?* with some attention to the metaphor of life as theater.

Wayne, Jane. "Huron Country Blues." *Books in Canada* 11, no. 8 (October 1982):9–12. Situates Munro in Wingham with some biographical data.

Index